DYLAN THOMAS

Dylan Thomas at nineteen

# DYLAN THOMAS

*His Life and Work*

JOHN ACKERMAN

St. Martin's Press
New York

St. Martin's Press, Scholarly and Reference Division,
175 Fifth Avenue, New York, N.Y. 10010

First published in the United States of America in 1996

Printed in Great Britain

ISBN 0–312–12903–3 (cloth)
ISBN 0–312–12905–X (paper)

Library of Congress Cataloging-in-Publication Data
Ackerman, John.
Dylan Thomas: his life and work / John Ackerman.
p.   cm.
Includes bibliographical references (p.   ) and index.
ISBN 0–312–12903–3 (cloth).— ISBN 0–312–12905–X (paper)
1. Thomas, Dylan, 1914–1953.   2. Poets, Welsh—20th century–
–Biography.   Wales—In literature.   I. Title.
PR6039.H52Z55   1996
821'.912—dc20
[B]                                                95–31678
                                                      CIP

TO MY MOTHER

# CONTENTS

# ACKNOWLEDGEMENTS

Grateful acknowledgements are due to the following: David Higham Associates Ltd. and J. M. Dent and Sons Ltd. for permission to quote from Dylan Thomas's published works and from Caitlin Thomas: *Leftover Life to Kill*; New Directions Ltd. (Dylan Thomas: *Adventures in the Skin Trade*); Atlantic-Little, Brown and Company (J. M. Brinnin: *Dylan Thomas in America*); Faber and Faber Ltd. (Vernon Watkins: *The Lady with the Unicorn, The Death Bell, Letters to Vernon Watkins*); Random House, Inc. (Karl Shapiro: *In Defense of Ignorance*); quotations also reprinted by permission of New Directions Publishing Corp., U.S.A.; and the Times Publishing Company (Dylan Thomas Obituary Notice).

# ILLUSTRATIONS

# PREFACE, 1996

The book offers an interpretation of Dylan Thomas's life and work in relation to his Welsh background, outlining the impact of social and literary traditions, in order to help the understanding of his poetry and focus his prose writing. I have considered biographical details valuable in so far as they illuminate the poetry and prose or the man who wrote it.

It was in his introduction to a poetry reading at the Massachussetts Institute of Technology, Boston, in 1952, that Dylan Thomas declared 'If I had been born and brought up in an igloo and lived on whales, not in it, about the same would be true, except that then it would have been extremely unlikely had I become a writer'; his pun whales/Wales signalling his witty comic vein. Thomas's own words are keys to his work, whether from his letters, reviews and articles or his replies to questions and introductions at his readings. 'My education was the liberty I had to read indiscriminately and all the time' he tells us in the same lecture, much of it no doubt 'in my father's brown study'. His father had gained a First Class Honours degree in English and was a notable teacher of English literature. In this large ground floor study Dylan shelved his own books (mainly poetry), and relates how he wrote 'before homework . . . the first botched scribblings of gauche and gawky heart-choked poems' and 'began to know one kind of writing from another, one kind of badness, one kind of goodness'. This is the poet's insight into his youthful creativity and his apprenticeship in the making of poems. Speaking of his schoolboy resolution he recalls his 'endless imitations . . . of whatever I happened to be galloping then, Thomas Browne, Robert W. Service, Stevenson, de Quincey, *Eskimo Nell*, Newbolt, Blake, Marlowe, the Imagists, the *Boy's Own Paper*, Keats, Poe, Burns, Dostoevsky, Anon. and Shakespeare. I tried my little trotters on every poetical form. How could I know the tricks of this trade, unless I tried them myself?' ('I am Going to Read Aloud' *The London Magazine*, vol 3, no. 9). He concluded with a flourish and caveat 'I couldn't trust the critics then—or now'. We see here something of the practice and mystery of early poetic self-discovery, albeit self-mockingly though amusingly remembered. The link between the mature poet's craftsmanship and the poem's final evolution is highlighted in discussion of manuscript versions of 'Poem on his Birthday' and 'Prologue', later in this book.

Dylan Thomas's great need throughout his life was a room apart from the family where he could write undisturbed, for he worked regular hours every day, broken only when broadcasting, on location during his war-time work on documentary films, and of course during his long American tours. He was the most disciplined and dedicated of poets, his later major poems taking months, often years, on their journey to completion, as his manuscripts show. In the late thirties his first sea-facing Laugharne homes of Eros and Sea View provided a room to write in. Staying in Richard Hughes's house near Laugharne Castle in May 1941 Thomas wrote enthusiastically to Vernon Watkins 'I have the romantic, dirty, summerhouse looking over the marsh [from the castle ruins] to write in.' In his 1949 broadcast reading of 'Poem in October' Thomas recalled his writing poetry 'in small rooms in Wales', certainly remembering the two stone cottages of Blaen Cwm, Llangain, owned by his mother's family and near Fernhill farm. He often stayed at Blaen Cwm in the thirties and forties. Here he finished 'Vision and Prayer', 'Poem in October', 'In my Craft or Sullen Art', 'Fern Hill', and re-wrote 'Unluckily for a Death,' in the summers of 1944 and 1945, all included in *Deaths and Entrances*. This quiet, remote, rural corner of West Wales was a place for poetry, undisturbed by his London's busy film world and work at this time. His writing-shed above the Boat House home that he called his 'water and tree room on the cliff', bird-haunted and from its windows vistas of Sir John's hill, the estuary, and on the opposite shore, of the hill farms and fields recalling his childhood visits, is now famous and fabled.

The one room studio flat in Manresa Road, Chelsea, just off the King's Road, where Dylan and Caitlin lived in 1943 proved especially cramped, particularly after their baby daughter Aeronwy was born in March. Their friends Theodora and Constantine Fitzgibbon came to the rescue: there was a spare room for Dylan in their nearby house in Godfrey Street and he went daily to write there. In October 1944 when living in their Newquay bungalow— again overlooking the sea, this time Cardigan Bay—Dylan apologises to Donald Taylor, the Director of Strand Films who employed him as a script writer during the war years, for his slow work on the film script *Twenty Years A-Growing*. He complained 'this little bungalow is no place to work in when there's a bawling child [the baby Aeronwy] . . . the rooms are tiny, the walls bum-paper thin.' But he then cheerily announces that 'Now, however, I have just taken a room in a nearby house: a very quiet room where I know I can work till I bleed.' During his time in Oxfordshire, he lived first in the one-room summerhouse of Margaret and A. J. P. Taylor's home in Oxford; he lamented  in a letter to Vernon Watkins in April 1946, when he was frequently reading and talking about poetry on the radio 'I want to write a poem of my own again, but it's hard here with peace and no room.' His generous patron Margaret Taylor provided him with a  gypsy caravan to work in. It followed him to the next Oxfordshire home she provided, Manor House in South Leigh, and finally to the garden of the flat she bought for him in Delancey Street, Camden Town (where I recently visited it!).

Few poets have been so badly served by their biographers: forty years after his death it is still fashionable to sensationalise any discussion of Thomas's life, and it seems unlikely this journalistic technique will be discarded. This is usually accompanied by the lack of interest in or low regard for Thomas's work such accounts display, often finding a failing inspiration and output in his last years to match their melodramatic picture of self-destruction. This is contrary to all the evidence. In his last three years Dylan Thomas completed the four major poems 'Poem on his Birthday', 'Do not go gentle into that good night,' 'In the White Giant's Thigh' and 'Prologue' as well as 'Lament'. His prose work included *Under Milk Wood* and short stories, nearly forty broadcasts, including several new talks like 'A Visit to America' and 'Laugharne', his thirty-fourth and last BBC script, his recording broadcast in Wales on 5 November 1953, the day he collapsed at the Chelsea Hotel, New York, and was taken to St Vincent's Hospital. 'A Story' now famously known as *'The Outing'* Dylan read on television in August 1953. It was enthusiastically reviewed ('almost a *tour de force*')— clearly he was discovering a new medium. But the need and drive to write poetry  was always with him despite the demands of films, broadcasting and lecturing. He was working on two potentially major poems when he died: 'In Country Heaven' which is a vision of God's world destroyed by nuclear warfare, and 'Elegy' for his father who died in December 1952 less than a year before Dylan's own death. This poem, unlike the previous one on his father's death 'Do not go gentle into that good night', is elegiac pastoral rather than protest. Sections of both are included in *Collected Poems 1934–1953*. And these were the years of the four American tours, when Thomas gave one hundred and seven lecture readings. His last engagement, the day after his thirty-ninth birthday, was a Symposium on 'Poetry and The Film'—he had written film scripts between 1941 and 1949. Recently editing Dylan Thomas's film scripts I was delighted to find fourteen war-time documentaries and nine feature scripts! The tragedy of Dylan Thomas's death, as his friend the novelist Richard Hughes came to reflect, was that it robbed us not of a promising young man, but of that much rarer thing, a promising middle-aged man. For indeed he died a great poet writing new poems, and successfully working in drama, broadcasting, films, television, and planning too the libretto of the opera Stravinsky was to compose.

Dylan Thomas has become a legendary figure also for his gift of comedy, his actor's self-dramatisation, and his unique skills as a reader of poetry—both his own and others. A reader of poetry should 'use *his* voice in the place of *your* eyes' (*Broadcasts* p.52) was the advice of this bardic poet who returned the importance of sound and rhythm to poetry. But the poet of tragic vision was also the born jester, Lear and the fool as one, in the words of his true friend Vernon Watkins. During the London blitz Dylan often stayed with Theodora Fitzgibbon in Chelsea, and though he was 'the most frightened of us all' his comic verve and wit took their minds off the bombing, she relates in *With Love*. Professional friends who worked with him paint the same picture of a gregarious, entertaining, entirely professional companion they loved to join in the pub afterwards. Hugh Griffith, who acted in Dylan Thomas's film *The Three Weird Sisters* spoke of him as 'a royal jester who was also the royal bard'; while Louis MacNeice, who directed him as reader and actor at the BBC, found him 'a comic genius – and the cause of comedy in others' (*Ingot* 1954). John Arlott produced many of Thomas's poetry programmes there and remembered him taking to production like a professional actor. Certainly Thomas liked to joke that the only language he knew was 'English, BBC Third Programme and saloon.' Arlott gives a vignette of him in the studio:

Round, with the roundness of a Tintoretto urchin – cherub, and in a large loose tweed jacket, he would stand, feet apart and head thrown back, a dead cigarette frequently adhering wispily to his lower lip, curls a little tousled and eyes half-closed, barely reading the poetry by eye, but rather understanding his way through it, one arm beating out a sympathetic double rhythm as he read. (*Adelphi* 1954)

Thomas's experience as a radio actor and reader contributed to the dramatic structure and verbal harmonies and rhythms of his radio 'play for voices', *Under Milk Wood*. But it is the great theme of nostalgia that is the light and shadow of his later prose, the call of 'Come back! Come back!', the cry of Captain Cat in *Under Milk Wood*. Dylan Thomas once described himself as 'Proustlike in my conservatory' (*Letters* p. 11), and this writing is a '*recherche du temps perdu*'. Again Thomas's own words best signal the artist's quest, no longer a young dog, for the knelled happiness in the seas and wood of his past, the poet dredging and rooting:

I am the kind of human dredger that digs up the wordy mud of his own Dead Sea, a kind of pig that roots for unconsidered truffles in the reeky wood of his own past. ('I am Going to Read Aloud')

'We have been there' is our collaborative cry on reading or hearing lines from *Under Milk Wood*, tales of Christmas and summers past or return journeys, and in poems like 'Fern Hill' and 'Poem in October' too, for these are rites of passage to lost happiness. Dylan Thomas spoke of 'the joyful poem, Fern Hill', whose words came 'out of a never-to-be buried childhood in heaven or Wales' (*Letters* 583), but he named it too 'a poem for evening and tears'. Paradoxically Thomas's poetry is often the most memorable, lines and phrases haunting us and, like his prose of nostalgia, touching a common heart. The words of a poem like 'Do not go gentle into that good night' have likewise joined the currency of common speech, like phrases in *Under Milk Wood*, probably the most popular and performed play of our time.

In her 1993 Introduction to *Portrait of the Artist as a Young Dog* Dylan's daughter Aeronwy Thomas observes that 'Words spoken, written or read aloud, were what he based his life on, even his relationship with his own family', recalling his reading aloud to her Grimm's *Fairy Tales* and nursery rhymes. Dylan Thomas liked to read aloud at home in the evening at the Boat House the poems or prose he was working on (often reading scenes from *Under Milk Wood* in the bath), repeating his reading aloud to himself earlier that day in what he called his 'word-splashed hut' during his working hours there (two till seven o'clock each day). For reading aloud was his final testing of word and rhythm, sentence and stanza.

I conclude this Preface with the comment on Dylan Thomas by his fellow Welsh poet R. S. Thomas that 'Dylan's primary importance derives from his concern with the great, simple images and symbols of life such as birth, death, sex and sin, together with his celebration of some of the greatest human virtues like love and faith.' (*Critical Quarterly* 1967). It is no coincidence that Wales has produced two of the great religious poets in English in this century, however different their style and doubt and celebration. A knowledge of the country and culture which produced Dylan Thomas is fundamental to a full understanding of the poet. This book shows he was the product of a particular place with living and inherited traditions, religious, cultural and political.

J. A.

# INTRODUCTION, 1990

## I

'Then (aged 15) I was arrogant and lost. Now I am humble and found. I prefer that other' said Thomas in America three years before his death there. Such comment, whatever its ironies, puts the legend in its place. When I wrote this book the major requirement in Dylan Thomas studies was an elucidation of his verse that would help readers to understand his poems, rather than pursuit of the legend and its sensationalism that had flourished in the ten years since his death. Secondly, an introduction to the increasingly popular prose works, famous through Thomas's records, broadcasts, and of course *Under Milk Wood* was needed. This book provides such a chronological account, tracing his development as poet and prose writer, and linking this for the first time with his Welsh background. This includes the formative influence of Swansea on the young poet; his family roots in West Wales and the childhood visits to Fern Hill farm and the nearby Blaen Cwm cottage; and finally the Boat House and Laugharne, both the village life and the inspiration of its now famous land- and sea-scapes. In addition to the importance of place, I also sought to show the impact of Welsh Nonconformity and the chapel, and the radical politics of Wales, both dramatically linked in the career of Thomas's grandfather's brother Gwilym Marles. They particularly influenced attitudes in Dylan Thomas's prose, and I was recently intrigued to come across his later comment (in America in 1952), 'Writers should keep their opinions for their prose' (*A Casebook on Dylan Thomas*, ed. J. M. Brinnin, p. 196). Elements in Welsh literature, such as the emphasis on sound in Welsh poetry and the Mabinogion's delight in animal life, offer their own perspectives on Thomas's verse. Anglo-Welsh literature is also introduced as an important context for Dylan Thomas's work, especially the poet Vernon Watkins, his close friend and closest poetic mentor, both assuming the bardic role of poet as singer and seer, and finding in nature the drive and metaphor of their vision. Dylan Thomas remains the most redoubtable dragon among the now many fiery Welsh intruders into English literature, following the trail Caradoc Evans blazed with *My People* in 1915. An important change today is the recognition of R. S. Thomas as a major twentieth-century poet in English, perhaps the greatest since Dylan Thomas. For all their differences in style, vision, and attitudes, both are fundamentally religious poets and poets of nature.

In both poets these two elements are inextricably linked. Describing how the role of priest and poet are united, R. S. Thomas's comments in 1969 are close to the pantheistic vision of his fellow Welsh poet who earlier spoke of 'the heron/Priested shore', of how 'a hill touches an angel' and declared 'the loud sun/Christens down the sky':

> The sacramental side is there at the root, I believe, I look upon the earth, for example, as something living. God created the whole, and therefore I feel when I act as a poet or when I act as a priest that I am doing the same work: conveying the sacrament of the earth, God's earth, to people.... That's the role of the poet, I believe; to glorify, to show the glory of life. (Quoted in translation by Tony Brown in *The Welsh Connection*, Ed. Tydeman, p. 165).

Introducing his projected 'long poem to be' 'In Country Heaven', including the completed 'In Country Sleep', 'Over Sir John's hill', and 'In the White Giant's Thigh', Dylan Thomas spoke of 'He, on top of a hill in heaven' and how 'when he weeps, Light and His tears glide down together, hand in hand' but concluding that 'the poem becomes, at last, an affirmation of the beautiful and terrible worth of the Earth. It grows into a praise of what is and what could be on this lump in the skies'. Such is the resurgent, optimistic pantheism that animates the last poems, whose pastoral landscapes and sea-chimes this book introduces.

Regrettably, accounts of his American visits, then and now, dwelt mostly on puffed up accounts of the poet's drinking between and particularly after his readings. Yet in his replies to questions from students and academics were the necessary insights into his poetry, often overlooked because they were expressed simply and literally, purged of academic and critical self-importance, and veined always with humour. These defensive, tart but self-revelatory comments, often asides and self-mocking, can be close to the heart of his poetic world. To the question (University of Utah, in *Dylan Thomas*, ed. Tedlock, p. 64) 'You always seem to put in your poetry just what you are seeing at the moment – the herons, and the birds near the estuary?' Thomas replied 'Yes – Yes. I wanted to write about the cliff, and there was a crow flying above it, and that seemed a good place to begin, so I wrote about the crow. Yes, if I see a bird, I put it in whether it belongs or not.' To the query 'Do you leave it there?' he answered 'If it is happy and at home in the poetry I do', humorously adding 'But really I should get a blind for my window.' Such oblique comment signposts 'the remoteness and quietude of his creative life' by the Laugharne estuary and Bill Read has recalled how 'at lunch time we ate around the old wooden table on the Boat House terrace, watching the movements of sea birds on the sand flats. One odd inky bird stood upright with both wings stretched out for minutes at a time perfectly motionless' (*A Casebook on Dylan Thomas*, p. 271). He recalls, too, how wild swans would fly in at high tide to the 'swanfood' basket. Such literal accounts highlight the poet's inspiration, so much more revealing than critical badinage on failing inspiration. Edith Sitwell rightly declared 'His is always the voice of Nature' (*Casebook*, p. 271).

Such early poems as 'The force that through the green fuse drives the flower' identify his own body and its senses with the cosmos, while his last poems evoke his unity with the life of nature moving before him on hillside and estuary, mortal but changing forms on their journey to death. In each case the driving force was his pantheism, initially obscurely pursued through his own 'small, bonebound island' (*Collected Letters*, p. 39), and later finding expansive lyrical and philosophic expression. His aim was always to re-establish the living organic connections with the cosmos. Throughout his verse is a celebration of the instinctive life. We would do well to remember that Whitman and D. H. Lawrence were two poets whose photographs were displayed in his hut, and while critical of Lawrence's sexual philosophy Thomas was particularly devoted to his volume *Birds, Beasts and Flowers* and a fine reader of these poems. Lawrence's affirmations in 'Apocalypse': 'I am part of the sun as my eye is part of me. That I am part of the earth my feet know perfectly, and my blood is part of the sea' are often echoed in phrase and image in Thomas's early poems, whether 'The secret of the soil grows through the eye/And blood jumps in the sun', or 'From poles of skull and toe the windy blood/ Slides like a sea' ('Light breaks where no sun shines').

'Poem on his birthday' was the last completed poem that focuses on the hill and estuary setting viewed from Thomas's writing shed, though here the scene is a timeless and panoramic one, as on his thirty-fifth birthday the poet meditates on his and nature's journey to death. Comparison of a working sheet of the ninth stanza (appropriately for a birthday poem there are twelve) with the final one demonstrates how the natural life of land, sea, and air weave this tapestry of mutability: heaven, illusory or not, being elemental as air, the souls of the dead though first seen as delicately wild as windflowers finally possessing the energy of the waves, those sea-horses that break before the poet's eyes. The sacramental heron with his familiar aloofness, who here marks nature's holy rites of change as he grieves them in 'Over Sir John's hill', is transformed to the druid heron:

> Who is the light of straight
> And gulling Heaven where souls grow wild
> As windflowers in the woods:

> Oh, may this birthday man by the shrined
> And aloof heron's vows
> Grieve until the night pelts down and then
> Count his blessings aloud!
> May he make, in his thirty-fifth death,
> His last sweet will and shroud.
> > (quoted in *Casebook*, p. 270)

> Who is the light of old
> And air shaped Heaven whose souls grow wild
> As horses in the foam:
> Oh, let me midlife mourn by the shrined
> And druid herons' vows
> The voyage to ruin I must run,
> Dawn ships clouted aground,
> Yet, though I cry with tumbledown tongue,
> Count my blessings aloud:
> > (final version in *Collected Poems*)

Significantly the poet who 'counts his blessings aloud' – the one unaltered line – lists them in the next stanza of the final poem as the four elements, the body's five senses, and his still deepening love and faith, despite death's ubiquity, in nature's undying energy and power, evident as 'the louder the sun blooms' and 'the tusked, ramshackling sea exults'. This poem, and the other manuscript worksheets are fully explored later in this book, yet we may note here, too, how Thomas has placed image and allegory in the mosaic of his pantheistic birthday tale. Importantly, too, notwithstanding verbal change, the final version keeps the exact syllabic count of the first, a pattern sustained throughout the poem.

Sound and incantatory chant was Thomas's distinctive method of conveying the intuitive and instinctive in verse: initially through his strongly rhythmic structures (that he latterly mocked for 'their vehement beat-pounding black and green rhythms like those of a very young policeman exploding'), and later the complex orchestrations of sound that induced the ecstatic note when read aloud, like 'Fern Hill', and 'Poem in October'. That this bardic delight in chant

and song invokes the romantic notion of the poet as
celebrator of ancient rites, with hints of the primitive and
magical, is inferred in the curious 'Note' to the *Collected
Poems*, with its pastoral reference to the shepherd who
makes ritual observances to the moon to protect his flocks.
Whatever irony may be in this note, there is no doubting
Thomas's lifelong insistence on the importance of the spell
poetry casts when read aloud, that reading is a skill and
craft; 'a practising interpreter' was Thomas's description of
himself as reader. Not surprisingly, his definition of poetry
emphasized its sound structure: 'memorable words-in-
cadence which move and excite me emotionally. And, once
you've got the hang of it, it should always be better when
read aloud than when read silently with the eyes. Always.'
(*Encounter VIII*, p. 23). Of course he was always ready to
mock even his own explanations, particularly in America
where his distrust of the intellectualism and jargon he met
in academic circles was always near the surface, so that to
the query 'Do you say the words aloud as you write them?'
he at once answered 'Yes. That's why I live in a hut on a
cliff.' (Utah, 1952). It was after his B.B.C. readings of poetry
and prose, as notable for their controlled and exact enuncia-
tion of word and phrase as their emotive power, that he
began to attract large audiences. And it was Dylan Thomas's
readings that rescued poetry from the lecture room and
élite gathering, for he often drew wide audiences, particularly in America, as had Dickens and Wilde on their tours.

'When I experience anything, I experience it as a thing
and a word at the same time, both equally amazing' Dylan
Thomas declared (*Dylan Thomas*, ed. Tedlock, p. 54),
emphasising the duality of experience and language for
him, especially of the individual word. It was the engine of
his method of composition, the amazing resonance of the
individual word, tried and tested for sound and colour,
meanings and texture before it found its place in the mosaic
of the poem. And its selection both contributed to and drew
from the emotional, physical, and intellectual life of the
poem, as is clear in the manuscript material of his last

completed poem 'Prologue'. The energy and inspiration of his composition were never stronger, evident in the word lists, words substitutions, word-building, word play – always the individual word, bringing to mind Thomas's comment to John Arlott that writing poetry was 'twisting and gnarling', however musical its rhythms and flow. Told in 1937 that Yeats wrote five lines a day, he replied 'I do three at the most.' As with Yeats, too, Thomas's manuscripts of all periods show that the first versions are easier to understand, often read like a paraphrase or crude summary of the final poem, as in the straightforward description of the Laugharne estuary in the notebook revision of 'On no work of words' (1938):

> For three lean months now, no work done
> In summer Laugharne among the cockle boats
> And by the castle with the boatlike birds.

Certainly these lines have a simple descriptive charm, but the finished poem was a more complex comment on 'the lovely gift of the gab'.

Rightly, Rayner Heppenstall said that Dylan Thomas was less 'finished' in 1953 than in 1939 or when he was nineteen, while 'the gargantuan collections' of work-sheets for 'Ballad of the Long-legged bait' show 'his unmatched and unreined imagination, the prodigality and massiveness of his sensual symbolism which would make a whole school of fleshly poets look like minnows' (D. Stauffer in *Poets at Work*, Edited by Charles D. Abbott, pp. 53–4). The process of reining and shaping that prodigal imagination is still richly active in the 1952 work-sheets of 'Prologue'. Thus we have such lists of similar sound but differing meaning as fold/foaled/shoaled, while 'The water tombed good lands' and the crossed out image of 'Animal islands, haunch to haunch' lead finally to:

> Across
> The water lidded lands,
> Manned with their loves they'll move
> Like wooden islands, hill to hill.

Likewise 'And   dark   floods   every   ringing   field'   and
      flood          holy   ~~feeling~~
'And the ~~dark~~ shoals every field'   becomes in the poetic
metamorphosis of verbal change 'And dark shoals every
holy field'. The poet's final choice of a 'clash' of anvils to
evoke his poetic labour was arrived at after listing and
considering the possibilities of 'percussion', 'cymballing',
'ringing', 'fanfare', 'flourish', 'concord', 'chiming'! The
poet's obsession with the word brings to mind his late-
morning habit of helping his father with the daily cross-
word before his own five hours of composition; while
Aeronwy Thomas remembers also her father's delight in
taking part in verbal games and charades, and relates that
'my father involved everyone in his overriding interest in
words' (*Christmas And Other Memories*, p. 14).

In the course of the poem the fable of the animals seeking
the poet's ark of love against the day's end and 'at poor
peace' invests a local setting with mythic as well as real
pastoral incident. In the manner of 'Over Sir John's hill',
'Prologue' offers a perspective of land and sea from a high
point, mingling description and meditation like John
Dyer's 'Grongar Hill', the first place poem in English and
one describing the scenery of the Towy as it flows to the sea,
its landscapes neighbouring Dylan Thomas's own Carmarthenshire home and haunts. 'Sir John's hill is a real hill
overlooking an estuary in West Wales' was Thomas's
introduction to his broadcast reading of 'Over Sir John's
hill', pointing out its topographical inspiration. 'Local
poetry of which the fundamental object is some particular
landscape ... with the addition of ... historical retrospection or incidental meditation' was Dr Johnson's description
of topographical verse, and certainly such poems as 'Over
Sir John's hill', 'Poem on his birthday' and 'Prologue' are
variously marked by retrospection and meditation as well
as allegory, so that a particular landscape may become
legendary.

In the last poems Thomas is seeking that 'quiet in the
soul' Dyer advocates through contemplation of landscape

and the natural life of woods and sea. In 'Grongar Hill' Dyer's bestiary includes raven, fox, thrush, and toad, while his observation that 'the shepherd charms his sheep' brings to mind the shepherd in Thomas's pastoral note to his *Collected Poems*. Some of Dyer's lines also prefigure the seaward journey at the day's and life's end in 'Prologue', with their hint of allegory:

> Wave succeeding wave they go
> A various Journey to the Deep,
> Like human life to endless sleep!
> Thus is Nature's Vesture wrought,
> To instruct our wand'ring Thought.

Contrastingly, however, Thomas's 'Prologue' offers animistic vision and stylistic vigour rather than picturesque rumination. Dylan Thomas knew the sounds and cries and calls of birds and animals, heard and saw them daily, and in this wittingly vociferous, mimetic poem their noisy presence ('hullaballoing clan', 'gabbing', 'cluck') salutes the poet's 'bellowing ark' and the 'flood ship's/Clangour' of his poetic labour. In the bravura and exact artifice of his last poem, written in three months, Thomas's bestiary of 'animals thick as thieves' in this 'kingdom of neighbours, finned/Felled and quilled' loudly and aptly introduce his *Collected Poems*. Thomas knew, too, the daily and sure sources of his poetry, for at this time in America he spoke of his home in Wales 'right by the sea' and humorously added 'I just sit . . . and unscientifically birdwatch, that is, I let the birds watch me' (Dartmouth College, May 1952). But we are with him back in the hut, 'that water and tree room on the cliff', its watery, bird-haunted vistas, hill and sheep-white farms his daily absorption and inspiration.

## II

Now that Thomas is accepted as a great twentieth-century poet and prose writer, the tides of sensationalism and denigration largely ebbed away, we can trace his professional commitment both in films and broadcasting that contributed to his later development, in poetry and prose, and also the ordinariness of his life, not only in Laugharne, but in its routines as film writer and broadcaster. His work in films, his career in radio, his fame as a reader now cast their perspectives, and are part of today's widening view of him and his work. We are increasingly aware, too, of the range of his enthusiasms and his interests, albeit the pub never far away. We should remember that there Dylan could be overflowing with charm, bonhomie and wit, as Jack Lindsay recalls, for half-drunk Dylan 'wove round himself delightful flights of fantasy and liked to reveal his remarkable powers as a mimic, a parodist, a pricker of all pomposities and falsities' he notes in *Meetings with Poets* (p. 25), significantly adding 'by reading his lighter stories and *Under Milk Wood* one can get some idea of what his improvised characterisations and his humorous inventions were like'. His broadcast recollections of his first Chelsea bed-sitter show this delight in humour and fantasy when he relates how the landlady Mrs Parsnip 'was always boiling cabbage downstairs', that 'the chimney huffed and puffed like a wolf' and surmised the 'tomcats lodging in the next room ... paid their rent with mice to Mrs Parsnip, for boiling'. Another never seen lodger living 'in a little leaking room off the stairs ... used to make a noise like a train going through a tunnel' (*Texas Quarterly*, vol. iv, no. 4, p. 57). Evidently Thomas's role as pub raconteur and entertainer was a feed and impetus to the later artist in comedy. Increasingly we now see that his later prose, albeit written on long rainy afternoons in his solitary 'word-splashed hut', on a Laugharne cliffside, belonged also to the affable, gregarious, actorly personality, always at home in the saloon bar, as well as such London haunts as the backbar of the Café Royal, the Savage Club in St. James's and the National Liberal Club – that he mockingly called The National Lavatory Club because of the striking architecture of its Gents. Dylan also probably heard the story of the famous advocate F. E. Smith who was in the habit of using the Club's lavatory until asked by the

door-man whether he belonged to the Club. Smith replied
'I thought it was the National Lavatory!' As so often,
particular reference lies behind Thomas's joke or comment.

Such film scripts as *These are the Men*, notable in the
directness and clarity of the prose and its narrative drive,
contributed to his later dramatic development. Its quick
evocation of people at their daily tasks anticipates *Under
Milk Wood*, though necessarily without its humour and
comic eccentricity of character: '(The mood of the opening
sequence is quiet and slow. From a height we look down on
to men baking bread, men going about their work quietly
and efficiently, men of no particular nationality, just working men. We see them in the bakery, in the fields at harvest
time, on the dockside, on a trawler, in an iron foundry.)

> Who are we? We are the makers, the bakers
> Making and baking bread all over the earth in
>     every town and village,
> In country quiet, in the ruins and wounds of a
>     bombed street
> With the wounded crying outside for the mercy
>     of death in the city,
> Through war and pestilence and earthquake
> Baking the bread to feed the hunger of history.'

(Quoted, *Meetings with Poets*, pp. 32–3)

Documentary scripts on war-time Britain and its bombed
cities, such as *Our Country* were part of his response to
the bombing and civilian deaths, leading to such poems as
'Ceremony After a Fire Raid'. Lindsay shrewdly writes that
'Dylan's politics were at root the immediate politics of a
clear-eyed and vigilant sympathy with one's fellows, a
characteristic of course of war-time solidarity and evident
in these lines from *These are the Men*:

> We are the makers, the workers, the farmers, the sailors,
> The tailors, the carpenters, the colliers, the fishermen,
> We dig the soil and the rock, we plough the land and the sea,
> So that all men may eat and be warm under the common sun.

In contrast, the film script *Twenty Years A-Growing*

(1944) illustrates Thomas's poetic and comic gifts and his liking for the child's eye-view. The evocation of morning certainly is a path towards *Under Milk Wood*:

> It is morning in the market town of Dingle. A cracked school bell is ringing. The main street is wide awake: a man leans at a corner, motionless, smoking. A woman stands at an open doorway, looking at the morning. A large pig crosses the road slowly, and enters a cottage. The school bell still rings....

While on contract to Gainsborough Pictures, 'I want to write the first original film operetta', wrote Dylan Thomas. 'Sidney's carte blanche as to freedom of fancy, non-naturalistic dialogue, song, music etc. is enormously encouraging' he added in a letter of 27 July 1948 about *Me and My Bike*, of which he completed only the opening sequence. But again it is a path to the late prose, for the script has songs in character with the various personalities as in *Under Milk Wood*, including one when 'Augustus and Georgina are on the lawn playing badminton and singing....

> Oh what a shuttle for
> Battlecock and shuttledoor!
> Oh what a battlecock!
> Back and fore.'

Georgina sings also melancholy songs for an absent lover; while in another scene 'through the open schoolroom windows, we hear the voices of the children reciting the alphabet', horse-racing references apt here, but a dramatic device later developed in the children's voices in *Under Milk Wood*:

> A for Ascot
> B for Bangor
> C for Caesarwitch
> D for Derby
> E for Epsom
> G for Galway races
> H for HORSE

The publication of *Me and My Bike* is accompanied by amusing and vivid illustrations, which is a feature of editions of Thomas's prose in recent years; for there are several illustrated versions of such popular tales as 'The Outing' and 'A Child's Christmas in Wales', and stories from *Portrait of the Artist as a Young Dog* published with illustrations include 'A Visit to Grandpa's', 'The Peaches', and 'Extraordinary Little Cough' among others. This is due to the strong visual appeal of his stories, with their rich flow of comic incidents and fantasy, as well as such poignant, dramatic episodes as his grandfather Dai Thomas standing on Carmarthen bridge with his black bag and red waistcoat, which closes 'A Visit to Grandpa's'. Similarly arresting is the closing scene of 'Extraordinary Little Cough' where George Hooping 'was lying fast alseep in the deep grass and his hair was touching the flames'. The appeal of several of the stories and broadcasts to children, and their use in schools, have also prompted these illustrated editions. Interestingly, too, critical writing on Thomas has developed a strong visual interest, due to the increasing awareness of the importance of place, and particularly his Welsh background, in his poetry, an approach initiated by Bill Read and Rollie McKenna and that I extended in *Welsh Dylan*, for it certainly helps the understanding of his poetry. And while Dylan and his famous scenes seem now to have been extensively photographed, Ceri Richards's illustrations of poetic themes in *Collected Poems* early on focused the haunting and mysterious role of nature, especially plants and animals, in the work. Surprisingly perhaps, Richards met Thomas only once. Looking at some of these illustrations when I met Ceri Richards in 1956, it was immediately apparent he shared Thomas's concerns with the cycle of Nature. Some of the drawings are reproduced in *Drawings to Poems by Dylan Thomas* (Enitharmon, 1980) and also in Roberto Sanesi's *Nella Coscia Del Gigante Bianco*. Especially notable are the fiery taloned hawk and fishing heron in 'Over Sir John's hill'; the 'Fern Hill' horses and farm-bearing owls; the

natural life of land, sea, and air that illustrates the opening
verses of 'Author's Prologue'; and the blown birds of
'Especially when the October wind'. The darker, more
obscure and more complex responses to such poems as 'The
force that through the green fuse drives the flower', with the
skull snug in the tree trunk among falling leaves and
flowers, and the crowded insects, birds, clouds, stars, fish
and windblown blossoms of 'Here in this Spring' uniquely
catch the conflated pantheism of the early verse. Undoubtedly Richards is an original, instinctive illuminator
of the character of nature in both early and later poetry, the
ubiquitous skull paradoxically one of the rites of passage in
the explosive energy of Thomas's pantheistic progress.

## III

A fascinating instance of the way in which seemingly
marginal professional commitments influenced Thomas's
development occurs in his poetry. In January 1942 he wrote
a linked sequence of verses, titled 'A Dream of Winter', as
captions to eight photographs of winter scenes. It opens:

Very often on winter nights the halfshaped moonlight sees
Men through a window of leaves and lashes marking gliding
Into the grave an owl-tongued childhood of birds and cold trees,

Or drowned beyond water in the sleepers' fish-trodden churches
Watching the cry of the sea as snow flies sparkling, riding,
The ice lies down shining, the sandgrains skate on the beaches.

Written probably at the end of 1941, these lines show the
loosening and opening up, both structurally and metaphorically, that led to the lyrical expansiveness of such verse as
'Poem in October', finished in 1944 but, Thomas significantly wrote to Vernon Watkins, 'contemplated for three
years'. 'A Dream of Winter' signals, I think, the later
pastoral mode. For language, feeling and rhythm recall
moments in 'Over Sir John's hill' ('windows of dusk and
water', 'a hoot owl/Hollows in the looted elms'), 'Poem on
his birthday' ('small fishes glide/Through . . . drowned/Ship

towns', 'This sandgrain day....') as well as 'A Winter's
Tale', rather than what he was writing in 1941. The
following lines of his response to a photograph of men in
snow-bound wastes are again resonant of his later style:

> And men may sleep a milkwhite path through
>     the chill, struck still waves
> Or walk on thunder and air in the frozen,
>     birdless wood....

while a London wharf setting in winter evokes the images
'The Ark drifts on the cobbles, the darkness sails in a fleet'.
A climbing scene in seemingly Alpine winter snows certainly
anticipates themes and images of his later snow-inspired
'A Winter's Tale':

> the snow-exploded hill
> Where the caverns hide the snowbull's ivory splinter,
> Fossil spire of the sea-boned seal, iceprint of pterodactyl.
> (*The Doctor and the Devils and other Scripts*, pp. 207–8)

Bill Brandt, who photographed the London scenes here
and was later to take the now famous photograph of Dylan
and Caitlin in their Chelsea flat, also for the popular war-
time numbers of *Lilliput*, wrote aptly that 'he (Dylan
Thomas) likes life at first hand, parodying it as he goes
along, dipping his pen in bars, suburbs, slums, and the
vitals of his native Wales, to which he owes so much' (*The
Bedside Lilliput*, p. 99). This valuably focuses Thomas's
openness and spontaneous response to the world around
him, whether in Wales, London, or his travels in America,
Italy, and Persia. Remembered later, he called such impressions 'the crumbs of one man's year', the title of the
broadcast (1946) that shaped such chance encounters –
though always of course looking back. Here he recalls an
August afternoon walking along a riverbank, a Guy
Fawkes' night, reflections on boarding a London bus on a
spring morning, or a passing moment on a 'street near
Waterloo station where a small boy, wearing cut-down
khaki and a steel helmet, pushed a pram full of firewood
and shouted, in a dispassionate voice, after each passer-by:

'Where's your tail?'. Evidently Thomas always 'felt a curious kinship for the despised and rejected. He collected their histories, their stories, their bits of information, as other men collected money' (A. T. Barker, *Esquire*, December 1957, p. 205). Not only were such tales and crumbs of experience from the bleaker edges of life a writer's treasure, but undoubtedly the poet, with his defiantly precarious lifestyle financially and materially, had a quick sympathy and some identification with such outsiders. Another unexpected side of Dylan is evident in the fact that he not only turned up at a meeting for the 'Author's World Peace Appeal' but 'dominated the discussion and all his amendments were agreed to', as Lindsay writes (*Meetings with Poets*, p. 38), noting that he appealed against committee jargon and for emotionally-direct statements. Typically, however, Dylan was to parody such a meeting in a letter to John Davenport, ending the letter by referring to a new poem as 'a kind of colloquial Lycidas set in the Rhondda valley'.

As in his broadcast talks, commissioned items however seemingly marginal to his main work at the time, both drew on his instinctive powers as a writer and promoted new paths. Relatedly, taking part in a symposium on films within days of his final collapse in New York, his contribution was notable for its experience and good sense, unlike the jargon and preposterous intellectualism of some of the other contributors, as he spoke of poetry in film:

> Now, this is a bit of poetry ... somebody coming down some murderous dark, dark, silent street, apart from the piano playing. Or it might have been a little moment when Laurel and Hardy were failing to get a piano up or down a flight of stairs. That always seemed to me the poetry – when those moments came.... I'm not at all sure that I want such a thing myself, as a poetic film.... I like stories, you know, I like to see something going on. I think the poet should establish a scenario and a commentary that would do that as well.

(Quoted in *Poetry and Film*, Gotham Book Mart, 1972).

With similar common sense, professionalism, and the knowledge that comes from practice as poet and reader rather than literary theorist, he replied to a student's query about whether the American new critics had stimulated an interest in poetry: 'I can "understand" poetry, but not the New Criticism, which seems to me to have all the obscurity for which modern poetry is condemned – and none of the occasional magic, none.' Again he has set down the traditional poet's defence of the art he practises. In a following question his reply to the flattering and over-simplified 'Have you in mind any large epic work?' is the great poet's humorous, lucid but true response, tempered by long wrestling with his 'craft or sullen art':

> Yes. But grandiose schemes are built in order that they may be dropped. If you have in mind the pattern of a great poem which one day you hope to write you will probably – as most Irish writers do – talk about it, in surprising detail, to barmen and other writers afflicted similarly – and of course never write it. But again, the weight of the idea of the great unwritten poem may help you in constructing some sunny and miserable love lyrics which possibly can be of deeper depth, and weight than all the unwritten greatness.

> (*Occident*, Spring 1952, University of California, p. 5.)

Such introductory comments were as arresting as his readings, the critical intelligence one would expect in a great poet usually hidden behind the mask of comedy and parody the poet wore not only as self-critic but as shield against academic pedantry, what he called 'earnest company' in his talk at the Massachusetts Institute of Technology, Boston, in 1952. He defends his dislike of explaining the meaning of his poems humorously but in words that point to their vigour and adolescent self-absorbed intensity:

> I couldn't ... say much if anything about what the poems might mean. In a few cases, of course, I didn't know myself – though that is true, I hope, only of certain of my earliest published poems, explosive outbursts of a boily boy in love

with the shape and sound of words, death, unknown love, and
the shadows on his pillow.

('I am Going to Read Aloud', London Magazine,<br>September, 1956, p. 15)

Such 'Introductions' were seemingly carefully prepared, so
exact is the choice of word – as the later singular and
startlingly true adjective in 'poems about . . . the jussive
grave'. Likewise with witty and graphic turn of phrase and
image Thomas humorously dismissed his youthful 'endless
imitations, though I never at the time of writing thought
them to be imitations but rather colossally original, things
unheard of, like eggs laid by tigers'. Crucially, he described
his writing as 'always experimental' and celebrated, too, his
boyhood pleasure in 'words, words, words . . . each of which
seemed alive forever in its own delight and glory and right'.
This Introduction entertains also with literary jokes, stories,
and dramatic fantasy, though Thomas before reading is
careful to avow to his College audience that 'all that matters
about poetry is the enjoyment of it, however tragic it may be.'
   In a 1949 broadcast talk, remembering his daily train
journeys from Oxford to London for his B.B.C. work,
Thomas offers vignettes of his fellow-travellers, barbed with
mockery and parody, as he watches from the 'tumbler-
circled counter in the bellying buffet-car':

> . . . all about me, chastely dropping, with gloved and mincing,
> just-so fingers, saccharine tablets into their cups of stewed
> Thames-water, or poising their cigarette-holders like blow-
> pipes, or daintily raising, the little finger crooked, a currant
> bun to the snapping flash of their long, strong teeth, tall and
> terrible women neighed: women inaccessible as goat crags,
> nowhere, on all this smacked and blossoming earth, at home
> except on lofty, cold bicycles with baskets at the front full of
> lettuce, library books and starchless bread, aloofly scything
> along the High, the wind never raising their sensible skirts, and
> their knitted pastel stockings full of old hockeymuscles.

(Quoted in *Fitzgibbon: The Life of Dylan Thomas*, pp. 340–1).

Satire blends with high comedy, Thomas obviously enjoying himself, parodying the life he sees as he moves along
the Oxford streets or London-bound train. Humorously,
too, he turns on the 'tiny, dry, egghead dons, smelling of
water-biscuit with finickety lips and dolls' bowties like
butterflies poisoned and pinned, [who] solved the cross-
word puzzles behind their octagonal glasses and smirked
their coffee up'. Nor has Thomas's burlesque finished with
the Oxford dons as he lampoons the 'gaunt and hairy horn-
rimmed lecturers in French who tapped their Gaulloise on
their Sartre and saw, with disdain, the pretty gasworks
ripple by ... red Reading fly by like a biscuit: they were
bent on an existentialist spree'.

Written for a broadcast from Scotland soon after his
return to live in Laugharne and titled 'Living in Wales',
Thomas's ridicule and jibes are fiercest at the expense of an
English snobbery he disliked. In needling and sharp satire
he relates how he was tired of 'living among strangers in a
dark and savage country whose ... tribal rites I shall never
understand, ... hearing, everywhere, the snobcalls, the
prigchants, the mating cries'. He laments 'the periodic
sacrifices of the young' and how he 'wanted to sit no longer
... in that narrow-vowelled jungle, alone as it seemed, by
my log fire — (a bright light keeps the beasts at bay) —
rolling the word Wales round my tongue like a gobstopper
of magical properties'. Speaking of Wales the tone now
becomes one of sentiment, nostalgia and comic fantasy,
unlike the young dog's Welsh-baiting satire of earlier years,
as he evokes 'the Welsh sea whose fish are great Liberals,
fond of laverbread and broth, and who always, on Sundays,
attend their green and watery chapels'. In America in 1952
Dylan Thomas revealingly declared, when asked did he
care less and less about prose, 'No, as you grow older they
are more and more separate is what you feel. When you are
young you are liable to write this bastard thing, a prose-
poetry. When you get a bit older you find they get
separated, and prose becomes more clean and spare' (*Casebook*, p. 196).

## IV

Finally, it cannot be too much emphasised that Laugharne always provided the safe womb for the poet, with its homely routines, the daily care of family and steadfast friends, morning and evening visits to the pub, a matter of gossip, beer, cards, and the Saturday night sing-song; so different from the exiled loneliness of America that led to despair and Bourbon. Conversations with Vernon Watkins in the middle fifties, with Caitlin and Mrs D. J. Thomas at the Boat House, as well as Mr and Mrs Richards at the Cross Inn, provided me with insights into Thomas's settled life there that still illumine. Min Lewis in her 1967 book *Laugharne and Dylan Thomas* confirms much of this picture, despite occasional sentimentality, with its description of Dylan in his 'unshapely baggy trousers' walking along the main street, never indicating he was a poet but his shy manner belying sympathetic yet shrewd observation of the locals. Very Welsh, too, and thereby how true they ring, are the reported comments, like that of Annie Jeremy, landlady of the 'Farmers Arms' that 'he only drank beer' and 'rarely spoke much and was always respectful' (p. 63) or that of Carl Eynon, publican as well as butcher who kept the 'Butcher's Arms' in nearby St Clear's, that 'he was a quiet likeable man who never caused trouble' – a name remembered for 'Butcher Beynon'. I too recall landlord Phil Richards's comment, 'Dylan was not the drinker people thought he was' though 'he didn't know the value of money' (p. 102). For when Dylan had money he readily spent it on others. Bertha Williams, who helped out in Sea View in pre-war days, remembered beer and stout, but no spirits, relates Min Lewis, and drinking friends were locals like Johnny Holloway, a notable gossip it seems, and Billy Williams who provided the taxi service there. Despite the tedium of winter months, it was a safe, small, friendly, feisty world. I offer this scenario since it's a cameo of Laugharne now gone, but one that tells us much of Dylan's last years as poet and dramatist. Not that Dylan Thomas ever forgot his beginnings, for in his introduction to the reading in Massachusetts in 1952 he recalled that 'Naturally, my early poems and stories, two sides of an unresolved argument, came out of a person who came willy-nilly out of one particular atmosphere and environment.' That atmosphere and environment was of course Swansea and West Wales. But that is where this book begins.

J. A.

# CHAPTER ONE

# THE WELSH BACKGROUND

I

'ONE: I am a Welshman; two: I am a drunkard; three: I am a lover of the human race, especially of women.'[1] This concise, humorous, and not untruthful account of himself was given by Dylan Thomas to an audience in Rome in 1947. It shows that he was aware of the extent to which his temperament and his imagination were the products of his Welsh environment.

With this remark we may compare two earlier statements made by Thomas: first,

I hold a beast, an angel, and a madman in me, and my enquiry is as to their working, and my problem is their subjugation and victory, downthrow and upheaval, and my effort is their self-expression;[1]

second,

Poetry, recording the stripping of the individual darkness, must inevitably cast light upon what has been hidden for too long, and, by so doing, make clean the naked exposure. Freud cast light on a little darkness he had exposed. Benefiting by the sight of the light and the knowledge of the hidden nakedness, poetry must drag further into the clean nakedness of light more even of the hidden causes than Freud could realize.[2]

The tone and substance are apocalyptic, self-conscious and rhetorical, showing the impact of surrealism and Freudian psychology on a young mind. But they represent attitudes the poet was to outgrow. Dylan Thomas grew 'from dragon's tooth to druid in his own land'.[3] The movement in his poetry was from a clinical towards a religious purpose.

Writing under the influence of early attitudes, Thomas often dissipated his prodigious energy. His work was too diffuse, and his imagination frequently lacked direction. With an increase in craftsmanship, a growing sense of purpose and dedication as a poet, came a widening, and at the same time a greater control, of theme and form. There is an extension of sympathy and understanding; the use of Christian myth and symbol; the emergence of a poetry of vision. But the potentiality of this development was present in his early work. The achievement represented by *Collected Poems* and *Under Milk Wood* indicates that Thomas, with an increasing sureness of instinct, came to make the best use of his poetic talent.

The progress of a writer depends, however, not only upon his own canalization of his energies, but also upon the prevailing climate of influence and taste. Thomas began publishing in the thirties, but from the beginning he was neither a political nor an intellectual poet. The first impact of *18 Poems* and, two years later, of *Twenty-five Poems*, lay in their originality: they were unlike any other poetry written in English at the time. Certainly there were few affinities with such poets as Auden, Spender, and Empson. His poetry was the product of a strongly individual imagination fostered by ways of thought and feeling Welsh in origin.

The distinctive characteristics of Thomas's work are its lyrical quality, its strict formal control, a romantic conception of the poet's function, and a religious attitude to experience. These are characteristics shared by other Anglo-Welsh writers. They were not qualities particularly current among English writers of the thirties. If we remember the difference between Thomas's use of Christian thought and symbol and T. S. Eliot's we need hardly seek any relationship there. Thomas's ideas derived from a different tradition. 'Religion, such as he knew it', writes Karl Shapiro, 'was direct and natural; the symbolism of religion, as he uses it, is poetry, direct knowledge. Religion is not to be used: it is simply part of life, part of himself; it is like a tree; take it or leave it, it is there'.[4] That is, it was part of the man; a way of feeling he inherited rather than acquired. The religious element in Thomas's poetry is the key to its correct interpretation. It was the most important result of Welsh influence. 'When he said he was a Puritan he was not believed; but it really was true.'[5] This fact is central to a full understanding of his work, for Puritanism had long directed Welsh life and thought. Its influence, for better or worse, was inescapable.

## II

The Welsh influence was present in three forms. First and foremost, there was the direct and inevitable influence of a particular community with particular traditions. Secondly, there was the influence of other Welshmen writing in English. These Anglo-Welsh writers helped to create a national consciousness, the sense of a life being lived that was peculiar to Wales: with them Thomas discovered a community of ideas and outlook. The third influence present in his environment was the tradition of culture existing in and through the Welsh language. Since he knew no Welsh this influence came through the two channels already mentioned: contact with Welsh-speaking relatives and friends, and through translations of Welsh poetry and prose.

As Geoffrey Moore writes in an article viewing the poet's work against his Welsh environment:

The national feeling engendered by so many hundreds of years of Welsh speaking survives now without the actual bond of language. The harp of Wales sounds in the ears of Welshmen whether they are archdruids from Bangor or boyos from the back streets of Cardiff. Without being hopelessly mystical about race, one can with some confidence assert that both it and environment have an effect on the nature of a people and the art that springs from them . . . the spirit of place and of country is an inescapable influence. To this degree, and to the degree that Dylan Thomas *opened himself* to the scenes and people and manners of the place in which he was born, it is meaningful to talk about the Welsh quality of his work.[6]

Welsh influence is, inevitably, present in his earliest work, but he was then less aware of it as such. It was when Thomas for the first time moved away from Wales that he began to see its life and traditions in perspective, and realized how they differed from the life and traditions of England. What was more important, he became aware of himself as belonging to this native culture, a culture which was becoming increasingly related to that of England but inescapably of different origin. His parents spoke Welsh, but he himself, though not Welsh-speaking, knew as much Welsh as do most of the inhabitants of South Wales. He was familiar with the more common phrases in use and well acquainted with the sound and verbal music of the Welsh tongue.

In his Note to the *Collected Poems* Thomas wrote:

I read somewhere of a shepherd who, when asked why he made, from within fairy rings, ritual observances to the moon to protect his flocks, replied: 'I'd be a damn' fool if I didn't!' These poems, with all their crudities, doubts, and confusions, are written for the love of Man and in praise of God, and I'd be a damn' fool if they weren't.

There is a bardic ring about this statement. Thomas is claiming a high function for the poet, though as usual there is a 'dog among the fairies' mocking wisdom, which, in the light of such apocalyptic and romantic claims, is a defensive irony. Frequently in his later poems he assumes the rôle of prophet, of a person mediating, in his art, between man and God. This is so, for example, in 'Author's Prologue' to the *Collected Poems*, 'Over Sir John's hill', and 'Poem on his birthday'. The poet here is a man endowed with special wisdom. In his statements about his work Thomas was very careful to support this myth already created in the poetry. This high estimation of the poet's place and function derives from specific traditions of Welsh life and thought. 'For an ancient Wales or Ireland a poet was not merely a professional verse-writer: he was acknowledged to exercise extraordinary spiritual power'[7]. A. G. Prys-Jones writes:

These influences had always been in his environment. . . . No one who has read his poems or heard him declaim them can fail to recognize his bardic affinities—or the racial sources of his headlong rhetoric, his passionate intensity, his powerful imaginative strength and his mystical, religious vision. In one very real sense, he belonged to the company of the great pulpit orators of Wales who were often bards . . .[8]

To this tradition can be attributed, in part, Thomas's confidence in his romantic and apocalyptic manner. General cultural movements such as surrealism and Freudian theories of art had, at best, clinical rather than religious or moral pretensions. It was his Welsh environment which offered a background of thought and culture fostering belief in the more primitive, mystical, and romantic conception of the poet.

### III

The Welsh eisteddfod, in its present form, was first established in 1789. There was also at that time a renewed interest in the religion of nature and in the cults of the druids. Iolo Morganwg, who sought to prove that these traditions had continued unbroken since druidical times in his native shire of Glamorgan, elaborated a ritual which purported to belong to the druids. On 21 June 1792 these fabrications were put into practice when he held the first *gorsedd* or esoteric coterie of bards, and they have been part of the eisteddfod programme ever since.[9] Therefore from this time in particular, due to the addition of allegedly primitive rites to the eisteddfod ceremony, certain mystical and recondite powers were attributed to the bard. Such ideas would obviously please the romantic imagination, but it must be remembered that the discipline of Welsh bardic poetry is among the strictest in any known literature. It was written in elaborate metres, and continues to be to the present day. Herein lies the paradox of the bardic tradition. The exuberance of the bardic personality, the liking for ceremony and elaborate ritual, co-exist with a most craftsmanlike devotion to composition. The picture of himself that Thomas gave to his public presents an interesting and not, I think, un-related parallel. There was on the one hand the flamboyant, larger-than-life part he played to the world; and on the other the painstaking pattern and discipline in his verse, which, during his life-time, generally passed unnoticed.

Another important feature of old Welsh poetry is an awareness of the dual nature of reality, of unity in disunity, of the simultaneity of life and death, of time as an eternal moment rather than as something with a separate past and future. The basis of this is a sense of paradox, or, in slightly different terms, a paradoxical conception of existence. Gwyn Williams, in the Foreword to his collection of early Welsh poetry, writes:

> I have entitled this book *The Burning Tree* to suggest an out-standing mood of the Welsh poet, the awareness at the same time of contrary seasons and passions, a mood in which the poet brings into one phrase the force of love and war, of summer and winter, of holy sacrament and adulterous love.

Matthew Arnold in his *Study of Celtic Literature* notes a passage from the *Mabinogion* as an instance of what he calls Celtic magic. 'And they saw a tall tree by the side of the river, one half of which was in flames from the root to the top, and the other half was green and in full leaf.' It was enough for Arnold to recognize this as magic, distinguishing it from the radiant, uncomplicated Greek way of handling nature, without prying into the mechanics of the image. Coleridge might have helped him here, for this Celtic tree is a hitherto unapprehended relation of things, an integration of spring and autumn such as Spenser expressed in a more English way and at greater length in the stanza beginning:

> There is continuall Spring, and harvest there
> Continuall, both meeting at one tyme . . .
> (*Faerie Queene* III. xlii)

A similarly startling juxtaposition of the unexpected occurs in Keats's phrase 'fairy lands forlorn', which Arnold also quotes and in which he finds the very same note struck. . . . It is the suddenness and success of this linking of the previously held to be incongruous that makes metaphysical poetry and distinguishes Dafydd ap Gwilym from Chaucer, John Donne from Ben Jonson, Dylan Thomas from W. H. Auden.

This introduces an important aspect of Thomas's poetry. A sense of paradox and, derived from this, a liking for the violent yoking of discordant images, a natural tendency to think of things in terms of their opposites, are characteristics of his early work. They direct his method of composition, for it must be remembered that his techniques were the result of a specific attitude to experience. This is shown in some detail in Chapter IV. Likewise, the art of composition in Welsh poetry owes much to this apprehension of the duality of existence. The poem itself tends to be a pattern of the experience, but given without a narrative design. Development of 'meaning' in the poem is concentric rather than linear. The relationship between the parts is total rather than consecutive, as in Thomas's 'Author's Prologue', 'Fern Hill', and 'Poem in October'. It is a whole experience, without actual end or beginning. Since the development of the poem depends to a lesser degree than is usual upon narrative outline or consecutive development of the thought, a greater emphasis is thrown upon formal qualities. The art depends upon a technical rather than intellectual discipline. There is extensive and subtle use of sound and rhythm; repetition of image, rhythm, and phrase; and a frequent use of parallel constructions. Emphasis on formal control often seems a substitute for intellectual application. Thomas, similarly, builds up his poems from an elaborate sound-structure, the basis of which is the stanza form. Such elaborate use of the stanza as he makes in 'Poem in October' and 'Fern Hill' is an example of his technical innovation as a poet. He was always as meticulously attentive to the sound of the words as to their meaning. There is evidence of this in his reviews of other poets.

I have stressed the importance of sound in Welsh poetry, and the consequent use of an elaborate prosody, but it must be remembered that this high estimation of the music of the verse does not preclude profundity or significance of content. It has few affinities with Swinburnian rhetoric. Thomas Parry in his *History of Welsh Literature* observed:

It is important here to recall the critical standpoint which determined Welsh poetry down to the end of the eighteenth century . . . *That standpoint is that sound is as important as sense; that metre and* cynghanedd, *the whole framework of verse, are as much a part of the aesthetic effect as what is said.** . . . The tendency of modern criticism has been to consider primarily the thought expressed in a poem; as for the rhythm, the rhymes, the alliteration, they are desirable no doubt but are regarded as an adornment of the verse. . . .[10]

Parry adds in a footnote:

This paragraph is so vital to a proper appreciation, and even to any real understanding, of Welsh bardic poetry that I have ventured to italicize the above sentence.* It is worth mentioning that Welsh criticism distinguishes *cerdd dafod* ('tongue song', i.e. poetry) and *cerdd dant* ('string song', i.e. music). Both are *cerdd,* song.[10]

The word *cynghanedd* means harmony, and in poetry is a means of giving pattern to a line by the echoing of sounds, consonantal and vowel. There are three main divisions of *cynghanedd: cynghanedd gytsain* consists of multiple alliteration; *cynghanedd sain* has alliteration and rhyme within the line; and *cynghanedd lusg* has internal rhyme only. An instance of *cynghanedd sain* in English would be: 'The road with its load of lads', where 'road' rhymes with 'load', and the 'l' of 'load' is repeated in 'lads'.[11]

The critic, when documenting the metrical patterns in Welsh poetry, approaches them from the outside. It would be misleading to think of the poet as working in a like manner. The bards were trained over a long period to use complex verbal patterns of sound and meaning. Hence it probably became an instinctive way of shaping their thought and feeling. It would be wrong to think of them labouring consciously for every alliteration, every thread in the pattern. Obviously the words, with their appropriate metrical relationships, often came unconsciously to the poet. Then he finished the pattern and co-ordinated the metrics of the stanza. Sound and image begin as an instinctive, natural impulse and it is only in the final organization of the parts that rational control enters. The poet's knowledge of the patterns of composition would, to some extent, subconsciously direct his writing. It is necessary to appreciate this fact in order to see Thomas's relationship to the Welsh metrical tradition in its right perspective. Obviously a rhythm, a sequence of sounds—such as 'young and easy', 'Adam and maiden', 'green and golden' from 'Fern Hill'— came to him separately, as a number of images might come. These Thomas builds into a longer sequence of verbal patterns (a whole poem) by conscious craftsmanship. Having begun with one rhythm he modifies it, starts another, goes back to the first, forming them into a pattern of sounds. I think it probable that in consciously organizing this structure of sound, he was aware of precedent for his patterns in Welsh poetry. The analysis of the sound-structure of 'Fern Hill' in Chapter IX shows how Thomas employs some of the techniques peculiar to Welsh prosody. In the latter there is a more elaborate and organic sound-structure than is usual in English poetry. Gwyn Jones considers Thomas to be 'Welsh in the cunning complexity of his metres, not only in the loose *cynghanedd*, the chime of consonants and pealing vowels, but in the relentless discipline of his verse.'[12]

In his essay on Welsh literature Matthew Arnold notes the emphasis on technique in Welsh verse:

the true art, the *architectonicé* which shapes great works, such as the *Agamemnon* or the *Divine Comedy*, comes only after a steady, deep-searching survey, a firm conception of the facts of human life, which the Celt has not patience for. So he runs off into technic, where he employs the utmost elaboration, and attains astonishing skill; but in the contents of his poetry you have only so much interpretation of the world as the first dash of a quick, strong perception, and then sentiment, infinite sentiment, can bring you.[13]

This is a censure which could be applied equally to twentieth-century Anglo-Welsh poetry and prose, with the possible exception of Thomas's own, where mastery of technique became increasingly allied to imaginative vision.

As a consequence of this technical dexterity, linked to a

quick and strong perception, the distinctive quality of Welsh
poetry is style. This aspect of Welsh literature Matthew
Arnold also commented upon:

> This something is *style,* and the Celts certainly have it in
> a wonderful measure. Style is the most striking quality of their
> poetry . . . by throwing all its force into style, by bending language
> at any rate to its will, and expressing the ideas it has with unsur-
> passable intensity, elevation, and effect.[14]

The success of Thomas's work is also primarily one of style:
his language is vigorous and exciting; his ideas impress
because of the intensity and elevation with which they are
expressed. From the beginning his genius lay more in
stylistic than intellectual originality. The ideas informing
his work are sometimes few and repetitive, but it is the force
and subtlety with which they are expressed that is remarkable. Likewise, since one of the distinctive qualities of
Thomas's poetry is its emphasis on technique, his development as a poet is characterized, in particular, by an increasing technical craftsmanship. The consummate artistry of the
later poems is in the tradition, whether by accident or design,
of Welsh verse.

IV

Welsh Nonconformity, since it stressed the importance of
'personal salvation' and was concerned with the personal
relationship between man, as an individual, and God,
created a climate of intense and introspective religious
fervour. It also encouraged the reading of the Bible. Two
important characteristics of Welsh life at the beginning of
the twentieth century were therefore determined: the
presence of an articulate, religious people; and in them the
existence of an introspective, Puritan and, at its most fertile,
divided conscience. The Bible is a most important influence
in Anglo-Welsh writing, and is the source of a great part
of Thomas's imagery. Likewise the Nonconformist ethic,
in its concern with the individual conscience, sin and

salvation, provides the moral tension that characterizes his work.

The popularity of the new religious movement was also due, undoubtedly, to its emotional appeal. The preaching festivals, the frequent impassioned revivals, and the great feasts of hymn-singing provided an emotional and passionate people with the excitement and inspiration that their hard lives otherwise denied them. Welsh hymn singing possessed the *hiraeth*, the other-worldly aspiration of an ancient race. Geraint Goodwin, in his novel, *The Heyday in the Blood*, has evoked the strange, yearning, overpowering emotion at the heart of Welsh hymn-singing:

> And then, like the wind gathering in a howl, came the slow, unearthly cadences of a hymn; it began, slow, inevitable, gathering strength just as the wind; as wild and pitiless as the wind. It had no place, like the wind. It began and it ended, but it gave nothing. It went in a whine, in fury, overhead, to the unreachable places. The human voice that had gone into it had become lost; the hymn had absorbed it, had taken it as the earth takes in its own growth. The hymn was beyond the choir, . . . beyond them all. It was like some dark, clouded flame, leaping up in its sombre beauty, remote and pure.[15]

The solitariness and the passion of Welsh hymnology are born of, and answer, a profound need in the Welsh character. One is reminded of Caitlin Thomas's comment on a service held after her husband's death:

> I shall never forget, after that futile church service: a mealy-mouthed compromise between literary preciosity and the overriding fear of making fools of themselves by too much musical pomp and ritual: when Dylan would have obviously preferred the typical blood and thunder Welsh hymns passionately shouted over him.[16]

From the Nonconformist movement came 'the great preachers of Wales, the seasonal preaching congresses reminiscent of bardic meetings, and that singing or chanting eloquence known as *hwyl*.'[17] This is a manner of speech much used by Welsh preachers, both in Welsh and English, and much loved by their congregations. T. Rowland Hughes, the Welsh novelist, has thus defined it:

> In preaching, or extempore prayer, sometimes even in descriptive speech, the speaker, under stress of emotion or deep conviction, instinctively and unconsciously lapses into this form of fervent declaration, which makes an instant appeal to the hearts of Welshmen.[18]

The chapel, while it maintained its control of Wales, shaped the Welsh temperament to a greater extent than the school; and it is not surprising that Anglo-Welsh writers should have found the influence of the pulpit an immediate one. Made sensitive, under its ever-present influence, to the sound of words, such a writer as Thomas found rhythm, incantation, the music of the line (whether in prose or verse) basic aids to expression.

An interesting example of the way in which Nonconformist, radical and popular sympathies in Welsh life tend to unite is found in the career of William Thomas, 1834-79. William Thomas was the brother of Dylan's paternal grandfather. He would seem to be celebrated in Dylan's middle name, Marlais, for he wrote under the name of Gwilym Marles, this being probably an older form of Marlais. Gwilym Marles came from north Carmarthen, as do both sides of Thomas's family, and Marlais is the name of a small river in Carmarthenshire. Gwilym Marles became a Unitarian minister in Cardiganshire, writing both poetry and prose in Welsh. He was especially famous for his radical writings, being a liberal in theology and a radical in politics, and was expelled from his living on account of his radical teaching.

I have outlined some of the traditions of the environment in which Thomas and his contemporaries grew up, and about which they were later to write. Of these eloquent and silver-tongued intruders into English literature, Gwyn Jones has written that 'this was the last generation that paid for emergence with its fathers' sweat and bruises; bible-blest and chapel-haunted, wrestle hard as we can, we stand con-

fessed the last, lost nonconformists of an Age'.[19] The picture
of Thomas as a lost Nonconformist, 'bible-blest and chapel-
haunted', wrestling with an inherited religion, is certainly
closer to the truth than many others that have been offered
of him.

# CHAPTER TWO

# THE INTRUDERS: INFLUENCES and RELATIONSHIPS

I

THE twentieth century has seen the decline of Welsh as the first language of Wales, and increasing numbers of Welshmen today speak only English. The period following the 1914-18 War saw the emergence of Welshmen writing in English, among them Dylan Thomas, who had little in common with English literary movements in the inter-war years. They were a different people, conscious of a different tradition. In his editorial to the first number of the *Welsh Review*, February 1939, Gwyn Jones writes:

It is perhaps the most spectacular manifestation of the mental activity of the district [South Wales] that the last few years have seen the emergence of a group of young writers (young in age or work) who for the first time are interpreting Wales to the outside world. They can be called a school only in the sense that Welsh blood, sometimes thickened to a mongrel brew, flows in their veins. They are as diverse as the land that gave them their rich if ragged heritage, but I believe firmly that they will soon be recognized as the most valuable leaven in English literature since the Irishmen opened insular eyes at the beginning of the century.

These notable intruders include Caradoc Evans, Dylan Thomas, Gwyn Jones, Vernon Watkins, Alun Lewis, R. S. Thomas, Gwyn Thomas, and Glyn Jones. They produce their best work when writing about Wales and the life they have known there. But it is a quality of style—fierce enthusiasm, energy and flexibility—that links and most distinguishes them. Other characteristics are a richness of metaphor, often not as precise or consistent as it might be; a dominantly sensuous, often sensual imagination; a delight in fantasy and the irrational; and a deep, pervading pathos. They begin with the word or phrase rather than the idea: their approach, even in prose, is that of the poet, and they tend to convey their meaning through the medium of the senses. This aptitude for sensory communication, combined with a Welsh inclination to eloquence and a natural tendency to speak in metaphor, can all too easily result in loose and high-flown rhetoric. However, a robust sense of humour and a liking for strict formal control guard against this disposition.

Another feature of Anglo-Welsh writing is that it tends to be subjective, and consequently introspective. It is characterized by permanent romantic attitudes: a posited belief in intuition, in the vitality of strong and passionate emotions, and in the influence of external nature. Its favourite themes are the exploration of childhood, death, and the sexual nature of man. We find also a conscious cultivation of the primitive, and a strong vein of comedy, based on observation of the more humorous aspects of Welsh life. The Anglo-Welsh writer, both in poetry and prose, moved away from interest in the sophisticated and intellectual. Thomas was aware of this tendency among his contemporaries. Stephen Spender, in his review of Thomas's *Collected Poems*, said:

Dylan Thomas represents a romantic revolt against this classicist tendency which has crystallized around the theological views of Eliot and Auden. It is a revolt against more than this, against the Oxford, Cambridge and Harvard intellectualism of much modern poetry in the English language; against the King's English of London and the South, which has become a correct idiom capable of refinements of beauty, but incapable of harsh effects, coarse texture and violent colours.[1]

Thomas wrote: '. . . this is now the clearest, most considered and sympathetic, and, in my opinion, truest review that I have ever seen of my writing. I mean, that your statement and understanding of my aim and method seems to me altogether true.'[2]

In this outline of Welsh influences and relationships in Thomas's work, it is also important to consider certain theological concepts which inform much Anglo-Welsh poetry. These ideas have shaped the religious attitude to experience. In particular, the celebration by the poet of all natural life, animal and vegetal, a celebration expressed usually in sensuous terms, is derived from specific theological concepts. The basis of this attitude is a sense of the unity of all creation, and this identity of all created forms is religious in character. The poet is aware of a sacramental universe in which the common things of life serve to illustrate profound mysteries. Hence all created things, whether blades of grass or sea-waves breaking on to the shore or 'the fishing holy stalking heron', are of themselves holy and are a witness to the Creator.

There is a Hebraic element in the Welsh character— probably the result of much Bible reading—from which stems the belief that everything in the world is, for its own sake, holy. 'They [the Welsh] did not like it when I told them the Welsh would make Hebrews of themselves very soon, if they didn't take to some other book than the Bible', observed Edward Thomas in a letter written from Amman-ford, Carmarthen. Platonic notions of the Idea behind external objects have, it might be claimed, hindered English poetry and English Christianity far too much. In the Hebraic conception of life each object is in itself holy. Each is part of a sacramental whole, not an imitation of some idea. Thus we have the peculiar 'inscape' and 'instress' of Hopkins, who sought the reality of each external object; for things exist and are important as they are, not as images of an ideal form. Hopkins's 'reality' was expressed in sensuous language that attempted to define the physical actuality of the thing. A concept of reality where every natural object contains the divine is obviously congenial to poetic creation. The Welsh character possesses a feeling of awe, a sense of the wonder of creation, to which is allied a sensitivity towards external nature and a sense of pristine innocence. In the formulation of this attitude to reality, contemporary Anglo-Welsh writers, including Dylan Thomas, have been influenced also by the work of Blake. When reading Thomas's poetry one is reminded constantly of Blake's 'For everything that lives is holy, life delights in life'.

The years 1900-36 brought South Wales into the main stream of world protest against poverty, inequality, and industrial materialism. The region produced one of the most intense expressions of revolt against the existing social order. The enthusiasm which had been aroused a few years earlier by the frequent religious revivals (*diwygiad*) was now turned to politics and literature. Gwyn Thomas has eloquently recalled the environment that fostered the South Wales writer in the twenties and thirties:

> Those Rhondda days are, for me, for ever bathed in a brilliant light; the tumult of political enthusiasms, the white-hot oratory of the people's paladins, the festivals of folk singing and hymn singing in the vast chapels, moving groups on the hillsides at night . . . their echoes can still fill my mind with an intense creative excitement. Then the hill-walks across to Llanwonno, or over to the Dimbath, the Beacons to the north, pulling us towards an even wilder solitude than we had ever known; and the Vale of Glamorgan to the South, tempting us to an ordered placidity which it would benefit our souls to cultivate. And between these two poles of attraction, the fermenting disquiet of the Valley streets, ringing with every note of pain and laughter contrived since man's beginning. In that small territory of land and feeling lay the whole world's experience. The years of study and experiment have driven convenient lines of communication through it; they have not enlarged its frontiers nor enriched the texture of its earth.[3]

Dylan Thomas remarked that

> out of the mining valleys of South Wales, there were poets who were beginning to write in a spirit of passionate anger against the inequality of social conditions. They wrote, not of the truths and beauties of the natural world, but of the lies and ugliness of the unnatural system of society under which they worked—or, more

often during the nineteen-twenties and thirties, under which they were not allowed to work.[4]

Poets spoke, Thomas continues,

in ragged angry rhythms, of the Wales *they* knew: the coal-tips, the dole-queues, the stubborn bankrupt villages, the children, scrutting for coal on the slag-heaps, the colliers' shabby allot- ments, the cheap-jack cinema, the whippet races, the disused quarries, the still pit-wheels . . . silicosis, little Moscow up beyond the hills.[5]

He probably had in mind Alun Lewis's poem 'The Moun- tain Over Aberdare' when he wrote this passage.[6]

The Anglo-Welsh writer found in South Wales at this time a background of creative vitality and social ferment. In his own work, however, Thomas was primarily concerned not with political, but with emotional, religious, and sexual man.

## II

To its first readers, Thomas's poetry seemed strange and difficult because they came to it with tastes developed by contemporary literature, and a knowledge of twentieth- century literature offered little aid to its understanding. The language and ideas to be found in Thomas's work had little in common with the imagery and ideas in the work of, say, W. H. Auden, T. S. Eliot or W. B. Yeats. Neither did it derive, to any great extent, from the nineteenth-century romantic poets. 'No poet of the English language had so hoodwinked and confuted his critics. None has ever worn more brilliantly the mask of anarchy to conceal the true face of tradition. . . . The most mistaken of his admirers were those who loved it [the poetry] for its novelty.'[7] The Anglo- Welsh writer A. G. Prys-Jones has suggested where this tradition lies: 'He was far more at home, I think, with Vaughan and Traherne, Blake . . . than with Freud and Marx, Kafka, Joyce and Proust.'[8] Indeed, contemporary Anglo-Welsh writing generally has been influenced by the religious poets of the seventeenth century. Thomas in particular has several important features in common with them: an interest in childhood as a state of innocence and grace; a deep sense of guilt and of separation from God, alternating with moments of vision; a liking for wit and paradox; and the use of Christian imagery and symbolism.

Dylan Thomas, like Donne, speaks with directness and passion on the theme of sex. His work shows the same mingling of sexual and religious themes, which results in a mingling of sexual and religious imagery. In both poets there is an intense consciousness of death. Donne preached a sermon, *Deaths Duell*, in his grave-clothes, and Thomas's poems show a similar obsession with the physical fact of death:

> I sit and watch the worm beneath my nail
> Wearing the quick away.[9]

In the analysis of Thomas's poems we shall find specific sources of theme and image in the work of Donne, and Thomas also is preoccupied with the relationship of divine and sexual love.

An important area of sensibility shared by the Anglo-Welsh poets of the twentieth century and the metaphysical poets of the seventeenth, one alien to the Romantic period, is the religious attitude to experience. This produced a poetry characterized by religious conflict and, on the positive side, religious vision. The religious mysticism in the work of Vaughan, Traherne, or Thomas is very different from the mystical aspiration in the poetry of Wordsworth or Shelley. The keen introspective analysis and extreme subjectivity which the seventeenth-century poets brought into literature is often revealed most satisfyingly in the poetry of religious vision.

The main characteristic of the introspective consciousness, then as today, is a profound sense of division, which reveals itself in various forms. Renan attributed to the Celt a defiance of all that comes from without; an unwillingness to acknowledge the reality of the objective universe. This is apt to express itself in literature by escape from reality into mysticism, longing, or romance. In Donne, Herbert,

Traherne, Vaughan, and Thomas the introspective consciousness is characterized by a deep sense of sin and of
separation from God. Donne's Holy Sonnets, Herbert's
*The Temple*, Thomas's 'Altarwise by owl-light', 'There
was a Saviour', and 'Vision and Prayer', all record the
attempt to heal this separation.

Expression of the sense of separation, however, sometimes
takes a different form, one that is less directly religious.
It is a feeling of distance from the original innocence of
childhood, and a desire to recapture the lost visionary
moments of that time of grace.

> Happy those early dayes! when I
> Shin'd in my Angell-infancy.
> Before I understood this place
> Appointed for my second race . . .
>
> But (ah!) my soul with too much stay
> Is drunk, and staggers in the way.
> Some men a forward motion love,
> But I by backward steps would move,
> And when this dust falls to the urn
> In that state I came return.[10]

Traherne, in his *Centuries of Meditations*, writes of childhood:

All appeared new, and strange at first, inexpressibly rare and
delightful and beautiful. I was a little stranger, which at my
entrance into the world was saluted and surrounded with
innumerable joys. My knowledge was divine. I knew by intuition
those things which since my Apostasy, I collected again by the
highest reason. My very ignorance was advantageous. I seemed
as one brought into the Estate of Innocence. All things were
spotless and pure and glorious: yea, and infinitely mine, and joyful
and precious. I knew not that there were any sins, or complaints
or laws. . . . I saw all in the peace of Eden; Heaven and Earth
did sing my Creator's praises, and could not make more melody
to Adam, than to me. All Time was Eternity, and a perpetual
Sabbath. . . .[11]

In this passage, the sentence 'and Earth did sing my Creator's
praises, and could not make more melody to Adam', sug-

gests that the author has the perception and privilege of the original Adam. Thomas often similarly assumes the identity of Adam or Christ in his poetry and prose. Extreme dependence on the experience of childhood, and the desire to recreate it is a major characteristic of both Anglo-Welsh poetry and prose. In such poems as 'Fern Hill' and 'Poem in October', this theme finds perhaps, in our own day, its most intense and beautiful expression.

III

The Anglo-Welsh poet whose work bears the closest relationship to that of Dylan Thomas is Vernon Watkins. Both have certain bardic qualities: they assume a prophetic rôle, an intuitive knowledge of existence. The eloquent language, religious (but not exclusively Christian) imagery, and rhetorical sweep of the verse, add to this impression of the bardic poet. Vernon Watkins, like W. B. Yeats and Dylan Thomas, reads his poetry aloud in a forceful, chanting manner. The music of the verse is given full value, unlike the fashionable kind of reading satirized by Thomas: 'There is the other reader, of course, who manages, by studious flatness, semi-detachment, and an almost condescending undersaying of his poems, to give the impression that what he really means is: Great things, but my own.'[12]

Linked with this bardic quality there is, in both poets, a fundamentally religious conception of existence. 'In our approach to poetry', writes Vernon Watkins, 'and in our method of composition we were unlike, but in our belief and findings there was a great affinity, and we became close friends.'[13] Where poetic technique is concerned there are, as Watkins claims, important points of difference—though there are, too, some interesting similarities—but undoubtedly Watkins's work had a most important influence on Thomas's development. They first met after the publication of *18 Poems*. From this time each regularly discussed his work with the other, and their close friendship lasted until Thomas's death.

I have said that Thomas came increasingly to think of

himself as a religious poet. It is interesting to find Watkins remarking that

a comparison between this early version [of the poem 'Unluckily for a Death'] which appeared, with two adjectival changes, in *Life and Letters Today* (October 1939) and the poem printed in *Deaths and Entrances* and finally in *Collected Poems* shows that all the changes made in its rewriting were movements away from ironical, and towards religious, statement.[14]

This movement characterizes the development of Thomas's poetry as a whole. Watkins has claimed that both he and Thomas sought a metaphysical truth in their work: for both poets natural observation was significant only in so far as it supported some deeper truth. In the Introduction to his edition of the letters he received from Thomas, Watkins states that his own themes were close to Thomas's, that they

were both religious poets . . . He [Thomas] understood, too, why I could never write a poem dominated by time, as Hardy could. This, in fact, was also true of Dylan, though some critics have mistakenly thought to find such poems in his work. It illustrates our affinity on a deeper level: his poems spoke to me with the voice of metaphysical truth; if we disagreed it was on a metaphysical issue, for natural observation in poetry meant nothing to us without the support of metaphysical truth.[15]

It was Watkins's personality and work which aided Thomas in his search for an expression of faith which escaped the domination of time.

# CHAPTER THREE

# EARLY YEARS

D YLAN MARLAIS THOMAS was born in Swansea in 1914. Dylan is an ancient Welsh name found in the *Mabinogion*:

She was fetched to him; the maiden came in. 'Maiden', said he, 'art thou a maiden?' 'I know not but that I am.' Then he took the magic wand and bent it. 'Step over this,' said he, 'and if thou art a maiden, I shall know.' Then she stepped over the magic wand, and with that step she dropped a fine boy-child with rich yellow hair. The boy uttered a loud cry. . . . 'Why,' said Math son of Mathonwy, 'I will have this one baptized'—of the rich yellow-haired boy. 'The name I will give him is Dylan.'

The boy was baptized, and the moment he was baptized he made for the sea. And there and then, as soon as he came to the sea he received the sea's nature, and swam as well as the best fish in the sea. And for that reason he was called Dylan Eil Ton (Dylan Eil Ton: Sea son of Wave).[1]

It was with a cannily prophetic note that Edward Thomas remarked of Swansea: 'If Wales could produce a poet he should be born in the hills and come here at the age of sixteen. He would have no need of Heaven or Hell.'[2] On another occasion Edward Thomas speaks of Swansea as that 'horrible and sublime town'[2] and observes that 'it is very large, but not, like London, so large as to be incomprehensible as a whole. It is all furnaces, collieries, filth, stench, poverty and extravagant show, the country and the sea at the very edge of it all.'[2] It is a description very similar to Dylan Thomas's: 'I was born in a large Welsh industrial town at the beginning of the Great War: an ugly, lovely town (or so it was, and is, to me) crawling, sprawling, slummed, unplanned, jerry-villa'd, and smug-suburbed by the side of a long and splendid-curving shore. . . .'[3] Both these writers remark upon the close proximity of industry, the countryside, and the sea. Swansea provided an epitome of Welsh life; for it was seaside resort, shopping centre, and scene of rugby and football matches for day-trippers from the surrounding mining valleys.

Dylan Thomas was never a strong boy,[4] and his capacity for getting into trouble was an additional source of worry to his parents. His mother relates, for example, how he fell off a builder's plank and was brought home unconscious, and on another occasion was dropped into a tub of lime by older boys.[5] He also slipped over the banisters in a friend's house and broke his nose. It is apparent that he was a venturesome, happy-go-lucky boy, grubby and curly-haired, full of life and high spirits. Yet from the beginning there was another side to his nature: the physically delicate, dedicated devotee to the art of poetry. 'He was a very sensitive boy', claims Mrs. D. J. Thomas. Due to recurrent illness—he suffered in his teens from a form of paralysis, and had tubercular symptoms that rendered him unfit for National Service in 1939 because of a scarred lung—he spent many months in bed. This gave him more time for reading and he was, from childhood, a voracious reader. He began writing verses when he was eight years old, entered the Grammar School at the age of eleven, and by his early teens had chosen his vocation: he was to be a poet. Academically, however, he was not a success. He regularly appeared near the bottom of his class in terminal reports and he passed no examinations. In one subject only was he interested: English. Mrs. D. J. Thomas recalls a conversation with her son on the subject of higher education:

I said, 'You know, you must try and get in to the University —what are you going to do? Anybody'd think you were a Keats or something.' He looked at me—and he wasn't the cheeky type, he wasn't even a big talker—and he said, 'I'll be as good as

Keats, if not better.' I went to his father and I said, 'I'll never tell him anything again.'[5]

Dylan Thomas's father taught English at Swansea Grammar School, where he was much revered for his enthusiastic and impassioned reading of literature. From the time Dylan could talk his father began to inculcate in him a love of the English language. David Thomas was himself a lover of poetry and had tried in his younger days to write it: he was, it seems, not easily reconciled to his lack of success. Caitlin Thomas speaks of

his father, that most unhappy of all men I have ever met; who did all the spade work of casting off the humble beginnings, bettering himself, assiduously cultivating the arts; and finished up a miserable finicky failure; while passing on to Dylan, on a heaped plate, the fruits of all his years of unrewarding labour.[6]

Dylan Thomas himself was aware of this debt to his father's patient efforts, a fact that J. M. Brinnin has recorded: 'I had learned from Dylan that much of his own early education had been more the result of his father's tutelage than of informed schooling.'[7] He spent much of his time in his father's study, which was particularly rich in its collection of English poetry, and in the evenings there were family readings from Shakespeare's plays and the English poets. By fifteen Thomas was, for his age, a competent critic, with a remarkable knowledge of both contemporary and earlier English poetry. That he was by no means the wild, untutored youth his own accounts of his childhood are apt to suggest, is well illustrated by an article on modern poetry written in 1929, when he was fifteen:

The most important element that characterizes our poetical modernity is freedom—essential and unlimited—freedom of form, of structure, of imagery and of idea. It had its roots in the obscurity of Gerard Manley Hopkins's lyrics, where . . . the language was violated and estranged by the efforts of compressing the already unfamiliar imagery. . . .
The freedom of idea can be found abundantly in any anthology.

Assuming that no subject is an unpoetical subject, the neo-Romanticists (headed by T. S. Eliot, and, in the majority of his moments, by James Joyce) give us their succession of sordid details, their damp despondent atmosphere, and their attraction for the gutter, 'the sawdust restaurants with oyster shells', 'the yellow smoke of streets', and 'cigarettes in corridors, and cocktail smells in bars'. . . .

It is the more recent poetry of to-day that shows the clearest influence of the war. The incoherence caused by anguish and animal horror, and the shrill crudity which is inevitable in poetry produced by such war, are discarded. Instead, we have a more contemplative confusion, a spiritual riot. No poet can find sure ground: he is hunting for it, with the whole earth perturbed and unsettled about him. Today is a transitional period. D. H. Lawrence, the body-worshipper who fears the soul; Edmund Blunden, who has immersed himself in the English countryside; Richard Church, the poet of detached contemplation; Ezra Pound, the experimental mystic, are only laying the foundations of a new art.[8]

Not all the observations are true; but the article as a whole does suggest an unusually knowledgeable grasp of the subject—and this in a person popularly thought of as addicted only to thrillers and cowboy stories. References to Thomas in the school magazine constantly offer the picture of a precocious, essentially serious-minded boy. There is, for example, the remark, under the heading 'Things We Cannot Credit', 'That D.M.T. should mispronounce a word.'[9] During these years, of course, he edited the school magazine.

Swansea was a lively, colourful town, and in his writing Thomas has registered his growing awareness of it:

Never *was* there such a town (I thought) for the smell of fish and chips on Saturday nights; for the Saturday after-noon cinema matinées where we shouted and hissed our threepences away; for the crowds in the streets, with leeks in their pockets, on international nights; for the singing that gushed from the smoky doorways of the pubs in the quarters we never should have visited; for the park, the inexhaustibly ridiculous and mysterious, the bushy Red-Indian-hiding park, where the hunchback sat alone, images of perfection in his head, and 'the groves were blue with sailors'.[10]

The park referred to is Cwmdonkin Park, which bordered Thomas's home. He was familiar with the factories, the chapels—he attended the local Nonconformist chapel as a child—the cinemas, the day excursions from the valleys, the dole-queues of the depression in which he grew up and, of course, the Park, which plays so important a rôle in his imaginative recreations of childhood.

Dylan spent long holidays in these childhood years on the farm in North Carmarthenshire belonging to his aunt, Ann Jones, and grew increasingly attached to the place. It is depicted in the story *The Peaches*, which opens the volume *Portrait of the Artist as a Young Dog*, and his description of the farm kitchen shows this affection:

Then a door at the end of the passage opened; I saw the plates on the shelves, the lighted lamp on the long, oil-clothed table, 'Prepare to Meet Thy God' knitted over the fire-place, the smiling china dogs, the brown-stained settle, the grandmother clock, and I ran into the kitchen and into Annie's arms.[11]

His childhood experiences on the farm became the source of inspiration for much of his later poetry and prose. In *The Peaches* he describes his nervous, boyish reactions as he waits for Uncle Jim (who has gone for a drink) to drive him home to the farm. The story records the perception of a highly-imaginative, sensitive child:

I began to whistle between my teeth, but when I stopped I thought the sound went hissing on behind me. I climbed down from the shaft and stepped close to the half-blind window; a hand clawed up the pane to the tassel of the blind; in the little, packed space between me on the cobbles and the card-players at the table, I could not tell which side of the glass was the hand that dragged the blind down slowly. I was cut from the night by a stained square. A story I had made in the warm, safe island of my bed, with sleepy midnight Swansea flowing and rolling round outside the house, came blowing down to me then with a noise on the cobbles. I remembered the demon in the story, with his wings and hooks, who clung like a bat to my hair as I battled up and down Wales. . . .[12]

I have so far been concerned with the sensitive, self-conscious side of Thomas's youthful personality. Possessing a hypersensitive nature, he soon found the need to acquire an outward assurance, and learned to hide away this vulnerable, private part of himself. He adopted the usual bohemian gestures, drinking, colourful clothes, the rôle of poet and *enfant terrible*. In his personality during these early years there is an instability that was to remain—though more effectively concealed. This imbalance is reflected in his early compositions. What is most noticeable about his contributions to the school magazine is the large amount of parody and humorous verse, which is much superior in quality to his serious poems at this time. Throughout his life Thomas maintained, both in his writing and in his talking, this liking for parody. *Portrait of the Artist as a Young Dog* was conceived as a parody of a familiar literary genre; in his poetry the pun is often a form of defensive parody, while in conversation he was always apt to joke at his own expense, parodying his favourite ideas and techniques. Often he jests at the more bardic, romantic claims in his major poems. The following example of his early parody, entitled *Children's Hour (or Why the B.B.C. Broke Down)*, was written when he was sixteen:

(Aunt Fanny is conducting an excursion into Arcadia. Imagine her voice to be high-pitched, mellow, and very endearing. In private life she is a Mrs. Waterberry, wife of Mr. Wilfred Waterberry, of Waterberry and Waterberry Ltd., whose sterling reputation I need hardly dwell upon.)

A.F.: Shall I transport you into the sylvan realms of Arcady, children, where the spring is twice as long as any other season, and where nymphs and shepherds, to say nothing of the dryads and other woodland denizens who infest the groves, dance, or rather frolic, for their dancing conforms to no ball-room regulations, the whole day through? Take my hand, then—no, not that one, the clean one—and let us drift together down the stream of time into that ageless place of revelry. Come, let us away. (Here several uncles make loud hissing sounds between their teeth, and a small boy, who seems bored with the whole proceedings, bangs a drum.) . . .

Come, children, let us away, after having enjoyed a real spot of Arcadia. (The boy bangs the drum and goes home.) Come, to the studio once more. Many happy returns to John Brown on his seventy-second birthday. Now, Johnnie, dear, there's a present for you in the sink, and another one under the bath. . . .[13]

The boy banging the drum refers, of course, to Dylan Thomas and is a typical example of the way in which he liked to dramatize himself. This is an effective satire on the B.B.C. Children's Hour manner—written, it is well to remember, in 1930. Among his many parodies of modern poetry at this time there is one of W. B. Yeats:

> A farmer's boy came up to me,
> (With a hey diddle diddle
>   The moon is my fiddle,
> And I play on the waves of the sea)[14]

Thomas left school at the age of seventeen, having passed no major examinations. He became a reporter on the *South Wales Evening Post*, a position he held for a year and a half. It was a time of rapid development, for as a reporter his knowledge of life was greatly extended, and during this period he started drinking. His experiences are recorded in *Old Garbo*, the penultimate chapter of *Portrait of the Artist as a Young Dog*. He was, however, an indifferent reporter, and spent most of his days strolling about Swansea, dawdling, arguing the toss with his friends, meeting people. Swansea at this time was a lively centre of artistic activity. Thomas's group of artist friends included the composer, Daniel Jones, and Alfred Janes, the painter. Their endless, adolescent discussions on 'music and poetry and painting and politics, Einstein and Epstein, Stravinsky and Greta Garbo, death and religion' Thomas fondly mocks in his *Return Journey* to the town.[15]

He discovered the pub to be his natural background, the

sounding-board for his wit, the place to meet people and to talk and also to listen, for Thomas was a good listener. He was also developing a sharp eye for provincial foibles, and was beginning to observe people realistically, ruthlessly, with a journalist's accuracy. Swansea was rich in vivid and interesting characters, and Thomas was learning to take full advantage of his environment. In his capacity as journalist he was beginning to turn his gaze outward, away from his own introspective obsessions, and always he was thinking of the stories he was to write:

I made my way through the crowds: the Valley men, up for the football; the country shoppers; the window gazers; the silent, shabby men at the corners of the packed streets, standing in isolation in the rain; the press of mothers and prams; old women in black, brooched dresses carrying frails; smart girls with shining mackintoshes and splashed stockings; little, dandy lascars, bewildered by the weather; business men with wet spats; through a mushroom forest of umbrellas; and all the time I thought of the paragraphs I would never write. I'll put you all in a story by and by.[16]

There are some interesting references in the passage. The word 'frail' is, in this sense, commonly used in this part of South Wales to describe a kind of woven, and very capacious, shopping bag, designed originally to carry fresh fish. They are often known as 'fish frails' and are particularly common in such coastal towns as Swansea. It is important to remember that Swansea was a seaport, and consequently had its dockside area and foreign population. The 'paragraphs' he would never write are, of course, conjectured newspaper articles.

The distinctive, varied life of Wales was leaving its mark on Thomas's experience. Later he was to turn these experiences to his needs as a writer, but for the present he was busy receiving impressions. The 'silent, shabby men at the corners ... standing in isolation in the rain', remind one it was 1931, the bitterest year of the depression in Wales, and though Swansea was no Merthyr, it also had its poverty and unemployment. Augustus John, a close friend in the thirties, wrote that Thomas in these years, 'like so many of his generation, discovered in himself a fellow-feeling for the under-dog'.[17] J. M. Brinnin detected his 'need for emotional identification with the lowest stratum of society', and concluded—correctly, I think—that his socialism had little to do with 'the *realpolitik* of the twentieth century'. Nevertheless, claims Brinnin, although Thomas did not associate himself with the political poets of the thirties, Auden, Spender, MacNeice, and Day Lewis, 'he was actually far more censorious of the *status quo* than any of the other British poets'.[18] Here Brinnin is referring to Thomas's political outlook in later years, but these opinions were rooted in his experiences during the years of depression in Wales. Welsh radicalism, a most important factor in this environment, left its impact upon the young poet. Its traditions were evangelical and liberal, rather than Marxist. Thomas did, in the early thirties, become a member of the Communist Party, but soon detached himself from it. Augustus John, with whom Thomas spent much time at Laugharne in the late thirties, wrote that 'At one time Dylan told me he joined the C.P., but, quite rightly, detached himself on finding that henceforth he would be expected to make his work a medium for propaganda.'[17] However, Thomas retained to the end of his life his left-wing attitude in politics. He was reported in the *Strand* magazine to have said in March 1947: 'One should tolerate the Labour Government because running down Labour eventually brings you alongside the Conservatives, which is the last place you want to be.'

The distressing social conditions were not, however, the only things in his environment that Thomas was beginning to react against. Like so many of his contemporary Anglo-Welsh writers and friends, he was becoming critical of the way in which Nonconformity was maintaining its restrictive influence on Welsh life. It was, indeed, inevitable that he should cross swords with Welsh Puritanism whose code he both mocked and feared. His intense nature, enjoying all the pleasures of life, was alien to its repressive doctrines. In an address to a Scottish Society of Writers in Edinburgh, delivered after he had moved from Wales to London, Thomas gave the reason for his exile:

> I am a Welshman who does not live in his own country, mainly because he still wants to eat and drink, be rigged and roofed, and no Welsh writer can hunt his bread and butter in Wales unless he pulls his forelock to the *Western Mail*, Bethesdas on Sunday, and enters public-houses by the back door, and reads Caradoc Evans only when alone, and by candlelight.[19]

Owing to Nonconformist teaching, 'the drink', as it is called, is still the arch-vice; so much so that deacons and chapel-members must still do their drinking in secret if they wish to be considered 'respectable'. Caradoc Evans was called 'the most hated man in Wales', and on one occasion had the distinction of having his books burned in the public incinerator. Thomas, needless to say, greatly admired his work. Their bitterness, when speaking on the subject of Wales, is shared by many Anglo-Welsh writers. It is due to the fact that those Welshmen who do not speak Welsh, and, what is even more heretical, write about Wales in English, are considered—and often treated—by their Welsh-speaking fellow-countrymen as foreigners irremediably lost to the English, forever beyond the pale. Thomas, in his address, went on to speak of his resentment at being denied his nationality by his own (Welsh-speaking) countrymen:

> Regarded in England as a Welshman (and a waterer of England's milk), and in Wales as an Englishman, I am too unnational to be here at all. I should be living in a small private leper-house in Hereford or Shropshire, one foot in Wales and my vowels in England. Wearing red flannel drawers, a tall witch's hat, and a coracle tiepin, and speaking English so Englishly that I sound like a literate Airedale, who has learnt his a's and e's by correspondence course, piped and shagged and tweeded, but also with a harp, the look of all Sussex in my poached eyes, and a whippet under my waistcoat.[19]

The reference to 'red flannel drawers' and tall black conical hat is a jibe at the traditional Welsh costume. An echo of the severe accusation that opens this address is found in

Thomas's film script, *The Three Weird Sisters*. This film is bitterly resented in Wales, since it dwells on the weaknesses of the Welsh in a manner reminiscent of Caradoc Evans. With a vitriolic bitterness that almost matches Evans's own, Thomas describes the Welshman as having 'a lie in his teeth and a hymn on his lips'.[19]

There was, however, a lighter side to Thomas's intransigent nature, and the desire to shock the orthodox Nonconformist taste is often given a more humorous expression, as in the opening of the story, *Where Taw flows*:

> Young Mr. Thomas was at that moment without employment, but it was understood that he would soon be leaving for London to make a career in Chelsea as a free-lance journalist: he was penniless, and hoped, in a vague way, to live on women.[20]

Marked out by the accusing finger of Welsh Nonconformity, no artist could feel more of a young dog than Dylan Thomas in Swansea; and, though being rebellious and defiant and aiming to shock, there was always an element of guilt lurking behind the bravado:

> The back room of 'The Three Lamps' was full of elderly men. Mr. Farr had not arrived. I leant against the bar, between an alderman and a solicitor, drinking bitter, wishing that my father could see me now and glad, at the same time, that he was visiting Uncle A. in Aberavon. He could not fail to see that I was a boy no longer, nor fail to be angry at the angle of my fag and my hat and the threat of the clutched tankard.[21]

Gwyn Jones has pointed out that Thomas owed to 'chapel-Swansea'

> more than he thought or admitted, both because of and despite the revolt and brisk irreverence he shared with many South Wales writers of his shaken generation. For one thing, Nonconformity made drink and pleasure so devilishly attractive.[22]

Most of the Anglo-Welsh writers rebelled against the severely restricted way of life that orthodox Nonconformity sought to maintain. They were not slow to hold up to ridicule and satire its many weaknesses, but the grip that Nonconformity

had upon these writers was much stronger than they sometimes realized in their youth. There was a racial Puritanism
that had been ingrained in the Welsh character over many
centuries. Even when the orthodox Nonconformist way of
life had been rejected, the Nonconformist conscience
remained. It could not, within the individual, be so easily
placated. The impact of regular attendance at chapel during
childhood, the memories of the preacher's eloquence, the
celebrated Welsh *hwyl*, have left their mark upon the Welsh
character. The Nonconformist tradition had, since the eighteenth century, insisted that each man should himself read
and interpret his Bible. Hence the chapels encouraged argument and dialectic; they urged men and women to think for
themselves rather than receive their beliefs from the minister.
Consequently, most Welshmen had a profound and exact
knowledge of the Bible, and this was, perhaps, an education
in itself.

A peculiar love-hate relationship towards Wales and its
Nonconformist background is characteristic of the Anglo-
Welsh writer. He begins by hating, but ends by loving.
Despite all his attacks on Welsh life and Nonconformity,
Caradoc Evans, not long before he died, said that he would
wish, given his life again, to become a preacher, and that for
two things only would he sacrifice his life: for his wife and
for Wales. There is a similar love-hate relationship in
Thomas's life and work. The quotations from his Edinburgh
address indicate his opposition to the narrower, more
fiercely nationalistic Welsh attitudes. He was not a Welsh
Nationalist:

> Dylan Thomas, having an educated and a quick mind, knew
> a little more [Welsh] than the average Southern Welshman,
> but he took no interest in the language—almost in fact
> deliberately turned away from it for to him it stood for Welsh
> Nationalism, and, as he once expressed it, 'F—— Welsh
> Nationalism'.[23]

During his time as journalist Thomas wrote several
articles of a historical and literary nature for the newspaper,
*Herald of Wales*, which contain a good deal of remote and

scholarly material. It is clear that he went to great pains in securing this information. The articles are factual rather than interpretative. They deal with the lives and work of local poets and with the visits of such celebrities as Landor, Borrow, and Edward Thomas to Swansea. Like Thomas's reviews in the *Adelphi*, written in his early twenties, they reveal unexpected erudition and critical judgement. One would hardly have thought him inclined to bring such seriousness of purpose to such a recondite field of interest. These writings reveal an attitude far removed from what one might expect after reading Thomas's portrait of himself as a reporter in *Portrait of the Artist as a Young Dog*. They represent a less familiar part of his many-sided personality and one, unfortunately, that has tended to be forgotten in the light of his later development. This painstaking, serious, almost scholarly aspect of himself he was disinclined to include in his public personality. Yet we shall see throughout his life other instances of his attention to detail and concern for accuracy. It seems that he inherited something of the family's pedagogic traditions.

There are several points of interest in these early news-paper articles. Thomas already exhibits a delight in the melodramatic, garish incident. He knew how to interest his readers: for example, his account of Llewelyn Prichard (the Swansea-born creator of the celebrated Twm Shon Catti, a popular figure in Welsh literature) concludes:

Prichard, coming home late one night to the cottage in Thomas-Street, attempted to write in his own room. But he soon fell asleep. The candle fell on to the papers surrounding him. His clothes caught fire. He was too drunk to know what to do, and died as strangely and as tragically as he had lived.[24]

Since, in these articles, Thomas was chiefly concerned with local poets writing in English, he has some interesting things to say about Welshmen writing poetry in English. It is evident he was himself much preoccupied with the subject:

It is curious that the wonders of Celtic mythology, and the inexplicable fascination that Welsh legends are bound to exercise

D

upon whoever takes enough trouble to become acquainted with
them, have not influenced the Anglo-Welsh poets more con-
siderably.

W. H. Davies, the most gifted Welsh poet writing in English
today, could, if he had chosen, have made something very great
out of the legends of his own country. He could have recreated
the fantastic world of the Mabinogion, surrounded the folk lore
with his own fancies, and made his poetry a stepping place for
the poor children of darkness to reach a saner world where the
cancer of our warped generation is no more than a pleasant itch.

But he preferred to follow in the direct line of the hedgerow
poets, leaning over some country stile with placid expression,
thinking of nothing more edifying than the brevity of life, the
green of the grass, and the inanity of personal expression.[25]

There is a caustic note in this criticism of W. H. Davies, but
the article does reveal that Thomas was giving thought to
the relationship between the Anglo-Welsh writer and his
inherited Welsh literary tradition. Thomas concludes: 'Only
a great writer can give this absurd country, full of green fields
and chimney stacks, beauty and disease, the loveliness of the
villages and the smokeridden horror of the towns, its full
value and recognition.'[25]

But Thomas's eyes were now turned towards London. He
had by this time written some of the poems that were to
be included in *18 Poems*, and was beginning to evolve that
distinctive and original style that characterizes his poetry.
He felt it necessary now to live in London: he must make a
name for himself as a poet; it was time to meet influential
people, to enjoy the company of other young writers. In any
case, he was beginning to find his bohemianism a little
difficult to maintain in Wales with his reputation as poet not
yet established. So he moved to London in the second half
of 1933 when he was approaching his nineteenth birthday.
He has left a vivid, humorous, and not entirely fanciful
picture of his public self in these days:

above medium height. Above medium height for Wales, I mean,
he's five foot six and a half. Thick blubber lips; snub nose;
curly mousebrown hair; one front tooth broken after playing a

game called Cats and Dogs, in the Mermaid, Mumbles; speaks
rather fancy; truculent; plausible; a bit of a shower-off; plus-
fours and no breakfast, you know; used to have poems printed
in the *Herald of Wales* . . . lived up the Uplands; a bombastic
adolescent provincial Bohemian with a thick-knotted artist's tie
made out of his sister's scarf . . and a cricket-shirt dyed bottle-
green; a gabbing, ambitious, mock-tough, pretentious young
man. . . .[26]

The public figure was already established, for there was a
strong theatrical impulse in Thomas's personality. His
picture, of course, is of his Swansea self, the provincial
bohemian. It was in something of this bohemian mood that
he left Wales for London with the comment: 'The land of
my fathers. My fathers can keep it.'[27]

# CHAPTER FOUR

# *18 POEMS*

*18 POEMS* was published in December 1934, when Thomas was just twenty and its sequel, *Twenty-five Poems*, followed in September 1936. In August 1939 appeared *The Map of Love*, which contained sixteen poems, together with seven short stories. These three books represent approximately one-half of Thomas's output as a poet. Since the earliest of his published poems dates, in manuscript, from December 1930, it is clear that this first half of his poetic work was written within the comparatively short space of eight years, the period of his adolescence and early manhood, from sixteen to twenty-four.

I have indicated the proximity of composition of these early poems because it seems to me that they share important and fundamental characteristics, and represent the first phase of Thomas's development. The second phase begins with the poems included in *Deaths and Entrances*, although, of course, there is not a distinct division, but rather a process of development. The early poems are the product of a young, obsessed mind and have a unity of theme, technique, and attitude.

The manuscript versions of the early poetry in Thomas's notebooks for the years 1930-4 throw some interesting light on this early work. The fact that these notebooks contain manuscript versions of just over half the poems eventually included in *18 Poems*, *Twenty-five Poems*, and *The Map of Love*, confirms one's impression of the unity of composition in the early work. In reading the first notebooks one enters the peculiar, distinctive world of the early poetry. It is dangerous, however, to make generalizations from these manuscripts about Thomas's development, because while in a poem such as 'Out of the sighs' the manuscript version closely resembles the final form the poem took, in others the early manuscript was hardly more than a source. The final poem is sometimes recognizable only by an occasional line or phrase. The manuscript versions are usually easier to understand and often read like rough, prose versions of the later poem.

What is most striking, at first sight, in Thomas's *18 Poems* is their appearance of complete originality. Vernon Watkins has commented on the violent nature of Thomas's personality:

> I quickly realized when we went for a walk on the cliffs that this cherub took nothing for granted. In thought and words he was anarchic, challenging, with the certainty of that instinct which knows its own freshly discovered truth.[1]

Glyn Jones, another Anglo-Welsh writer, was a close friend in these early years and they often discussed their work together. In a conversation with me Glyn Jones recalled how impressed he was from the beginning by the originality and the violence of Thomas's poetry. How was it that Thomas within a year or two turned from competent school-magazine versifier into an original poet? This, I think, is a problem which will puzzle critics for some time. Also interesting is the fact that the style so triumphantly established in *18 Poems* remained fundamentally the same throughout his life —though of course there was development of theme and technique. His work does not show the kind of development found, for example, in Shakespeare or Yeats, where there is a real change in the style of the poet: though Thomas's later poetry is generally more lucid.

Thomas's manuscript poems written in the years 1930-4 help to explain this discovery of an individual style, for it was something he was always working towards. In making his selection for *18 Poems, Twenty-five Poems, The Map of Love,* and indeed throughout his later poetic career, he was careful to omit all poems which did not conform to this basic style. Vernon Watkins has written that Thomas had developed at school a passionate feeling for language which was sharpened and intensified by an acute destructive judgment. He took no reputation for granted. He approached the great masters of his art with an impudent suspicion.[2]

This acute, destructive judgement Thomas brought to his own compositions. From the beginning he was as severe upon himself as he was upon others. In these years, in a very real sense, his energy was destructive. He was rigorously critical of his own work. Perhaps his individual style was achieved at some expense, for it is somewhat narrow in its intensity and deliberately limited to specific capabilities.

The manuscript poems reveal an adolescent sexual pre-occupation and their originality lies in the occasional striking image. One is immediately aware of the characteristically sensuous, often sensual use of language. It soon becomes clear that Thomas's most urgent concern was with the more introspective, obsessive, sexual, and religious currents of feeling. The Puritanism that was to inform all his later writing soon appears as a directing force in the manuscript work, and his Nonconformist conscience is seldom silent. This conscience is an integral part of Thomas's Welshness. It is reflected in his disparagement of London in one of the letters to Vernon Watkins: he criticizes London life because it lacks, he claims, a sense of good and evil.

I've just come back from three dark days in London, city of the restless dead . . . its intelligentsia is so hurried in the head that nothing stays there . . . there's no difference between good & bad.[3]

The Puritanism at the heart of Welsh life produced in Thomas a literature of conflict. The attitudes in his poetry are sometimes Christian, sometimes anti-Christian: but even when the feeling is anti-Christian in attitude it is religious in temper, for the strong, racial Nonconformist spirit had given him a religious sense of profane existence. In his early poems he often speaks of himself as damned. He seems to be quarrelling with God and His Church, but belief in the reality of God and Christ is always there. It is something that, try as hard as he will, he cannot lose.

Thomas's poetry is also informed by the perception of a radical relationship between human and natural life. This sometimes leads to a mystical sense of the unity between all forms of life, a sensitivity towards animal and vegetal life much more profound than the conventional 'love of nature'. A related concern in his poetry is the attempt to fit this sense of the unity of human and natural life into the developing pattern of religious thought and feeling.

T. S. Eliot has observed that 'individual writers can be understood and classified according to the type of Protestantism which surrounded their infancy, and the precise state of decay which it had reached'.[4] In Thomas's case the Protestantism had continued to have a profound and dominating influence on the way of life. It was an influence too deeply rooted to be more than superficially dismissed. Thomas was, of course, open to many secular influences in his environment, but, as T. S. Eliot has suggested, 'what is still more important is unity of religious background'.[5] And this unity, for Thomas, was an inescapable reality. He was a Puritan and 'he did not believe there was such a thing as a comfortable conscience'.[6]

What, we may ask, were the other major aspects of this personality that found such individual expression in *18 Poems*? Undoubtedly Thomas was an extremely sexual man; he possessed, too, what may be called a sexual imagination, one quick to create imagery and perceptions basically sexual in their connotations. He had also a tremendous faith in himself, allied to unusual will power and a somewhat intransigent nature. He had the courage of his emotions, was always ready to rebel against orthodoxy, and was determined to stick to his own beliefs. He would be on the side of the devil, if he couldn't be on the side of God. Such a nature was bound inevitably to come into conflict with the environment that produced it. In Thomas's poetry, however, the conflict was not expressed in external terms, but in a more terrible, self-destructive form. In his early poems he tended to dismiss the reality of the outside world, and was himself the universe of *18 Poems*, *Twenty-five Poems* and,

to a lesser extent, *The Map of Love*. God, Christ and the
devil, sin and redemption are potentialities, in a sense
realities, within his own being.

> I hold a beast, an angel, and a madman in me, and my
> enquiry is as to their working, and my problem is their subjuga-
> gation and victory, downthrow and upheaval, and my effort
> is their self-expression.[7]

On the subject of the impact of this Welsh Puritanism on
Thomas's life, Caitlin Thomas has observed that 'though
Dylan imagined himself to be completely emancipated from
his family background, there was a very strong puritanical
streak in him, that his friends never suspected.'[8]

Puritanism tends to be characterized by introspection and
guilt, and in a very real sense the Puritan's relationship is an
egotistical and solitary relationship with God. In the traditions of Welsh Nonconformity, a strong emphasis is placed
upon the relationship of the individual with God, and there
is a deep-set belief in 'personal salvation'. V. S. Pritchett
writes in words that are true of Thomas's own development:

> the inner life of the Puritan was not only filled with dramas of
> power and guilt but these were exotically coloured by his reading
> of the Bible. He can even be said to have become too absorbing
> and too interesting to himself. He was living alone a life of inner
> violence. . . . Puritanism or its conflicts are strong in our auto-
> biographical writing. . . . The Puritan is present in all the worry
> that goes on in the English novel, the dramas of guilt and con-
> science. Seeing things as either Right or Wrong has made our
> novelists poor in psychological interest.[9]

Thomas, under the impact of a strong Puritan tradition in
Wales, brought into poetry a drama of guilt and conscience,
of Right and Wrong. His Puritanism, it will be seen, is
very different from that, say, of D. H. Lawrence, who has
little perception of religious experience in the Christian
sense, little of the sense of original sin that informs Thomas's
work.

Before looking at some of the poems from *18 Poems*, one
other facet of Thomas's personality needs explanation. It

has already been suggested that from the beginning he possessed a certain destructive energy. This was due, in part, to his profound distrust of the intellect. He seems to have feared the influence of intellectual upon emotional and sensory experience, and consequently is reluctant to impose too rigorous a cerebral control upon his emotional perceptions and upon his imagery. If an experience recorded in one of the poems is confused or conflicting he accepts that obscurity and wildness.

In his early poems he seems to be arguing rhetorically with himself on the subject of sex and death, sin and redemption, the natural processes, birth and decay. At times he writes about religion as if he and the Druids, Christ and Adam, the chapel preachers and the devil were contemporaries. His themes, however, are relatively few and simple. What is remarkable is the originality and intensity with which they are expressed. Difficulty occurs when the density of image embodies a depth and subtlety of emotional and sensory perception that the mind, in conceptual terms, cannot follow. 'The force that through the green fuse drives the flower', one of the first successful poems, illustrates his technique at this stage.

The theme of the poem is that all human, animal, and vegetal life is subject to the same creative and destructive forces. Characteristically, Thomas relates this perception to himself. Emphasis is laid upon the process of creation as a biological creative-destructive continuum, and the subjugation of man to the forces of cosmic destruction is the theme of the opening lines:

> The force that through the green fuse drives the flower
> Drives my green age; that blasts the roots of trees
> Is my destroyer.
> And I am dumb to tell the crooked rose
> My youth is bent by the same wintry fever.

Thomas's attitude to death and the consequent physical decay is closely paralleled in the work of another Anglo-Welsh writer, Margiad Evans:

Walking between the oak tree and the stile, I thought of death, as I do every day and every hour. Not death with its kneeling, and service, and decay; but of short corruption to cleanness, and the white bone in its starry beauty on the turf.[10]

Thomas identifies the vitalizing processes in man and the vitalizing processes in nature: both are subject to the same life, the same death. There is the characteristic paradox: 'crooked rose', signifying the co-existence of death and life. The word 'green' is used in the first and second lines with a different emphasis in meaning, causing the reader to re-identify the particular meaning of each use. For Thomas 'green' is symbolic of potential or recently created life. Hence, in the first line the word refers both to the life-giving force in the flower and, of course, to the green colour of the stem; in the second it defines the youth and innocence of the poet. The second and third stanzas elaborate the expression of the basic theme by the use of image. The final stanza reveals, however, a greater development and attains some degree of resolution:

> The lips of time leech to the fountain head;
> Love drips and gathers, but the fallen blood
> Shall calm her sores.
> And I am dumb to tell a weather's wind
> How time has ticked a heaven round the stars.

The meaning of these lines is that time itself, as man conceives it, is subject to this creative principle existing before and after human time. It is the power of love which remains as the vindication of life and survival: the fact that the processes of life go on, that the process of generation in man and nature never fails, and that the seasons change, is itself witness of some beneficent will at the heart of the universe. I do not think, however, 'the fountain head' can be interpreted in any positive way as being a Christian concept in this poem. The positive acceptance of Christian theology comes later. It is human time, says the poet, which has imagined a heaven, an immortality other than a biological concept of a return to the first elements. All Thomas is certain of at this stage in his life is this process of creation and destruction. He is determined to be honest with himself in these poems and will write only of what he knows. There is a note, however, of sacrificial theology in the sentence: 'but the fallen blood Shall calm her sores', but as regards a Christian interpretation of life, the poem remains non-committal. It closes on a note of bitterness and frustration at the mortality of individual life:

> And I am dumb to tell the lover's tomb
> How at my sheet goes the same crooked worm.

The paradox 'crooked worm' echoes the earlier image, 'crooked rose'. The worm itself makes possible the processes both of life and death, being a living symbol of both states. Particularly effective in this poem are the careful construction, the use of repetition, and compulsive rhythm. The images cohere to form a comprehensible pattern of sound and meaning.

From this poem we can learn, also, something of Thomas's aims when revising his work. I have set out below phrases altered after the poem's first publication in the *Sunday Referee*, 29 October 1933, for publication in *18 Poems*:

|            | Sunday Referee      | 18 Poems                           |
| ---------- | ------------------- | ---------------------------------- |
| v.4, l.3   | make her well       | calm her sores                     |
| v.4, l.4   | the timeless clouds | a weather's wind                   |
| v.4, l.5   | That time is all    | How time has ticked a heaven round the stars |

The ideas behind the images remain the same, but they are given more forceful expression: superficially, however, there is less clarity, for the informing idea is more difficult to grasp. In the second revision, where 'the timeless clouds' becomes 'a weather's wind', Thomas has used a characteristic verbal technique. In terms of meaning little has been added, but the second phrase is more suggestive of associations and has also an effective alliteration: 'a weather's wind' has the quality and strangeness of new poetic life. The sensory perception registered is keener and more original, as in the

third change, where 'That time is all' becomes 'How time
has ticked a heaven round the stars'.

There is much emphasis in these early poems on the processes of human, as well as natural life. An important
though comparatively simple poem, 'Before I knocked', is
written on the subject of birth. Thomas deals with the fact of
birth from the standpoint of immortality: life begins before
personality (that is, human form) and continues after the
death of personality. In this poem Thomas characteristically
identifies man with Christ, a device related to the seven-
teenth-century poets' use of Christian mythology and
symbol. Donne, for example, wrote:

> We think that *Paradise* and *Calvarie*,
> *Christs* Cross, and *Adams* tree, stood in one place;
> Looke Lord, and finde both *Adams* met in me;
> As the first *Adams* sweat surrounds my face,
> May the last *Adams* blood my soule embrace.[11]

By assuming this identity, Thomas in his early poems is
seeking to define the relation between immediate reality and
archetypal religious symbols. 'Before I knocked' opens:

> Before I knocked and flesh let enter,
> With liquid hands tapped on the womb,
> I who was shapeless as the water
> That shaped the Jordan near my home
> Was brother to Mnetha's daughter
> And sister to the fathering worm.

Here the poet is speaking of existence before it takes the form
of human life. Thomas assumes, as so often, the rôle of
ambassador: here, an ambassador between the life that
begins with conception in the womb and previous existence
in nature. He sees all life as part of an organic whole; existence is a unity which is broken when life is conceived, but to
which the body returns at death. In imaging the experience
of life in the womb the poet sees himself as both male and
female ('was brother . . . and sister'). The reference to the
Jordan suggests the identification of man and Christ. The
'fathering worm' is a compressed expression of Thomas's

view of life as a progress towards death, or—stated paradoxically—life makes death possible. The child in the womb
is aware of the journey to death it must make and already
feels within itself the seed of destruction:

> My heart knew love, my belly hunger;
> I smelt the maggot in my stool.

It is 'time' that casts forth this child into life, because once
mortal the child is subject to time, and it is necessary for the
child to live and sip 'the vine of days':

> And time cast forth my mortal creature
> To drift or drown upon the seas
> Acquainted with the salt adventure
> Of tides that never touch the shores.
> I who was rich was made the richer
> By sipping at the vine of days.

The elaboration of image 'Of tides that never touch the
shores' seems to have in it no thematic development, and the
power of that line to lie entirely in the sensory appeal of its
language. The next stanza continues:

> I, born of flesh and ghost, was neither
> A ghost nor man, but mortal ghost.
> And I was struck down by death's feather.
> I was a mortal to the last
> Long breath that carried to my father
> The message of his dying christ.

Here Thomas speaks in the person of Christ, who, in terms
of the Virgin Birth was in a real sense born both of the flesh
and ghost. His incarnation was neither entirely human nor
entirely divine. The line 'And I was struck down by death's
feather' means, simply, that Christ was subject to death.
The source of his image is the Bible, for 'death's feather' is
the feather from the wing of the Angel of death; and the
'father' reference is to God, since Christ did in fact die. The
relatedness of all life, of man, of Christ, of natural life, is an
important concept in the poem.

In the final lines Thomas speaks in his own person, but on

behalf of all men. He asks all believers to *remember* mankind, which he, being mortal, represents, and to *pity* Christ because of His sacrifice in partially taking on human form. Christ is said to have 'doublecrossed' His mother's womb because of the doctrine of the Virgin Birth. 'The point of view is explicitly that at which Crashaw only hinted, that Incarnation represents a vicious joke played by a malicious God on Christ, Mary and mankind.'[12]

> You who bow down at cross and altar,
> Remember me and pity Him
> Who took my flesh and bone for armour
> And doublecrossed my mother's womb.

In Thomas's poetry, the sexual process in man is important because it leads to regeneration. Likewise the natural world, it is implied, also repeats this sexual process:

> And yellow was the multiplying sand,
> Each golden grain spat life into its fellow.

Man, through his sin, has created death, yet that same sexual process by which life goes on Thomas tends to equate with sin. This would seem to be the subconscious impact of his Puritan upbringing. His thought runs in what might be called a vicious, though poetically fertile, circle.

In his early poems and stories, 'Thomas moves between sexual revulsion and sexual ecstasy, between puritanism and mysticism, between formalistic ritual . . . and irresponsibility'.[13] Contrary to the popular idea of his attitude to sexual love, there is at times in his writing a very real and terrible horror of the flesh:

The world is ripe for the second coming of the son of man, he said aloud.

But it was not the ripeness of God that glistened from the hill. It was the promise and the ripeness of the flesh, the good flesh, the mean flesh, flesh of his daughter, flesh, flesh, the flesh of the voice of thunder howling before the death of man.

That night he preached of the sins of the flesh. O God in the image of our flesh, he prayed. . . .[14]

Surrounded by shadows, he prayed before the flaming stack, and the sparks of the heather blew past his smile. Burn, child, poor flesh, mean flesh, flesh, flesh, sick sorry flesh, flesh of the foul womb, burn back to dust, he prayed.[15]

On one occasion, after three days of riotous celebration, 'Dylan said, "To be able to tear off my flesh—to get rid of this awful, horrifying skin we have—to get at the bone, and then to get rid of that! What a wonderful thing!" He tore at his hands, really scratching them, and his eyes blazed in anger and wretchedness.'[16] His Puritan conscience did not live in harmony with his animal, human self. The poem 'If I were tickled by the rub of love' is a release of these conflicts.

> If I were tickled by the rub of love
> A rooking girl who stole me for her side,
> Broke through her straws, breaking my bandaged string,
> If the red tickle as the cattle calve
> Still set to scratch a laughter from my lung,
> I would not fear the apple nor the flood
> Nor the bad blood of spring.

The basic image in the poem, 'rub', is, of course, Shakespearian and carries echoes of Hamlet's soliloquy, with its theme of death and sexual disgust. It is, in its everyday usage, a word with sexual associations. The poet speaks of sexual love in terms of bitterness and frustration: 'tickled', 'to scratch a laughter'. If, says the poet, he could believe in sexual love and celebrate it in his work he would not fear the loss of innocence (the apple), or the punishment that follows this loss (the flood), or 'the bad blood of spring'. The last phrase refers both to the regeneration which the spring season brings—'bad' because it inherits original sin even at its creation—and to the misery of the poet's own adolescence, with its religious and sexual frustration and fear. The line 'A rooking girl who stole me for her side' is again a very impersonal, almost contemptuous designation of the beloved: the lover is thought of as a robber ('rooking', 'stole'). Like the apple and the flood, this idea also derives from Genesis —in this case ii.22–23:

And the rib, which the LORD God had taken from man, made he a woman, and brought her unto the man. And Adam said, This is now bone of my bones, and flesh of my flesh: she shall be called Woman, because she was taken out of Man.

One is reminded of Thomas's later line, 'Sin who had a woman's shape', which is also based on the Genesis story of the Fall. There is, of course, a certain subconscious conflict in Thomas's opening stanza: he *is* tickled by the rub of love, sex *is* desirable, but with it come associations of fear and guilt and death. He is aware that what attracts him also repels him: and cannot come to terms with himself.

Because Thomas is an uncivilizable puritan and a hardshell fundamentalist of some undefinable kind, the puritanism sets up the tension in his poetry—a tension based upon love and fear of love—the basic sexual tension, the basic theological tension.[17]

In the second stanza Thomas writes of the moment of conception in the womb and relates his emotions and conflicts to that stage of life. The images move around these emotions and conflicts, defining them:

> Shall it be male or female? say the cells,
> And drop the plum like fire from the flesh.
> If I were tickled by the hatching hair,
> The winging bone that sprouted in the heels,
> The itch of man upon the baby's thigh,
> I would not fear the gallows nor the axe
> Nor the crossed sticks of war.

If he were again an unborn child, the poet says, he would not fear death, whether by execution or in war, but of course the point is that he *does* fear all these things, though he wishes he did not. From the stage of life in the womb, with the sexual appetites peculiar (according to the poet) to it, Thomas passes to the sexual appetites of adolescence:

> I would not fear the muscling-in of love
> If I were tickled by the urchin hungers
> Rehearsing heat upon a raw-edged nerve.
> I would not fear the devil in the loin
> Nor the outspoken grave.

Here the poet deals with another aspect of sexual development, masturbation: 'Rehearsing heat upon a raw-edged
nerve.' If he could accept these appetites he would not fear
'the muscling-in of love'. The phrase 'devil in the loin' again
associates the ideas of sex and sin, while the metaphor 'the
outspoken grave'—that is the grave which everywhere
announces its victory—dramatically evokes his obsession
with the fact of death.

In stanza five the poet speaks directly of himself and casts
aside the subjunctive of condition used in the earlier verses:

> This world is half the devil's and my own,
> Daft with the drug that's smoking in a girl
> And curling round the bud that forks her eye.
> An old man's shank one-marrowed with my bone,
> And all the herrings smelling in the sea,
> I sit and watch the worm beneath my nail
> Wearing the quick away.

In this poem there is profound moral conflict as well as
subconscious conflict in Freudian terms. The poet tells us he
is in love, but this is not the customary poetical convention of
'love-madness'. He is 'daft with the drug that's smoking in a
girl': that is, the drug of sexual desire makes him 'daft'. The
poet sees the intoxicating drug in the girl's eye: is there
perhaps an echo of the popular slang 'give him the glad eye',
implying sexual invitation? He sees her anatomically, not
in pretty, romantic terms. There is probably a pun in the
'eye' image whereby 'forks her eye' carries a sexual interpretation. Olson suggests an association with the pointed fork
of the devil with whom the poet shares his world. In both
associations there is further attraction and repulsion. In his
sexual desires he shares his world with the devil; and this is
half of the real world, which is composed both of Good and
Evil. The drug has been planted in the girl by the devil: she
is not responsible for her sexual nature. At this moment of
repulsion and attraction the poet thinks of the process of age
and death that is already in him. Are there also, in Freudian
terms, intimations of impotency in old age—'an old man's
shank'? The line 'And all the herrings smelling in the sea'

conveys a sense of the corruption and lechery inherent in his personality. Faced with these emotions and conflicts Thomas turns to the one overwhelming reality: death. Death, not sex, is the major obsession in his poetry:

> I sit and watch the worm beneath my nail
> Wearing the quick away.

Death, concludes the poet, is the only rub that tickles. The sexual act, the love of the mother for her child, the romantic devotion of lovers: all these modes of love come to nothing before the fact of death. Six feet of earth, the 'rubbing dust' is the supreme fact. The final stanza brings together the emotions and conflicts around which the poem has moved, and there is the familiar combination of sexual and religious imagery:

> And what's the rub? Death's feather on the nerve?
> Your mouth, my love, the thistle in the kiss?
> My Jack of Christ born thorny on the tree?
> The words of death are dryer than his stiff,
> My wordy wounds are printed with your hair.
> I would be tickled by the rub that is:
> Man be my metaphor.

In the reference to 'Death's feather on the nerve' (see also p. 47) Thomas is registering the presence of death in every fibre and impulse of the body. The 'thistle in the kiss' continues the imagery of attraction and repulsion: 'a little probing reveals not a liberated body but an obsessed mind', so that 'it seems evident that Thomas's allegiance to Freud has not resulted, in his poems, in the cleansing of sexuality from the Old Testament sense of sin'.[18] It must be concluded, I think, that the poet's interpretation of sex is closer to the Old Testament than the psychology of Freud. 'My Jack of Christ' is a daring, though typical, image of sexual and religious frustration. The 'hair' reference brings us back to the lover. The poem ends with a verbal gesture ('Man be my metaphor') but no resolution of its themes. It is a statement of conflicts, an imaging of the 'womb of war':

Out of the inevitable conflict of images—inevitable, because of the creative, recreative, destructive and contradictory nature of the motivating centre, the womb of war—I try to make that momentary peace which is a poem. I do not want a poem of mine to be, nor can it be, a circular piece of experience placed neatly outside the living stream of time from which it came; a poem of mine is, or should be, a watertight section of the stream that is flowing all ways.[19]

Matthew Arnold suggested that complexity of image and emotion, a startling juxtaposition of the unexpected producing a kind of magic—so different from the lucid, uncomplicated Greek way of handling nature—characterized the Celtic imagination. Similarly in his book, *The Burning Tree*, Gwyn Williams has continued this line of thought and indicated that a sense of paradox, deriving from a paradoxical conception of existence, was a feature of Welsh literature. As I have attempted to show, the relationship between the parts, in such compositions as 'If I were tickled by the rub of love', is total rather than consecutive. It is a whole experience, without actual end or beginning. For this reason Welsh literature tends to impose a strict metrical and rhythmic control on the experience, rather than a thematic organization of the parts. The form in such poetry derives from sound and verbal structure rather than the consecutive development of the thought. Thomas's definition of his method, quoted above, does very emphatically stress the paradoxical process at the centre of his composition—a destructive-creative continuum—and the impossibility, for him, of a consecutive handling of experience. This is because he tends to view experience as a process of flux, of continual change, wherein each thing contains its opposite. For Thomas, nature, or, let us say, reality, is the 'stream of time . . . that is flowing all ways'.

Defining his method of composition, in a letter to Henry Treece, Thomas relates his technique, whereby image begets image, to his concept of reality:

When you say that I have not Cameron's or Madge's 'concentric movement round a central image', you are not accounting

for the fact that it consciously is not my method to move con-
centrically round a central image. A poem by Cameron *needs*
no more than one image; it moves around one idea, from one
logical point to another, making a full circle. A poem by myself
*needs* a host of images, because its centre is a host of images. I
make one image—though 'make' is not the word; I let, perhaps,
an image be 'made' emotionally in me and then apply to it what
intellectual and critical forces I possess—let it breed another,
let that image contradict the first, make, of the third image bred
out of the other two together, a fourth contradictory image,
and let them all, within my imposed formal limits, conflict.
Each image holds within it the seed of its own destruction, and
my dialectical method, as I understand it, is a constant building
up and breaking down of the images that come out of the central
seed, which is itself destructive and constructive at the same time.

What I want to try to explain—and it's necessarily vague to
me—is that the *life* in any poem of mine cannot move concen-
trically round a central image; the life must come out of the
centre; an image must be born and die in another; and any
sequence of my images must be a sequence of creations, recreations,
destructions, contradictions. I cannot . . . make a poem out of a
single motivating experience; I believe in the simple thread of
action through a poem, but that is an intellectual thing aimed
at lucidity through narrative.[20]

This is an extremely interesting, and, when interpreted,
informative statement of poetic method. It is a little difficult,
however, to determine its exact meaning because it mingles
two different aspects of Thomas's poetry, and talks of them
as the same. It is, ostensibly, a definition of technique—of
the technical devices by which Thomas creates a poem. It is
not, it would appear, about his ideas and his emotions—the
content of his poetry. It seems to deal with structural rather
than philosophic ends, but this is not the case, for in defining
his technical process Thomas uses philosophic terms. That
is to say, his technique properly derives from the nature of
what he has to say, from his conception of life. Hence it is
important to bear in mind that the definition is not exclusively one of technique. It is an account, primarily, of
Thomas's concept of the nature of life; only secondarily—in

so far as this directs his technique—of his use of language. There is no apparent reason, for example, why one image should bear the seeds of its own destruction, or breed a contradictory image, except of course in terms of Thomas's attitude to experience. Hence, in this definition, we are constantly passing from a technical to a philosophic explanation. I think, therefore, this definition is illuminating only if the relationship between technique and theme is made clear. We may deduce, then, that in so far as each particle of existence has in it the seeds of its own destruction (a basic idea in Thomas's poetry) so does each image bear its own destruction. Each image 'breeds' another: the sexual terminology is significant. The new image contradicts the previous one, because, for Thomas, experience (which the images seek to create) itself is in the nature of paradox, in which the constituent parts contain their opposite. Let all these images *conflict*, says Thomas, not *unify*. It is interesting to see him insist that the image is made emotionally. The imposed formal limits of the poem are, of course, the rhythmic and stanzaic structure and in all Thomas's poetry there is an important sound structure. His technique suggests that his mind was not analytical. His aim was not so much the isolation and precise definition of a particular experience as a re-creation, by sensation, of the welter and unity of all experience. It had to be created in words in all its conflict and paradox. His mind worked from the one perception to the many, and for him the nature of truth lay in paradox. Everything tends to its opposite. Rational analysis of experience was no good because, in the end, it was self-defeating in its mistaken effort to see things in separation. This attitude to reality occasions much of the obscurity in Thomas's work. The images, however, are usually grouped by a sturdy advancing rhythm and an elaborate sound structure—that is the imposed formal control.

This definition of his method is closely paralleled in a letter to Vernon Watkins, where Thomas criticises a poem by Watkins because it is too 'literary' and lacks the 'inevitability' and quality of 'action' that he himself looks for in poetry.

> I can see the sensitive picking of words, but none of the strong, inevitable pulling that makes a poem an event, a happening, an action perhaps, not a still-life or an experience put down, placed, regulated; the introduction of mist, legend, time's weir, grief's bell . . . seem to me 'literary', not living. They seem, as indeed the whole poem seems, to come out of the nostalgia of literature. . . . A motive has been rarefied, it should be made common. I don't ask you for vulgarity, though I miss it; I think I ask you for a little creative destruction, destructive creation: 'I build a flying tower, and I pull it down' . . . But . . . it is a poem so obviously written in words; I want my sentimental blood: not Roy Campbell's blood, which is a red & noisy adjective in a transparent vein, but the blood of leaves, wells, weirs, fonts, shells, echoes, rainbows, olives, bells, oracles, sorrows.[21]

Thomas's concern with the quality of 'action' in a poem— with the poem's existence as an action and not as a regulated, set-down experience with beginning and end—again recalls Gwyn Williams's remarks on the presentation of experience in Welsh literature: namely, that it is a whole experience whose relationships are total rather than consecutive. It is clear, therefore, that Thomas's poetry shares certain characteristics peculiar to Celtic literature: it accepts a paradoxical concept of reality; it offers an immediate, sensuous, and conflicting image of nature; it imposes an elaborate formal structure upon an emotional handling of experience.

In defining his method of composition, Thomas claims to apply to the image what intellectual and critical forces he possesses. This, I think, is true in his successful poems, but in some of the early ones he fails to organize all the parts into a coherent form. Without a narrative outline his writing lacks lucidity; reminding one of Matthew Arnold's observation that the Celt, though possessing an intense and original emotional perception, fails to bring to this adequate intellectual control and a sense of measure. Thomas's early poetry contains many instances of profound and striking images surrounded by an incomprehensible density of language. At this stage he had still to learn how to organize and relate his perceptive insights. It is interesting to find that in most cases these images are rich in Biblical associations:

> My fuses timed to charge his heart,
> He blew like powder to the light
> And held a little sabbath with the sun.[22]

> For we shall be a shouter like the cock,
> Blowing the old dead back.[23]

> A cock-on-a-dunghill
> Crowing to Lazarus the morning is vanity.[24]

> This was the god of beginning in the intricate seawhirl,
> And my images roared and rose on heaven's hill.[25]

These sentences, in isolation, have the potency of the highest poetry, but unfortunately their lucidity is not representative of the poems in which they occur.

A poem which exhibits the most coherent pattern of Thomas's experience at this time is 'Especially when the October wind'. The background to the poem is a particular Welsh setting. The poem also reveals certain important aspects of Thomas's personality and ideas. He was always apt to view experience, sensory, emotional, and intellectual, in terms of words, and was aware of the reality of language. His consciousness of himself was always conditioned by this sense:

> There, playing Indians in the evening, I was aware of me myself in the exact middle of a living story, and my body was my adventure and my name. I sprang with excitement and scrambled up through the scratching brambles again.[26]

Often his eye was less on the object than on the word, and as this poem illustrates, he tended to see experience in terms of verbal patterns:

Especially when the October wind
With frosty fingers punishes my hair,
Caught by the crabbing sun I walk on fire
And cast a shadow crab upon the land,
By the sea's side, hearing the noise of birds,
Hearing the raven cough in winter sticks,
My busy heart who shudders as she talks
Sheds the syllabic blood and drains her words.

The punishing by 'frosty fingers' is an original evocation of
the feeling of the wind blowing through the hair. The sun is
referred to as 'crabbing' since it casts a crab-like shadow of
the body (as suggested in the later image, 'shadow crab'),
and also because Thomas often thinks of the sun, in this
early poetry, as destroying the human body: hence the
image 'crabbing', with implications of seizing, taking hold
of. He sees the sun as a power which brings about the old-age
and mortality of the flesh. In these early poems it is a basic
image of life-destroying forces, but one which undergoes an
important change in its associations in the later work. The
words 'on fire' mean that the poet feels the heat of the sun,
and also refer to his inspiration of the moment. He is writing
about the mood of inspiration, of the moment when the
creative impulse in him makes itself felt.

The reference to the sea suggests the scene of the poem.
Swansea rises from the sea in hill formations rather like an
amphitheatre, and Thomas's home was on the hillside high
above the town. Facing this was Cwmdonkin Park, with its
birds in the leafless trees ('winter sticks')—for the time of the
poem is early winter. Swansea bay would have formed his
whole horizon as he looked down to the town. From his
earliest childhood in his colourful provincial home he was
exposed to the sights and sounds of country and sea.

The closing lines of the first stanza develop the theme of
poetic inspiration and composition. The words 'busy heart',
'syllabic blood' suggest the emotional and personal nature of
Thomas's approach to poetry.

In the second stanza he moves from a direct description
of the scene and deals with his isolation as a poet. He

talks of his attempt to create this life about him in terms of language:

> Shut, too, in a tower of words, I mark
> On the horizon walking like the trees
> The wordy shapes of women, and the rows
> Of the star-gestured children in the park.
> Some let me make you of the vowelled beeches,
> Some of the oaken voices, from the roots
> Of many a thorny shire tell your notes,
> Some let me make you of the water's speeches.

He adopts a derangement of the senses in these lines, by which the normal outline of objects is blurred. Human and natural life is blurred into association by the power of the word: human forms being given the attributes of vegetal life, and vice versa. Even the sea is spoken of in sensory terms ('the water's speeches') peculiar to a human being. This is more than the conventional poetic technique of personification, for so strong was Thomas's sensory perception that he could imaginatively enter into the life of nature. There is a similar sensibility in the work of Margiad Evans:

> I would see as the light sees. I would know as the earth knows when it feels the grass pulled by the sheep, when it rounds the rabbit's nest, when the blow of the hoof shoots to its heart. I would feel as the water feels round the rocks and the roots and the breasts of the swans. It seems to me that there must be a feeling of touch along the horizon and the meeting of the clouds must mean sensation.[27]

The park referred to in Thomas's poem is of course Cwmdonkin Park. The epithet 'star-gestured' suggests the outstretched legs and arms of the children hilariously at play, and bears associations of heaven and innocence (related to Thomas's idealization of childhood). The 'thorny shire' refers to the other places and lives of which the poet is aware, lives that are not always easy and happy. 'Thorns' is, of course, a Biblical symbol rich in Christian ideas of sacrifice and suffering, and is used in this context for its relevance to the artist who writes from the 'syllabic blood' that he sheds.

Stanza three considers the everyday world and the world
of the poet in relation to time:

> Behind a pot of ferns the wagging clock
> Tells me the hour's word, the neural meaning
> Flies on the shafted disk, declaims the morning
> And tells the windy weather in the cock.
> Some let me make you of the meadow's signs;
> The signal grass that tells me all I know
> Breaks with the wormy winter through the eye.
> Some let me tell you of the raven's sins.

The poet first considers man-made, mechanical time,
artificially measured by clocks and calendar. He is inside the
house, looking out of the window at the church clock and
weather vane ('the windy weather in the cock'). It is a
chiming clock ('neural meaning', 'declaims'). The poet
now advances to a more significant concept of time as
measured by nature—the seasons ('the meadow's signs').
'The signal grass that tells me all I know' is an example of
Thomas's unremitting honesty: he will claim knowledge
only of those things he learns from experience. He can see in
external nature ('the signal grass') the process of growth and
decay, of life and death, which is the one certain and important ('signal') fact he knows. This is a more significant
concept, he claims, than that of time artificially measured by
man. 'Wormy winter' is a characteristic paradox, implying
that the worm, being both a creative and destructive force,
is symbol both of life and death. Thus the winter itself is a
part of the creative organ of life. One is again reminded of
Margiad Evans's writing.

The sting of the dying nettle, the prickle of an autumn weed, the
sprout of a seed, each told me something. Under the leaves, under
the branches, rotting, germinating, preparing, a hundred years
were there to come. . . . Although the nettles are going down into
the earth, and the hardiest weeds are yellowing . . . it is the
month of germination . . . the first era of growth. I can taste
germination on my tongue and at the back of my throat. . . .
Not only in thrusting forth, but in decaying and folding back are
the processes begun.[28]

The third stanza closes with a reference to the raven, traditionally a bird of death and ill-omen, which suggests the original sin that is part of the created world. The poem ends with a bringing-together of its themes.

> Especially when the October wind
> (Some let me make you of autumnal spells,
> The spider-tongued, and the loud hill of Wales)
> With fists of turnips punishes the land,
> Some let me make you of the heartless words.
> The heart is drained that, spelling in the scurry
> Of chemic blood, warned of the coming fury.
> By the sea's side hear the dark-vowelled birds.

The 'loud hill of Wales' is, on one level, that overlooking Swansea where the poet lived: it is 'loud' with his words. With an effective use of cadence the poem moves to its close as the poet's inspiration passes. The *furor poeticus* is gone, the 'scurry of chemic blood' eased. Lines 6 and 7 of this stanza also suggest an underlying sexual meaning. In his early poems Thomas often associates the act of writing—poetic inspiration—with sexual experience. 'Especially when the October wind' ends on a note of reconciliation that is sad rather than joyous, the one-syllable words creating a heavy, subsiding sound-pattern. It is as though the sea itself has now become still, and only the birds call above the retreating waves: 'By the sea's side hear the dark-vowelled birds'.

As with 'The force that through the green fuse drives the flower' and 'If I were tickled by the rub of love', there is no resolution of theme or image on an intellectual level. At the close of the poem there is only a dying of the experience. The resolution is one of sound and action, a return towards emotional stillness. Another feature of this poem is the way in which Thomas's imagery is directed by the particular scene before him. The influence of an actual background, whether associated with place or person, helps him to organize his conflicting emotions and perceptions. Wales, with its much-loved landscape and distinctive way of life, was the major influence in Thomas's movement towards clarity and control of emotion and image.

# CHAPTER FIVE

# TWENTY-FIVE POEMS

TWENTY-FIVE POEMS continues the rebellious, self-questioning themes of *18 Poems*. The dominant mood is still of impassioned introspection, showing an obsessive concern with death, sex, sin, and the isolation of the individual. There is, however, more definition in the feelings as the poet begins to cast off his more adolescent emotional attitudes. His mind, turning outward, creates more objective patterns of feeling, and there is a deepening of his religious attitude to experience. The informing ideas in the poems remain, nevertheless, basically few and simple. Biblical thought and imagery remain the real foundation of the poetry.

He continues to interpret Biblical narrative in terms of a personal mythology, as in the poem 'Incarnate devil', where he restates the Genesis story of God's creation of good and evil. It was first entitled 'Poem For Sunday', and begins:

> Incarnate devil in a talking snake,
> The central plains of Asia in his garden,
> In shaping-time the circle stung awake,
> In shapes of sin forked out the bearded apple,
> And God walked there who was a fiddling warden
> And played down pardon from the heavens' hill.

'The circle' that the snake 'stung awake' is the circle of life and death that came about after the Fall. Before Adam yielded to temptation there was no death. The reference to God as 'fiddling' is typical of Thomas's witty, though sometimes blasphemous, handling of Biblical legend. The poem follows the Biblical account of Eden closely:

> The wisemen tell me that the garden gods
> Twined good and evil on an eastern tree.

The wisemen are, of course, authors of the Genesis story. The term 'garden gods' is used since the poem speaks of God's creation (the 'shaping-time') of the world and, in particular, the Garden of Eden. The source of the poem would seem to be Genesis ii. 8–9:

> And the LORD GOD planted a garden eastward in Eden; and there he put the man whom he had formed. And out of the ground made the LORD GOD to grow every tree that is pleasant to the sight, and good for food; the tree of life also in the midst of the garden, and the tree of knowledge of good and evil.

The poem closes with a typical pun: 'A serpent fiddled in the shaping-time', where the repeated word 'fiddled' carries on the play of wit.

Thomas possessed a dual attitude towards religious myth and symbol, for, despite the influence of Christian thought and language on his writing, he often yields to the temptation of blasphemy when dealing with religious themes. One is reminded of Yeats's comment that 'only the true believer dare blaspheme'. Thomas cannot resist the pun, the joke, the daring conjunction of sexual and religious implications in the one image. In the sequence of Christian sonnets, for example, which contains some of the most moving religious verse he ever wrote, he refers to God the Father as an 'old cock from nowheres', and describes the Angel Gabriel as a 'two-gunned cowboy'. In these sonnets, Thomas draws his imagery from films of the Wild West:

> And from the windy West came two-gunned Gabriel,
> From Jesu's sleeve trumped up the king of spots,
> The sheath-decked jacks, queen with a shuffled heart;
> Said the fake gentleman in suit of spades,
> Black-tongued and tipsy from salvation's bottle.[1]

The state of salvation is referred to as a state of drunkenness. Such writing, I think, lacks the certainty of metaphysical wit. It is a young man's attempt at blasphemy. There is

something too obviously 'clever' about it, yet the attitude
behind such composition is sincere.

The eighth sonnet is much more certain in its emotional
effect than the section from the fifth already quoted. Thomas
is trying to image Christ's experience on the Cross:

> This was the crucifixion on the mountain,
> Time's nerve in vinegar, the gallow grave
> As tarred with blood as the bright thorns I wept;
> The world's my wound, God's Mary in her grief,
> Bent like three trees and bird-papped through her shift,
> With pins for teardrops is the long wound's woman.
> This was the sky, Jack Christ, each minstrel angle
> Drove in the heaven-driven of the nails
> Till the three-coloured rainbow from my nipples
> From pole to pole leapt round the snail-waked world.
> I by the tree of thieves, all glory's sawbones,
> Unsex the skeleton this mountain minute,
> And by this blowclock witness of the sun
> Suffer the heaven's children through my heartbeat.

The opening lines describe the crucifixion scene on the hill
('mountain') of Calvary. This is seen as the most intense,
sensitive, and painful moment of time ('Time's nerve in
vinegar'). It is a symbol of the death of all mankind; 'gallow
grave' suggests the gallows scene, punishment and death.
Thomas, as usual, creates a conflict of image, so that the
thorns in Christ's crown are an image also of his tears. The
place itself was as 'tarred with blood' as were the thorns
about his head. Thomas claims that the whole world was
Christ's wound; and likewise, since all creatures are identified (we shall see later that Christ is identified with Every-
man in 'Jack Christ'), God shares Mary's grief. The 'long
wound' is the eternally repeated wound of child-bearing and
also suffering, and Mary is said to belong to suffering (the
'wound'), so complete is her agony. The nails were 'heaven-
driven' because the crucifixion was brought about by God's
will; 'minstrel angle', a pun on 'ministering angels', also
imparts this idea. As a result of His crucifixion and sacrifice,
Christ in three days rises from the dead to immortality ('the

three-coloured rainbow'). Immortality is now possible for other men. The world has awakened slowly from its death ('the snail-waked world'), and in the closing lines Thomas speaks in the person of Christ once more. It is interesting to find him insisting that death unsexes and therefore makes immortal the human form; thus by implication associating sex with sin. He speaks of a 'mountain' minute because it is the most significant moment in all time, and because of the particular hill-top scene. Christ's sacrifice destroyed the power of time by creating immortality. It was a 'blowclock' witness since time (the clock) was defeated, 'blown' to pieces. Christ, through His agony, suffers 'heaven's children' to come to Him. It is characteristic of Thomas that he should define the Christian state of grace by reference to child-hood, his view of which derives from Matthew xviii. 3–4:

> And [Jesus] said, Verily I say unto you, Except ye be converted, and become as little children, ye shall not enter into the kingdom of heaven. Whosoever therefore shall humble himself as this little child, the same is greatest in the kingdom of heaven.

The imagery in this poetry follows specific Christian doctrines, but the poem's first impact is in terms of strikingly sensuous, rhythmic language. An important part of this impact depends upon surprise. Thomas's liking for shock tactics, his use of the daring image, the unusual reference, pun, and double-meaning, has certain affinities with the seventeenth-century religious verse of Donne and Vaughan.

Such expressions, however, as 'bird-papped', 'Jack Christ', 'the tree of thieves', 'glory's sawbones', and 'Unsex the skeleton' represent an attitude very different from the con-ventional piety of much religious verse. As well as the seven-teenth-century influence in Thomas's religious verse there is an important racial strain. Stanford has commented upon this, taking his example from Thomas's prose writing:

> In the *Portrait of the Artist as a Young Dog*, there is one passage, particularly, which reveals the Cymric or Celtic spirit in Thomas. Its essence consists of what we may term a familiarity with the divine, and its method of sudden surprising contrast.[2]

In illustration of this attitude Stanford refers to the following passage from the short story *The Peaches*. Gwilym, the young poet's cousin, who is studying for the ministry, practises preaching in his father's barn:

'O God, Thou art everywhere all the time, in the dew of the morning, in the frost of the evening, in the field and the town, in the preacher and the sinner, in the sparrow and the big buzzard; Thou canst see everything, right down deep in our hearts; Thou canst see us when the sun is gone. . . . Thou canst see and spy and watch us all the time. . . . Thou canst see everything we do, in the night and the day, in the day and the night, everything, everything; Thou canst see all the time. O God, mun, you're like a bloody cat.'[3]

Stanford writes of this passage that 'Not to accept the sincerity of this unanticipated descent would be to miss the racial element here. It is a peculiarly Welsh property.'[2] What he is hinting at is the ability to think of God and Christ in easy, colloquial terms. There may be a parallel in the way that Welshmen sing hymns in the pub on Saturday night with all the fervour they brought to their childhood chapel-singing and eisteddfodau. Such an attitude may lead to blasphemy, as sometimes in Thomas's writing, but it does always posit a basic religious feeling. In a similar way, Thomas's father would growl on a rainy day, 'It's raining, blast Him!' or exclaim wryly on a pleasant day, 'The sun is shining—Lord, what foolishness!' Karl Shapiro writes of Thomas's work:

The main symbol is masculine love, driven as hard as Freud drove it. In the background is God, hard to identify but always there, a kind of God who belongs to one's parents rather than to the children, who do not quite accept him.[4]

This sums up well Thomas's relationship with the Nonconformist tradition. The belief in God and Christ and the Fall was there and he could not escape from it, try though he might, at the beginning, to rid himself of this religious imagination. As a young man he was apt to rebel hilariously

against this background, and one is reminded of T. S.
Eliot's observation:

> Where blasphemy might once have been a sign of spiritual
> corruption, it might now be taken rather as a symptom that the
> soul is still alive, or even that it is recovering animation: for the
> perception of Good and Evil—whatever choice we may take—is
> the first requisite of spiritual life.[5]

Thus, sometimes Thomas's attitude is Christian, and
sometimes he seems to aspire to the image of Antichrist.
The poem 'I have longed to move away' deals with his
conflicts in matters of religious belief:

> I have longed to move away
> From the hissing of the spent lie
> And the old terrors' continual cry
> Growing more terrible as the day
> Goes over the hill into the deep sea;
> I have longed to move away
> From the repetition of salutes,
> For there are ghosts in the air
> And ghostly echoes on paper,
> And the thunder of calls and notes.

There is in these lines a strong impulse to reject the conventional Nonconformist religious beliefs ('the hissing of the spent
lie'). There is, too, the desire to escape from the fear of death,
a fear that increases with the passing of time. The imagery
of approaching death ('as the day Goes over the hill into the
deep sea') has perhaps an echo of Revelation xx. 13: 'And
the sea gave up the dead which were in it.' Thomas
frequently associates the sea with death; for example in
*Under Milk Wood*: 'and from the larrupped waves the lights
of the lamps in the windows call back the day and the dead
that have run away to sea'.[6]

The poet goes on to relate how he has longed to move
away from the conventional rituals of belief, but the second
stanza reveals that he cannot utterly reject the religious traditions of his environment. They may yet contain some life:

F

> I have longed to move away but am afraid;
> Some life, yet unspent, might explode
> Out of the old lie burning on the ground,
> And crackling into the air, leave me half-blind.

Nevertheless, he will not accept a too-easy belief that is maintained only by fear of death:

> Neither by night's ancient fear,
> The parting of hat from hair,
> Pursed lips at the receiver,
> Shall I fall to death's feather.
> By these I would not care to die,
> Half convention and half lie.

The last two lines in particular satirize conventional and— to the poet—hypocritical ('half lie') Nonconformist church-going. For Thomas, as for so many other Anglo-Welsh writers, its traditions are spiritually spent: it is a convention and a lie and he will not meet death armed only with its beliefs. He feels the need of a more regenerate, honest, spiritual condition. Throughout the poem there is specific reference to the formalities and conventions of belief that the poet wishes to avoid: 'the repetition of salutes', 'the parting of hat from hair'—to him the Nonconformist religious traditions are as polite and meaningless as the accompanying handshakes and raising of the hat. At the end of a chapel service, it is the duty of the deacons to shake hands with the worshippers as they leave the chapel.

Nevertheless, this seems to me a poetry of half-belief. The mood is conditional: 'I have longed to move away . . . *but*'. For Thomas, the facts of religion are there, but he is torn by conflicting moods of acceptance and rebellion. He is always reluctant to place his trust, and would seem to suffer from a certain personal instability, a split in temperament. Karl Shapiro has suggested that

there are two minds working in Thomas, the joyous naturally religious mind, and the disturbed, almost pathological mind of the cultural fugitive or clown. On every level of Thomas's work one notices the lack of sophistication and the split in temperament.[7]

Shapiro has half perceived, I think, an important racial aspect of Thomas's personality. For him it was the intensity of the passion of the moment that counted and he believed, like most Welshmen, with the strength of his emotions, rather than his intellect. Consequently, in a mood of celebration and acceptance, Thomas would write with all the conviction of that mood. He might on another occasion write under the inspiration of a different emotional attitude, because thought and attitude were derived from personal convictions essentially emotional in character. All depended, therefore, upon the strength and direction of his emotions at a particular moment. As a result, throughout his whole poetic career, there are poems Christian in feeling followed by poems more pagan in outlook. Poetry of celebration is closely followed by poetry of bitterness and rejection. The feeling may move from pagan stoicism to a Christian belief in immortality, but this is not to say that either attitude was not deeply held at the time.

I have already suggested that in *Twenty-five Poems* Thomas is increasingly concerned with religious themes. One of the most important poems in this collection is 'This bread I break', which shows a more positive use of Christian imagery, being based on the service of the Eucharist:

> This bread I break was once the oat,
> This wine upon a foreign tree
> Plunged in its fruit;
> Man in the day or wind at night
> Laid the crops low, broke the grape's joy.
>
> Once in this wind the summer blood
> Knocked in the flesh that decked the vine,
> Once in this bread
> The oat was merry in the wind;
> Man broke the sun, pulled the wind down.

> This flesh you break, this blood you let
> Make desolation in the vein,
> Were oat and grape
> Born of the sensual root and sap;
> My wine you drink, my bread you snap.

Here the poet's sense of the unity of all creation has become religious in character. The elements of the Eucharist, the forms of natural life, and mankind itself, are identified with Christ.

The poem registers a sense of the sacramental nature of the universe: the common things of life serve to illustrate profound mysteries, which are themselves witness to, and celebrate, the Creator. An important Eucharistic concept is the idea that a part can represent the whole; a part that is consecrated can refer to a consecrated whole. The concept of divinity lies in the accepted physical reality of the bread and the wine, not in some notion of the Idea behind external objects: consequently, each particle of life contains the divine. This idea of a sacramental universe profoundly influences Thomas's later work. Such a concept of reality, which places emphasis on the physical actuality of the thing —like Hopkins's concern with the 'inscape' and 'instress' of objects—demands for its expression a sensuous rather than philosophic use of language. Thomas, in this poem, stresses that the flesh and blood were 'oat and grape Born of the sensual root and sap'. Again, in these verses, he speaks in the person of Christ. As man harvested the crops, so did he shed, and therefore partake of, Christ's blood.

There is in Thomas's poetry a strong racial feeling which Matthew Arnold has called 'Titanism'; a deep-set pessimism and sense of nostalgia, veined sometimes with bitterness and frustration. Arnold considered it a significant feature of Celtic literature:

The Celts, with their vehement reaction against the despotism of fact, with their sensuous nature, their manifold striving, their adverse destiny, their immense calamities, the Celts are the prime authors of this vein of piercing regret and passion—of this Titanism in poetry.[8]

This impassioned pessimism, regret, and longing, are beautifully conveyed in Thomas's reading of his own poems;
notably 'Should lanterns shine', which conveys his despair
of ever finding lasting convictions. Love, reason, and the
power of the body ('the pulse') all seem to end in frustration.
He is left only with the hope of change and a profound
nostalgic longing:

> I have been told to reason by the heart,
> But heart, like head, leads helplessly;
> I have been told to reason by the pulse,
> And, when it quickens, alter the actions' pace
> Till field and roof lie level and the same
> So fast I move defying time, the quiet gentleman
> Whose beard wags in Egyptian wind.
>
> I have heard many years of telling,
> And many years should see some change.
>
> The ball I threw while playing in the park
> Has not yet reached the ground.

In these lines Thomas, as usual, related his despairs to the
one certain fact of death, imaged here as Time, 'the quiet
gentleman Whose beard wags in Egyptian wind'. This, with
its associations of pyramids and the ageless desert, is a powerful metaphor but the thought is a simple one: the complexity
lies in the original way it is conveyed to the senses. The
elaboration of the image in sensuous terms has no accompanying extension of meaning on the poem's narrative level.
    Another important theme which is developed in *Twenty-
five Poems* is the isolation of the individual, and in particular
the artist. In these early poems Thomas is apt to relate all
experience to himself. In this his art, at this stage, may be
said to be limited. He does not write of experience outside
the orbit of his own personal emotions, but seems also, at
times, to be anxious to hide his naked inner self: 'make me a
mask and a wall to shut from your spies'. Perhaps the most
successful statement of his feeling of isolation is the poem
'Ears in the turrets hear', where he speaks of himself as an

island visited by ships and sailors. He is unsure whether to welcome other people:

> Beyond this island bound
> By a thin sea of flesh
> And a bone coast,
> The land lies out of sound
> And the hills out of mind.
> No birds or flying fish
> Disturbs this island's rest.

We shall find that a major development in *The Map of Love* is his increasing awareness of the condition of other people. He begins to move away from the introspective obsessions of his previous work.

In 1937 he married Caitlin Macnamara. Since his first departure from Wales he had stayed for short periods in London, Cornwall (he was married in Penzance Registry Office), and Ringwood, but he was forever returning to Wales. London was for him the place to meet people, the place for parties, and the place to establish literary contacts. When writing poetry he needed increasingly to be in Wales, remote and alone. Sometimes he returned to his mother's home in Swansea; sometimes he stayed in Laugharne, which was already known to him. Lawrence Durrell has recalled that he 'tried to get him to visit . . . Paris and then return to Corfu for the summer. But he steered off the Continent and did not seem to have any interest in France, or anywhere but his beloved Wales.'[9] Thomas's first home in Laugharne, soon after his marriage, was Eros, a cottage facing the estuary, within sight and sound of the sea-birds, fishing boats, winds, and weathers of the bay. His sea-world knocked at his doorstep.

# CHAPTER SIX

## THE MAP OF LOVE

*T*HE *MAP OF LOVE*, which was published in 1939, marks the beginning of that deepening and exten- sion of poetic sympathy and personal vision that characterizes Thomas's later work. Vernon Watkins has written of the poems in *The Map of Love*:

> Each is an experience perceived and controlled by the religious sense and each answers its own questions. He [Thomas] has pared his imagery without losing any of its force.[1]

In this collection Thomas offers a more profound and con- trolled exploration of the themes that inform his earlier work. He is able to see in perspective his earlier adolescent attitudes and emotions.

Before examining the poems in this volume, it is necessary to consider Thomas's relationship with the surrealist move- ment, whose influence is most discernible in his early short stories. Its impact upon his poetry has been over-emphasized, as becomes apparent when it is set beside a truly surrealist poem such as 'The Very Image' by David Gascoyne. This first appeared in the Surrealist Number of *Contemporary Poetry and Prose*, and is representative of English surrealist verse.

> An image of my grandmother
> her head appearing upside-down upon a cloud
> the cloud transfixed on the steeple
> of a deserted railway-station
> far away

An image of an aqueduct
with a dead crow hanging from the first arch
a modern-style chair from the second
a fir-tree lodged in the third
and the whole scene sprinkled with snow.

From 1933 to 1935, when Thomas was forming his own personal style, there was little available surrealist material which he might have read, for surrealism was essentially a European cultural movement. He would have instinctively reacted against anything at once so 'literary' and so propagandist. Karl Shapiro saw him as

the young poet of natural genius and expansive personality who recoils from the ritual of literary tradition [literary, that is, in the worst sense: belonging to the 'arty' and 'bohemian' traditions] and who feels himself drawn into it as into a den of iniquity. (This is both the puritanism and the provincialism of Thomas.)[2]

He remained essentially provincial in outlook and certainly his attitude to London literary life and its cosmopolitan culture—though he was ready from time to time to avail himself of its favours and pleasures—was apt to be critical. Keidrych Rhys, Editor of *Wales* and a close friend of his, has said that Thomas hated the London literary world.

Thomas was very annoyed that Treece associated his name with the surrealist movement, for he was always anxious to maintain his integrity and individual status as a poet. Though he co-edited an early number of *Wales* with Keidrych Rhys, and though he was willing to fill its numbers with his own work, he refused to allow his name to appear on the magazine as co-editor. As the magazine had gone to press, however, his name had to stand. He would not put his name to any collective enterprise and deeply resented his inclusion, later, in both surrealist and Apocalypse manifestos. David Richards, one of Thomas's friends at Laugharne, recalls that

Thomas most emphatically disagrees with the surrealist creed and spent at least ten minutes during one of our conversations denouncing it. His ideas come from his inner-most mind but before they reach paper, he says, they must go through the rational processes of the intellect, unlike the Surrealists who put their words down on paper exactly as they emerge from chaos, as it were, without shaping them or putting them in order, as Thomas does; for them chaos is the shape of order.[3]

What conclusions then are to be drawn concerning Thomas's relations with the surrealist movement? I think he was in general sympathy with certain surrealist attitudes, though it is more likely that such English surrealist and apocalyptic writers as Treece and Hendry were influenced by Thomas, than he by them. The surrealists encouraged the break with rational control, the use of imagery from the subconscious mind, and the application to art of Freudian psychology; three things of which Thomas approved. The obsession with sex, the accepted conflict of image, and the release of emotions were aspects of Thomas's poetry that the surrealist literary theories seemed to justify. In purpose, however, Thomas's poetry differed entirely from the work of the surrealists, who aimed to break down order and reject all positive values, since such values were considered false. There was little concern with the objective standards of art, since an objective critical approach to matters of form and structure, had no meaning for the surrealists. Thomas has himself stated, however, that once an image arises 'I . . . apply to it what intellectual and critical forces I possess.'[4] His attitude to experience was far from anarchic and he sought in his poetry to create values, rather than image a world devoid of them. His art may show uncertainty and doubt—the signs of an unremitting honesty—but it was directed by racial feelings that made such an amoral outlook impossible for him.

'After the funeral', which seems to me the finest of Thomas's early poems, reveals the extent to which his work was directed by Welsh traditions of thought and feeling. It was written in memory of his aunt, Ann Jones, who was very dear to him, and on whose farm in North Carmarthenshire he spent many of his happiest childhood days.

He describes such a childhood holiday in the story *The Peaches*. In 'After the funeral', for the first time in his poetry, Thomas's emotional range was extended beyond his own subjective world. With a perception and self-critical awareness critics are apt to deny him, he observed of 'After the funeral':

> The next poem I'll read is the only one I have written that is, directly, about the life and death of one particular human being I knew—and not about the very many lives and deaths whether seen, as in my first poems, in the tumultuous world of my own being or, as in the later poems, in war, grief, and the great holes and corners of universal love.[5]

Thomas, in these lines, suggests the development his work shows: in his early poetry all experience is seen in terms of his subjective world, but in the later work his imagination and impassioned interest is extended beyond the frontiers of his own personality. *The Map of Love* marks the beginning of this later development.

The opening lines of 'After the funeral' set the scene. We are given a series of impressions registering bitterness, almost hysteria; 'mule praises', 'brays', 'windshake of sailshaped ears'—the implied image is that of a mule, to which the mourners are compared in their attitudes:

> After the funeral, mule praises, brays,
> Windshake of sailshaped ears, muffle-toed tap
> Tap happily of one peg in the thick
> Grave's foot, blinds down the lids, the teeth in black,
> The spittled eyes, the salt ponds in the sleeves.

The poet, is, nevertheless, describing the funeral scene in the light of his own emotions. The vain chatter of the people, the incidents of the burial evoke in him reactions mainly of horror and rejection, and he speaks satirically of the mourners' 'spittled eyes' (as though the mourners have been spitting on their eyes to feign tears), and 'the salt ponds in the sleeves' (another image of assumed grief). He is also embittered by the facile and—to him—inadequate acquiescence

of the bereaved, who find sufficient balm in the theology of
their conventional Nonconformist beliefs. Thomas protests
against this, rejecting the attitudes of conventional piety.
The poem continues:

> Morning smack of the spade that wakes up sleep,
> Shakes a desolate boy who slits his throat
> In the dark of the coffin and sheds dry leaves,
> That breaks one bone to light with a judgment clout.

The boy is the poet who, having spent much of his childhood
at Ann Jones's farm, has at this moment of her death special
childhood memories. Faced with his aunt's death, he thinks
himself a boy again. With the paranoic fantasy of a child he
imagines himself dead in the coffin: 'and sheds dry leaves' is
an important and difficult image that has, I think, two
related planes of meaning. It refers to the merging again of
human and natural forces—a favourite idea of Thomas's.
Since vegetal life continues, the fact that the human body
rejoins the natural forces ensures a kind of immortality. The
phrase also refers to the child's fruitless tears. Vernon
Watkins has told me that Thomas, discussing the poem with
him, suggested these lines might show surrealist influence.

At this point in the poem the poet returns to the scene in
the house. He is standing, it would seem, in the parlour from
which the body has just been taken. It is the familiar, little-
used, Welsh parlour, the holy of holies, used only for funerals
and on Sundays. It contained the best furniture, was apt to
be dusty, and seemed always—so solemn its atmosphere—
to be anticipating a funeral:

> After the feast of tear-stuffed time and thistles
> In a room with a stuffed fox and a stale fern,
> I stand, for this memorial's sake, alone
> In the snivelling hours with dead, humped Ann
> Whose hooded, fountain heart once fell in puddles
> Round the parched worlds of Wales and drowned each sun
> (Though this for her is a monstrous image blindly
> Magnified out of praise; her death was a still drop;
> She would not have me sinking in the holy

Flood of her heart's fame; she would lie dumb and deep
And need no druid of her broken body).
But I, Ann's bard on a raised hearth, call all
The seas to service that her wood-tongued virtue
Babble like a bellbuoy over the hymning heads,
Bow down the walls of the ferned and foxy woods
That her love sing and swing through a brown chapel,
Bless her bent spirit with four, crossing birds.

When writing this poem Thomas was anxious to take his images from common everyday, domestic things and not to move from the humble origins and familiar simplicities of his aunt's life and home. It is interesting to compare his description of the same parlour in his story *The Peaches*. Here once again are the stuffed fox, the fern, a Bible; it is a typical Welsh parlour of this period:

The best room smelt of moth-balls and fur and damp and dead plants and stale, sour air. Two glass cases on wooden coffin-boxes lined the window wall. You looked at the weed-grown vegetable garden through a stuffed fox's legs, over a partridge's head, along the red-paint-stained breast of a stiff, wild duck. A case of china and pewter, trinkets, teeth, family brooches, stood beyond the bandy table; there was a large oil lamp on the patchwork tablecloth, a Bible with a clasp, a tall vase with a draped woman about to bathe on it, and a framed photograph of Annie, Uncle Jim, and Gwilym smiling in front of a fern-pot. . . . The fireplace was full of brass tongs, shovels, and pokers. The best room was rarely used. Annie dusted and brushed and polished there once a week, but the carpet still sent up a grey cloud when you trod on it, and dust lay evenly on the seats of the chairs. . . .[6]

This room, now 'fiercely' in mourning, becomes the scene of the poem.

The line 'After the feast of tear-stuffed time and thistles' illustrates the techniques of association that Thomas employs. He has said that his poetry can often be taken on its literal level. The period of bereavement has been one of tears ('tear-stuffed time'), but the word 'feast' suggests there was a certain enjoyment of the grief. In Wales, to this day, a

funeral is referred to as 'beautiful', and usually involves a
long procession of mourners, tiers of flowers, and fervent
hymn-singing. Familiar with adversity and violent death,
the Welshman has learned to enjoy sorrow. The word
'thistles' denotes the pain that has been present in this
bereavement. The whole line, moreover, has a secondary
play of associations: 'feast' refers to the 'funeral meats' of
the repast which follows the burial ceremony and is as
important a social occasion as a wedding. In the phrase
'tear-stuffed time' the poet has in mind the familiar herb—
an association which 'stuffed' corroborates: 'thistles' extends
the vegetable metaphor. In this way, the word 'feast' is used
both literally and metaphorically: similarly, the word
'stuffed' is both descriptive of the funeral repast and applied
metaphorically to the mourners.

The phrase 'snivelling hours' censures the ineffectual
weeping and continues the satiric note. Ann's heart is spoken
of as a fountain, bringing love to the 'parched worlds of
Wales', so that it 'drowned each sun'. But, we may ask, why
'hooded' fountain heart? He is thinking of the hood of a nun,
with its associations of devotion and dedicated love, and
perhaps also humility and sacrifice. He is aware that Ann
would have been too humble to accept such praise: to her
it would be a 'monstrous image blindly Magnified out of
praise'. The 'flood' of her love is holy, he says, introducing
an image, which is a development of the earlier fountain
image, and significant in that in his later work the word
'flood' is increasingly used as an image of love. Another
important image is that of the druid, the ancient Welsh
poet, prophet, and priest, to whom was attributed supernatural and divine powers that made him a mediator
between man and the gods. Thomas, in his rejection of
conventional Nonconformist doctrine and in his attempt to
create a mythology of Ann Jones's love, implicitly compares
himself to the ancient druid. As a poet, he has a similar
mediating task and refers to himself as 'Ann's bard on a
raised hearth'. Her virtue is 'wood-tongued' because it is
meek and does not speak of itself. I think there is a slightly

contemptuous note in the chapel mourners' 'hymning heads',
over which Ann's virtue babbles like a bellbuoy. The reference to the 'fox' and the 'fern' is very important, for these
items in the rather shabby home are, at the close of the poem,
the symbols used to transcend reality. They are in themselves a familiar enough part of the Welsh home, and Ann
Jones lived on a farm, which perhaps explains the many
stuffed animals. It is, on Thomas's part, a characteristic
choice of symbol, the one an animal, the other a plant.

His aunt's love is compared to a bell in the line 'That her
love sing and swing through a brown chapel'. The 'four,
crossing birds' make a cross and a kiss of blessing, an image
whose origin could be an echo of Revelation iv. 6–8:

And before the throne there was a sea of glass like unto crystal:
and in the midst of the throne, and round about the throne,
were four beasts. . . . And the four beasts had each of them six
wings about him . . . and they rest not day and night, saying,
Holy, holy, holy, Lord God Almighty, which was, and is, and
is to come.

Certainly the sea image occurs earlier ('call all The seas to
service'). It is likely, I think, that at such a time Thomas
would have been reading the book of Revelation, and its
imagery would have remained in his mind. The poem
continues:

> Her flesh was meek as milk, but this skyward statue
> With the wild breast and blessed and giant skull
> Is carved from her in a room with a wet window
> In a fiercely mourning house in a crooked year.
> I know her scrubbed and sour humble hands
> Lie with religion in their cramp, her threadbare
> Whisper in a damp word, her wits drilled hollow,
> Her fist of a face died clenched on a round pain;
> And sculptured Ann is seventy years of stone.

The poet insists again on the humility of the dead woman,
but nevertheless it is a 'skyward' statue he is creating.
Throughout the poem he emphasizes the physical ugliness
of her death ('scrubbed and sour . . . hands') and its menial

surroundings; and he contrasts with these things the image
of her love he is building, druid-like, 'on a raised hearth'.
Effective irony is obtained by a subtle device in the lines 'I
know her scrubbed . . . in their cramp', where the implied
predicating of 'hands' and 'religion' with 'lie in their cramp'
passes judgement on the impoverished Nonconformist
religious attitude. Thomas dismisses the ugliness of her death,
the inadequacy of her conventional religious attitude to
death. The lines that describe the dead body move heavily,
until suddenly a quickening cadence seems to enact a trans-
figuration: 'And sculptured Ann is seventy years of stone'.
Physical ugliness is replaced by marmoreal serenity. The
closing lines continue this transformation:

> These cloud-sopped, marble hands, this monumental
> Argument of the hewn voice, gesture and psalm,
> Storm me forever over her grave until
> The stuffed lung of the fox twitch and cry Love
> And the strutting fern lay seeds on the black sill.

'Sopped' satirizes the conventional idea of heaven, which the
'cloud' suggests. The adjective 'hewn' indicates the poet's
attitude to his craft: poetry, like stone, is 'hewn' only with
great effort.

The poem is resolved by dialectical method. The implication at the close is, of course, that the fox *will* cry Love, that
the fern *does* ensure a kind of immortality. The belief in the
immortality ensured by the biological processes of returning
life is characteristic of Thomas. To choose the fox as a symbol
of love is a particularly powerful vindication of faith in love:
one remembers the rite of 'blooding' children with the fox's
blood after it has been hunted down. This assertion of faith
in spiritual love is a new element in his work. Conventional
attitudes to death and religion are dismissed in favour of the
idea of re-immersion in the natural process of creation, and
of a belief in love as the supreme spiritual force.

'After the funeral', then, is a formal elegy: its protagonists
are the poet, the mourners, and Ann Jones, whose body is
asleep in death. The mourners themselves are spiritually

asleep, as also is the poet until the terrible reality of death
wakens him with the 'Morning smack of the spade that wakes
up sleep'. Alliteration and assonance play an important part
in the poem: blinds . . . black; spittled . . . salt . . . sleeves;
stuffed . . . stale; humped . . . hooded; worlds . . . Wales;
broken . . . body; humble . . . hands; babble . . . bellbuoy.
The running echo is part of the rhythmic compulsion of the
poem, and sound it seems suggested the next image, which
was then accepted or rejected as it suited the sense.

'If my head hurt a hair's foot' illustrates how closely
Thomas's poetry was allied to his personal experience. It
was written in the spring of 1939, when Caitlin Thomas was
expecting her first child, on a subject that would attract
Thomas's compassionate, sexual imagination. In the opening
stanzas the child about to be born addresses its mother:

> 'If my head hurt a hair's foot
> Pack back the downed bone.

Let me perish rather than cause you pain, says the child; the
theme is elaborated in a succession of images:

> 'All game phrases fit your ring of a cockfight:
> I'll comb the snared woods with a glove on a lamp.

'The bed is a cross place', the child continues: 'cross' having
associations of pain and anger as well as Christian implications of suffering and sacrifice. It is also a rustic word for
sexual intercourse. The mother, however, replies that there
is no escape, for her or for the unborn child, from the joy and
the anguish, the life and the death, that she carries:

> The grain that hurries this way from the rim of the grave
> Has a voice and a house, and there and here you must couch
>    and cry.

> 'Rest beyond choice in the dust-appointed grain,
> At the breast stored with seas. . . .
> The grave and my calm body are shut to your coming as stone,
> And the endless beginning of prodigies suffers open.'

Even at the child's birth the grain of life 'hurrying from the
rim of the grave' is 'dust-appointed': that is, it must return to

dust. In such a concept of existence all life is, at every moment, dying. Thomas echoes Donne both in thought and imagery:

> In the wombe the dead *child* kills the *Mother* that conceived it, and is a murtherer, nay a *parricide*. . . .

> But then this *exitus a morte*, is but *introitus in mortem*, this *issue*, this deliverance *from* that *death*, the death of the *wombe* is an *entrance*, a delivering over to *another death*, the manifold deathes of this *world*. Wee have a winding sheete in our Mothers wombe, that growes with us from our conception, and wee come into the world, wound up in that *winding sheet*, for wee come to *seeke a grave*; And as prisoners discharg'd of actions may lye for fees; so when the wombe hath discharg'd us, yet we are bound to it by cordes of flesh, by such a *string*, as that wee cannot goe thence, nor stay there. Wee celebrate our owne funeralls with cryes, even at our birth.[7]

Thomas's image, 'the worm of the ropes round my throat', owes a debt to Donne's 'cordes of flesh'. Both poets are obsessed with the idea of the worm: '*Miserable riddle*, when the *same worme* must bee *my mother*, and *my sister*, and *my selfe*.'[8] Thomas ends his poem on a religious note: birth is miraculous. Though the grave and the mother's body are shut to the child's coming as stone, by the miracle of recurring life (maintained by God's Grace) 'the endless beginning of prodigies suffers open'.

In Anglo-Welsh literature, as I suggested earlier, there is an emphasis on sensory experience: the writer seeks to convey the physical nature of things. Thomas's poem, 'When all my five and country senses see', deals with this theme. He tells us that as 'the youth becomes more self-conscious, his virginal sensuous delight in the world about him decays . . . but that the poet's emotional energy will restore and vivify his responsiveness',[9] producing a state of innocence founded on love. This will come to pass by an improvement of sensual enjoyment. One is reminded of Blake's claim that: 'If the doors of perception were cleansed every thing would appear . . . infinite'.[10] This emphasis on sensory and emotional experience has an important influence on Thomas's later

G

visionary poetry. 'When all my five and country senses see' registers the first, virginal state of innocence, before moving to the consciousness of experience through words and the inevitable loss of innocence with the increase in self-know-ledge, when 'wounds are mended bitterly'. The poem finally suggests the visionary experience, founded on love, which the poet may attain: the song of innocence has become the song of experience:

> When all my five and country senses see,
> The fingers will forget green thumbs and mark
> How, through the halfmoon's vegetable eye,
> Husk of young stars and handfull zodiac,
> Love in the frost is pared and wintered by,
> The whispering ears will watch love drummed away
> Down breeze and shell to a discordant beach,
> And, lashed to syllables, the lynx tongue cry
> That her fond wounds are mended bitterly.
> My nostrils see her breath burn like a bush.
>
> My one and noble heart has witnesses
> In all love's countries, that will grope awake;
> And when blind sleep drops on the spying senses,
> The heart is sensual, though five eyes break.

Thomas here asserts that experience is gained by an improve-ment of sensual enjoyment: his final statement is that 'the heart is sensual'. When writing his poetry 'Dylan worked upon a symmetrical abstract with tactile delicacy; out of a lump of texture or nest of phrases he created music, testing everything by physical feeling . . .'[11] An important theme developed in *The Map of Love*, and one that had long troubled Thomas's questioning mind, was the theme of art as illusion, of religion as illusion. Allied to his religious nature was an unwavering honesty: he always questioned the validity of his experience, probing what were for him the fundamental truths of art and religion. The poem 'It is the sinners' dust-tongued bell' examines these themes. There are Yeatsian echoes in

> Moonfall and sailing emperor, pale as their tide-print,
> Hear by death's accident the clocked and dashed-down spire
> Strike the sea hour through bellmetal.

'The moon, its reflected light, its sea-flux influence, is symbolic of the seeming, but illusory, transcendence of death by the artist, the Christian, the lover.'[12] In another poem Thomas contrasts the 'undying artifact' of the carved bird on a steeple tower with the miraculous and holy life of actual living birds:

> The spire cranes. Its statue is an aviary.
> From the stone nest it does not let the feathery
> Carved birds blunt their striking throats on the salt gravel.[13]

But these 'built' birds 'fly with winter to the bells'—that is, they possess no real life:

> Those craning birds are choice for you, songs that jump back
> To the built voice, or fly with winter to the bells,
> But do not travel down dumb wind like prodigals.

Thomas was deeply disturbed by the contrast between the vitality of living things and the utterly different vitality that belonged to art. The poem is inspired by the same scene as 'Especially when the October wind': contemplating the carved birds on the steeple, the poet contrasts the fixity of art with the life of the birds flying in Cwmdonkin Park.

It is most apt that the volume *The Map of Love* closes with the poem 'Twenty-four years', for this is a compact and urgent summary of the attitudes and ideas that inform Thomas's early work. It reviews life as a progress to death. The image of the tailor represents the world of the flesh in contrast to that of the spirit; the world of mortal time as against that of eternity. The poem might well be prefaced by a passage from Donne:

> Whilest wee are *in the body*, wee are but in *a pilgrimage*, and wee are *absent from the Lord*. . . .

Our *youth* is *worse* then our *infancy*, and our *age worse* then our *youth*. Our *youth* is *hungry and thirsty*, after those *sinnes*, which our *infancy knew not*; And our *age* is *sory* and *angry*, that it *cannot pursue* those *sinnes* which our *youth* did. And besides, al the way, so many deaths, that is, so many deadly calamities accompany every condition, and every period of this life, as that death it selfe would bee an ease to them that suffer them.[14]

Thomas's lines are perhaps the most compact he ever wrote:

> Twenty-four years remind the tears of my eyes.
> (Bury the dead for fear that they walk to the grave in labour.)
> In the groin of the natural doorway I crouched like a tailor
> Sewing a shroud for a journey
> By the light of the meat-eating sun.
> Dressed to die, the sensual strut begun,
> With my red veins full of money,
> In the final direction of the elementary town
> I advance for as long as forever is.

It is a birthday poem, like many others deriving its inspiration from an event of personal significance or a particular observed scene.

The 'tears' of the opening line refer to the suffering that is the condition of living. The 'dead' of the second line are on one level of interpretation the dead fears, hopes, and despairs of life. Bury them, says the poet, lest they multiply upon each other. He turns to the subject of birth: 'the groin of the natural doorway' is clearly the womb in which the child is accurately said to be 'crouched like a tailor'. Even while in the womb the poet was preparing for death ('sewing a shroud for a journey'). The sun is called 'meat-eating' because it brings about man's age and is the directing force in his progress towards death. As we have seen, Thomas tended, in such of his early poems as 'Especially when the October wind', to use the sun as an image of destruction. 'Dressed to die' is a variation of the slang expression 'dressed to kill': life's journey, a 'sensual strut', is a continual destructive conflict between the spirit and the flesh. The 'red veins full of money' represent the sensual potentiality of man that he must 'spend' during this journey. Thomas frequently uses 'money' as an image of sensuality, corruption, and worldliness. The 'elementary town' has several connotations: it refers to the return to the first elements, and has associations of simplicity and innocence. The last line has a personal emphasis, in that 'forever' surely applies to the duration of Thomas's existence. He refers all experience, all time, all resolution to his own personal condition, for he is himself the universe of his poems.

As Thomas developed, he emerged from his early intro-spective obsessions and outgrew certain of his adolescent attitudes. Negative emotions of self-destructive despair and frustration gave way to a more lucid and serene acceptance of the human condition. His later poetry is essentially a poetry of reconciliation. He believed that each man should work out his own salvation, his personal relationship with God; he should also be his own psychiatrist and confessor: 'I've always wanted to be my own psychiatrist, just as I've always wanted everybody to be their own doctor and father.'[15] The cost of this effort is registered in his early poems. What also strikes one forcibly here and in the later poems is the obsession with death that is even stronger than the obsession with sex. Thomas's terrible awareness of mortality was probably due in part to his tubercular con-dition. Inevitably this and his early attack of paralysis left its impression upon him. His energy, like that of Keats, is sometimes a febrile energy.

It might be said with justification that Thomas brought English poetry in the twentieth century back to the aural tradition, and in his reviews, written for the *Adelphi* between 1934 and 1936, he continually emphasized the place of sound in poetry. He criticizes the tendency of modern poetry to value cerebral rather than aural craftsmanship:

> The true future of English poetry, poetry that can be pronounced and read aloud, that comes to life out of the red heart through the brain, lies in the Celtic countries. . . .

> 'The Death of the Ear' would be an apt subtitle for a book on the plight of modern poetry. . . .

> . . . this lack of aural value and this debasing of an art that is primarily dependent on the musical mingling of vowels and consonants. . . .[16]

He is reacting against the intellectual, cosmopolitan, and cerebral traditions represented by the work of T. S. Eliot and Ezra Pound:

Wales, Ireland . . . Scotland, are building up, from a tradition of ballad, folksong . . . a poetry that is as serious and as genuine as the poetry in Mr. Pound's Active Anthology.[16]

Thomas's most elaborate and mature craftsmanship occurs in the later work, but the early poems exhibit an unusually accomplished verbal technique. From his early youth he compiled word lists, made up alphabetically. This explains, in part, his use of strange, esoteric words such as 'hyleg', 'scut', 'stammel', and 'parhelion'. Any new word that he came across in his voracious reading he made note of. It would seem, in his early work, that when he required a word to complete a line, he was apt to choose the most obscure and odd. In this way he always avoided hackneyed expression, though sometimes at the expense of intelligibility. From the beginning, his technique of composition was essentially one of verbal patterning. A poem was built up from the individual word or phrase or line. As he grew older, his critical sense developed and he wrote less. Lawrence Durrell wrote of Thomas's method of composition in the early years:

I was disappointed [one wonders why] to find that he wrote slowly and with difficulty and went on mutating his nouns and adjectives until he got his colours sharp enough to carry the effect he wanted.[17]

Vernon Watkins says of the poem, 'I make this in a warring absence', which was the second poem in The Map of Love: 'I saw this poem at many stages on its way to completion. It took roughly a year to finish. A single line would occupy him for many days.'[18] In his later work Thomas perfected his craftsmanship, creating a poetry of religious vision and philosophic insight that was maintained by what might be called a ritual of form.

Many of his poems, and particularly the later ones, were written in and concerning Laugharne, to which he became deeply attached: his references to it are always tinged with nostalgia and affection. Vernon Watkins writes:

Just before the war I stayed with Dylan frequently in Laugharne. The peace and beauty of this small sea-town beyond Carmarthen, a fishing village at the end of the world, represented for him the last refuge of life and sanity in a nightmare world, the last irregular protest against the regularity and symmetry of madness.[19]

These sentiments are echoed by Thomas himself in his letters to Watkins:

We'll be back in Wales, I hope, at the end of February. Certainly in March. Laugharne will be beautiful in the Spring. You must come often.[20]

I hope we can stay here [Laugharne] for a good bit: I have the romantic, dirty summerhouse looking over the marsh to write in.[21]

Rooted also in Thomas's love of Wales are the sometimes buoyant, sometimes morbid, but always impassioned early stories, where the Welsh wizard chants over his devilish brew while the Welsh jester sets fire to the page.

# CHAPTER SEVEN

# A PROSE INTERLUDE: THE EARLY STORIES

Unlike his method of composition in poetry, Thomas wrote prose very rapidly. He thought it less important than his poetry, but throughout his career his prose composition was closely linked with his development as a poet. The prose work is made up of the following: early stories, some of which were included in *The Map of Love*; *Portrait of the Artist as a Young Dog*; *Under Milk Wood*; broadcast talks, which were published under the title, *Quite Early One Morning*; some later stories, included in *A Prospect of the Sea*; *Adventures in the Skin Trade*, an unfinished novel; several film scripts, one of which, *The Doctor and the Devils*, has been published in book form; and, finally, a large collection of letters, including the volume, *Letters to Vernon Watkins*. The early prose, written up to 1939, includes the early stories, *Portrait of the Artist as a Young Dog*, and the first chapter of *Adventures in the Skin Trade*, entitled *A Fine Beginning*.

Thomas's prose is essentially a poet's prose—eloquent, sensuous, strongly rhythmic, and rich in metaphor. It shares the usual Anglo-Welsh attitudes: it is nostalgic, impassioned, personal, and apocalyptic. The writing draws much upon Biblical thought and imagery, and childhood is a dominant theme. Its style owes much to Welsh pulpit oratory and, for its full subtlety, must be read aloud. Sometimes, it must be admitted, the magic of the word and the emotions of the author get the better of the sense.

This chapter considers the early stories written between

1934 and 1939, which differ significantly from the stories in
*Portrait of the Artist as a Young Dog*. In both theme and technique these early stories are closely related to the early
poetry. It seems that Thomas had, at this stage, yet to
discover the dividing line between prose and poetry. The
stories are introspective and subjective to an unusual degree,
and only occasionally do they possess a dramatic form.
*After the Fair*, probably the first story that Thomas wrote, has
an unusually clear narrative outline. It begins:

The fair was over, the lights in the coco-nut stalls were put
out, and the wooden horses stood still in the darkness, waiting
for the music and the hum of the machines that would set them
trotting forward. One by one, in every booth, the naphtha jets
were turned down and the canvases pulled over the little gaming
tables. The crowd went home, and there were lights in the
windows of the caravans.[1]

The story opens poignantly, with the closing of the fair, and
the central character is a young girl who has left home:

Nobody had noticed the girl. In her black clothes she stood
against the side of the roundabouts, hearing the last feet tread
upon the sawdust and the last voices die in the distance. Then, all
alone on the deserted ground, surrounded by the shapes of
wooden horses and cheap fairy boats, she looked for a place to
sleep. Now here and now there, she raised the canvas that
shrouded the coco-nut stalls and peered into the warm darkness. . . . Once she stepped on the boards; the bells round a
horse's throat jingled and were still; she did not dare breathe
again until all was quiet and the darkness had forgotten the
noise of the bells. . . . But there was nowhere, nowhere in all
the fair for her to sleep.

The prose is lucid and musical. At the close of the story the
girl, together with the Fat Man she has made friends with
and a baby she tries to comfort, are described fantastically
and irrationally riding, in the night, the speeding roundabout:

As the roundabout started, slowly at first and slowly gaining
speed, the child at the girl's breast stopped crying and clapped

its hands. The night wind tore through its hair, the music jangled in its ears. Round and round the wooden horses sped, drowning the cries of the wind with the beating of their hooves.

And so the men from the caravans found them, the Fat Man and the girl in black with a baby in her arms, racing round and round on their mechanical steeds to the ever-increasing music of the organ.

In his early stories Thomas often tends to move from realism to fantasy, from a disciplined handling of experience to a freer registering of emotions. *A Prospect of the Sea* is a further illustration of this. It opens in a style characteristic of Anglo-Welsh prose at its best:

It was high summer, and the boy was lying in the corn. He was happy because he had no work to do and the weather was hot. He heard the corn sway from side to side above him, and the noise of the birds who whistled from the branches of the trees that hid the house. Lying flat on his back, he stared up into the unbrokenly blue sky falling over the edge of the corn. The wind, after the warm rain before noon, smelt of rabbits and cattle. He stretched himself like a cat, and put his arms behind his head. Now he was riding on the sea, swimming through the golden corn waves, gliding along the heavens like a bird; in sevenleague boots he was springing over the fields; he was building a nest in the sixth of the seven trees that waved their hands from a bright, green hill.

The imagery is poetic ('the unbrokenly blue sky falling over the edge of the corn'), and the forms of natural life are blurred by a derangement of the senses ('swimming through the golden corn waves', 'trees that waved their hands').

Now he was a boy with tousled hair, rising lazily to his feet, wandering out of the corn to the strip of river by the hillside. He put his fingers in the water, making a mock sea-wave to roll the stones over and shake the weeds; his fingers stood up like ten tower pillars in the magnifying water, and a fish with a wise head and a lashing tail swam in and out of the tower gates. He made up a story as the fish swam through gates into the pebbles and the moving bed.

This is a communication of sensory experience, remarkable for its originality of perception. A little later in the story there is a typically Anglo-Welsh celebration of natural life:

> The boy sent a stone skidding over the green water. He saw a rabbit scuttle, and threw a stone at its tail. A fish leaped at the gnats, and a lark darted out of the green earth. This was the best summer since the first seasons of the world. He did not believe in God, but God had made this summer full of blue winds and heat and pigeons in the house wood. There were no chimneys on the hills with no name in the distance, only the trees which stood like women and men enjoying the sun; there were no cranes or coal-tips, only the nameless distance and the hill with seven trees. He could think of no words to say how wonderful the summer was, or the noise of the wood-pigeons, or the lazy corn blowing in the half wind from the sea at the river's end. There were no words for the sky and the sun and the summer country.

Clearly Thomas has in mind the first splendour of creation. His description moves to an ecstatic idealization of the countryside of youth in which the chimneys, cranes, and coal-tips of industrial Swansea have no place. The landscape is witnessed in a vision: it is a summer country.

Towards the close of the story, as the poet describes the dying of the afternoon, again there is a tendency to blur the outlines of experience:

> The afternoon was dying; lazily, namelessly drifting westward through the insects in the shade; over hill and tree and river and corn and grass to the evening shaping in the sea; blowing away; being blown from Wales in a wind, in the slow, blue grains, like a wind full of dreams and medicines; down the tide of the sun on to the grey and chanting shore where the birds from Noah's ark glide by with bushes in their mouths, and to-morrow and to-morrow tower over the cracked sand-castles.

The reference to Noah's ark is important, for the story ends on an apocalyptic, religious note, recalling Vernon Watkins's observation that Thomas's 'early stories explored the relation between immediate reality and archetypal symbols':[2]

A raven flew by him, out of a window in the Flood to the blind, wind tower shaking in to-morrow's anger like a scarecrow made out of weathers.

'Once upon a time,' said the water voice.

'Do not adventure any more,' said the echo.

'She is ringing a bell for you in the sea.'

'I am the owl and the echo: you shall never go back.'

On a hill to the horizon stood an old man building a boat, and the light that slanted from the sea cast the holy mountain of a shadow over the three-storied decks and the Eastern timber. And through the sky, out of the beds and gardens, down the white precipice built of feathers, the loud combs and mounds, from the caves in the hill, the cloudy shapes of birds and and beasts and insects drifted into the hewn door. A dove with a green petal followed in the raven's flight. Cool rain began to fall.

Such prose is very close to the style of Thomas's poems. There is little narrative outline and much of its meaning is implicit in the associations of the words, the strong rhythmic compulsion, and the sensory power of the language. The passage suggests the sacramental unity of all life, a unity that is outside time. This is the same creation, the same hope of regeneration as in the original story of the Flood. Contemporary life is interpreted in the light of traditional Christian mythology, and the dove and the raven are symbols, respectively, of redemption and regeneration ('with a green petal'), death and sin.

Another story which closely follows Old Testament mythology is *The Tree*, and here again the narrative outline is blurred at times. Its three characters—gardener, child, and idiot—possess a larger-than-life, primeval quality that recalls the work of Caradoc Evans. They inhabit a strange, impassioned world:

The gardener loved the Bible. When the sun sank and the garden was full of people, he would sit with a candle in his shed, reading of the first love and the legend of apples and serpents. But the death of Christ on the tree he loved most. . . . He would sit in his shed and read of the crucifixion, looking over the jars on his window-shelf into the winter nights. He would think that love fails on such nights, and that many of its children are cut down.

The gardener tells the child the Bible stories:

'Where is Bethlehem?'
'Far away,' said the gardener, 'in the East.'
To the east stood the Jarvis hills, hiding the sun, their trees drawing up the moon out of the grass.

The idiot is introduced in a manner reminiscent of Caradoc Evans's narrative style:

There was an idiot to the east of the country who walked the land like a beggar. Now at a farmhouse and now at a widow's cottage he begged for his bread.

Thomas suggests the idiot's innocence and holiness and the Welsh scene is identified with that of Christ's childhood:

'Bethlehem,' said the idiot to the valley, turning over the sounds of the word and giving it all the glory of the Welsh morning. He brothered the world around him, sipped at the air, as a child newly born sips and brothers the light. The life of the Jarvis valley, steaming up from the body of the grass and the trees and the long hand of the stream, lent him a new blood. Night had emptied the idiot's veins, and dawn in the valley filled them again.
'Bethlehem,' said the idiot to the valley.

There is a poet's delight in the sound of the word. It is significant that Thomas identifies the life of the idiot with the natural life around him ('He brothered the world around him'). On Christmas morning the idiot walked into the garden:

'Let me be,' said the idiot, and made a little gesture against the sky. There is rain on my face, there is wind on my cheeks. He brothered the rain.
So the child found him under the shelter of the tree, bearing the torture of the weather with a divine patience, letting his long hair blow where it would, with his mouth set in a sad smile. . . .
'Where do you come from?' asked the child.
'From the east,' answered the idiot.

The story moves to an apocalyptic, dramatic finish in which the Biblical past superimposes its image on the present:

'Stand up against the tree.'

The idiot, still smiling, stood up with his back to the elder.

'Put out your arms like this.'

The idiot put out his arms.

The child ran as fast he could to the gardener's shed, and, returning over the sodden lawns, saw that the idiot had not moved but stood, straight and smiling, with his back to the tree and his arms stretched out.

'Let me tie your hands.'

The idiot felt the wire that had not mended the rake close round his wrists. It cut into the flesh, and the blood from the cuts fell shining on to the tree.

'Brother,' he said. He saw that the child held silver nails in the palm of his hands.

In this story Biblical narrative has been interpreted in modern and personal terms, as in Thomas's early poetry. His idiot is in the romantic tradition of Wordsworth's idiot boy.

Some of the stories draw upon the magical, mystical, and primitive elements in Welsh folk-lore, and Thomas works out his violent themes of sin and death, revenge and redemption against a heavily coloured, almost Old Testament background. In his story *The Enemies* Mr. and Mrs. Owen emerge as vital, life-giving forces in a valley that is seen as primeval and barren:

Up came the roots, and a crooked worm, disturbed by the probing fingers, wriggled blind in the sun. Of a sudden the valley filled all its hollows with the wind, with the voice of the roots, with the breathing of the nether sky. Not only a mandrake screams; torn roots have their cries; each weed Mr. Owen pulled out of the ground screamed like a baby. In the village behind the hill the wind would be raging, the clothes on the garden lines would be set to strange dances. And women with shapes in their wombs would feel a new knocking as they bent over the steamy tubs. Life would go on in the veins, in the bones, the binding flesh, that had their seasons and their weathers even as the valley binding the house about with the flesh of the green grass.

There is a similar perception of the germination of natural life, and of empathy with natural life, in the writing of Margiad Evans:

Sifting the golden hazel and dark copper willow leaves, I saw and touched the earth. . . . It smelt of fermenting juices. Touching it I felt its clinging, living coldness mounting the veins of my arm, drawing me down into it. Under the dead bracken, the ivy, the celandine, and fox-glove it lay, lapping minute birth, minute decay. I saw the berry's kernel, the emptied broken nutshell, the flex of the shrivelled grass root like a nerve exposed.[3]

The visitor to the valley in Thomas's story is old, afraid of death, and unable to accept the life-process in the way that Mr. and Mrs. Owen, more primitive characters, have accepted it:

'He is frightened of the dark,' thought Mrs. Owen, 'the lovely dark.' With a smile, Mr. Owen thought: 'He is frightened of the worm in the earth, of the copulation in the tree, of the living grease in the soil.' They looked at the old man, and saw that he was more ghostly than ever. . . . Suddenly Mr. Davies knelt down to pray. . . . He stared and he prayed, like an old god beset by his enemies.

Both Thomas's poetry and prose attempt to define similar modes of thought and feeling, and such sentences and phrases from these stories as 'felt desolation in his veins',[4] 'desireless familiars',[5] occur later in the poetry as 'Make desolation in the vein',[6] 'A desireless familiar'.[7]

These stories, to a greater extent than the poetry, owe something to surrealist techniques. Many of the unpublished stories are about lust, insanity, cruelty, and fear. They involve their author in a release of emotion, but whereas the surrealist creed encouraged merely the release of subconscious emotions, Thomas's interpretation of these emotions is essentially religious in character. T. S. Eliot has said that

Yeats's 'supernatural world' was the wrong supernatural world. It was not a world of spiritual significance, not a world of real Good and Evil, of holiness or sin, but a highly sophisticated lower mythology summoned, like a physician, to supply the fading pulse of poetry with some transient stimulant.[8]

Unlike Yeats's supernatural world, the strange world of Thomas's stories is composed of Good and Evil—though, admittedly, the sense of evil tends to dominate.

Perhaps the most successful of these stories is *The Burning Baby*. It is more dramatic in its emotions, more complex in its themes than the others, and it has a firmer narrative outline. I am indebted to Mr. Glyn Jones for information concerning the source of this story. On a visit to Aberystwyth to meet Caradoc Evans he told Dylan Thomas the story of Dr. Price of Llantrisant. The doctor, who died in 1893 at the age of ninety-three, defied in a most exhibitionist fashion the legal, religious, and moral conventions of his time. He called himself a druid and, on his public appearances, dressed in weird and highly-coloured costumes. He chanted pagan addresses to the moon and boasted of supernatural powers. His much-loved illegitimate son, whom he named Iesu Grist (Jesus Christ) and believed destined to recover the lost secrets of the druids, died at the age of five months. Price carried him to the top of a hill in Caerlan fields and, chanting wild laments over the body, burned it.[9]

Thomas listened to this story lounging on his bed at their Aberystwyth hotel and by the end, Glyn Jones recalls, the bed-sheet was riddled with cigarette burns. Thomas's mind seized upon the incident of the child's cremation for *The Burning Baby*, which opens:

> They said that Rhys was burning his baby when a gorse bush broke into fire on the summit of the hill. The bush, burning merrily, assumed to them the sad white features and the rickety limbs of the vicar's burning baby. What the wind had not blown away of the baby's ashes, Rhys Rhys had sealed in a stone jar. With his own dust lay the baby's dust, and near him the dust of his daughter in a coffin of white wood.[10]

In the second paragraph the vicar's elder son enters the story.

> They heard his son howl in the wind. They saw him walking over the hill, holding a dead animal up to the light of the stars. They saw him in the valley shadows as he moved, with the motion of a man cutting wheat, over the brows of the fields. In a sanatorium he coughed his lung into a basin, stirring his fingers delightedly in the blood. What moved with invisible scythe through the valley was a shadow and a handful of shadows cast by the grave sun.

One is reminded of Thomas's own tubercular symptoms. After these vigorous and dramatic paragraphs which set the scene, the narrative begins: 'It was, they said, on a fine sabbath morning in the middle of summer that Rhys Rhys fell in love with his daughter.' Thomas is morbidly obsessed with the corruption of the flesh:

He moved his hand up and down her arm. Only the awkward and the ugly, only the barren bring forth fruit. The flesh of her arm was red with the smoothing of his hand. He touched her breast. From the touch of her breast he knew each inch of flesh upon her. Why do you touch me there? she said.

The vicar's son finds a dead rabbit and, as so often in these stories, a mutilated animal is used to release feelings of cruelty and horror.

The rabbit's head was riddled with pellets, the dogs had torn open its belly, and the marks of a ferret's teeth were upon its throat. He lifted it gently up, tickling it behind the ears. The blood from its head dropped on his hand. Through the rip in the belly, its intestines had dropped out and coiled on the stone.

The boy is a changeling, an idiot, with long green hair. He, too, has been subject to strange sexual adventures, for his sister 'was to him as ugly as the sowfaced woman of Llareggub who had taught him the terrors of the flesh. He remembered the advances of that unlovely woman.' It is interesting to see the name Llareggub, that was to reappear as Llaregyb in *Under Milk Wood*, first coined in these stories of the mid-thirties. The earlier version is more suggestive of the word's etymology, a device employed also in Samuel Butler's title, *Erewhon*.

Rhys Rhys's daughter conceives a child by him, and it is this child which Rhys Rhys burns alive:

Surrounded by shadows, he prayed before the flaming stack, and the sparks of the heather blew past his smile. Burn, child, poor flesh, mean flesh, flesh, flesh, sick sorry flesh, flesh of the foul womb, burn back to dust, he prayed.

Significantly, Thomas makes a minister of religion the central character in the story; as in such other tales of lechery, fear, and cruelty, as *The Horse's Ha*, *The School for Witches*, and *The Holy Six*. Hypocrisy is the chief target of his ferocious satire:

> That night he preached of the sins of the flesh. O God in the image of our flesh, he prayed.
>
> His daughter sat in the front pew, and stroked her arm. She would have touched her breast where he had touched it, but the eyes of the congregation were upon her.
>
> Flesh, flesh, flesh, said the vicar.

The instinct to wound the Nonconformist clergy was as deeply rooted in Thomas as in Caradoc Evans. To attribute perverse desires to the religious and 'respectable' is a simple but effective method of attack, and Thomas is not slow to exploit its possibilities:

> Rhys Rhys sat in his study, the stem of his pipe stuck between his flybuttons, the bible unopened on his knees. The day of God was over, and the sun, like another sabbath, went down behind the hills. . . . Merry with desire, Rhys Rhys cast the bible on the floor. He reached for another book, and read, in the lamplit darkness, of the old woman who had deceived the devil. The devil is poor flesh, said Rhys Rhys.

The use of the Welsh background in the story *The Holy Six* is again imaginative rather than realistic. Thomas seeks to convey an atmosphere of primitive, sensual claustrophobia:

> The Holy Six of Wales sat in silence. The day was drawing to a close, and the heat of the first discussion grew cooler with the falling sun. All through the afternoon they had talked of nothing but the disappearance of the rector of Llareggub, and now, as the first lack of light moved in a visible shape and colour through the room, and their tongues were tired, and they heard the voices in their nerves, they waited only for the first darkness to set in. At the first signs of night they would step from the table, adjust their hats and smiles, and walk into the wicked streets. Where the women smiled under the lamps, and the promise of the old sickness stirred in the fingertips of the girls in the dark doorways, the Six would pass dreaming, to the scrape of their boots on the pavement, of the women throughout the town smiling and doctoring love. To Mr. Stul the women drifted in a maze of hair,

and touched him in a raw place. The women drifted around Mr.
Edger. He caught them close to him, holding their misty limbs
to his with no love or fire. The women moved again, with the
grace of cats, edging down the darker alleys where Mr. Vyne,
envious of their slant-eyed beauty, would scrape and bow. To
Mr. Rafe, their beauties, washed in blood, were enemies of the
fluttering eyes, and moved, in what image they would, full-
breasted, fur-footed, to a massacre of the flesh. He saw the red
nails and trembled. There was no purpose in the shaping wombs
but the death of the flesh they shaped, and he shrank from the
contact of death, and the male nerve was pulled alone.

I have quoted at some length in order to indicate themes and
technique that are typical of these stories. The Holy Six are
at once clerical gentlemen and symbols of the same order as
the mediaeval Seven Deadly Sins. The name Stul is an
anagram of 'lust'; Edger of 'greed'; Vyne of 'envy'; and
Rafe of 'fear'. In this paragraph Thomas suggests the various
reactions of these characters towards sex: they are, respectively, reactions dominated by lust, greed, envy, and fear.
Thus, to Mr. Rafe the women represent a 'massacre of the
flesh': 'he saw the red nails and trembled'. For him 'the
shaping wombs' meant 'the death of the flesh' and 'the male
nerve was pulled alone'.

The link between these early stories and the early poetry
is, very obviously, a fundamental one, both in theme and
attitude. While *The Holy Six* deals with the subject of sexual
man, *The Horse's Ha* is concerned with death in the form of a
plague which enters a town. Again the language closely resembles that of the early poems, not least in its Biblical echoes:

What is death's music? One note or many? The chord of
contagion? Thus questioned the undertaker, the cup three-
quarters empty in his gloved hand. He who marks the sparrow's
fall has no time for my birds, said ApLlewellyn. What music is
death? . . .

So Mr. Montgomery was left alone, by the desolate church,
under a disappearing moon. One by one the stars went out,
leaving a hole in heaven. He looked upon the grave, and slowly
removed his coat.

The emotional and moral attitudes behind such writing are conditioned by an essentially religious view of experience.

Thomas's early stories are essentially a by-product of his poetry. Their obsession with sexual themes, with cruelty, with death and decay has, in its total possession of the personality, something adolescent about it. The prose is distinguished more by its intense sensual power than by its subtlety. In the main tradition of Anglo-Welsh prose-writing, Thomas aims at an imaginative—rather than a realistic— recreation of sensory experience, and packs his language with metaphor. He well understood what Rimbaud called 'the Alchemy of the word'. The stories, however, remain obsessively personal. They are solipsistic: each story brings the reader back to Thomas's own emotional conflicts, fears, and desires. They are imaginative projections of his own intuitions and feelings, bearing little relationship with the everyday, external world. He is hardly concerned with human relationships at all, for his interest in human life is essentially personal and isolated. He writes of the facts of love, death, happiness, and sorrow as they confront indivi- dual man. His concern with experience is not social but personal, not psychological but religious. The tales have the intensity and strangeness, in their wildest moments, of nightmare: and that nightmare, that phantasmagoria of images and perceptions, is offered as reality.

I have already suggested that Thomas was quick to draw upon the more arcane fantasies that the Welsh background and Welsh folk-lore presented to him. It is interesting to see, too, that in his stories, he usually put Welsh names in the final draft: thus, in *The Visitor*, the name Millicent was changed to Rhiannon; and in *The Orchards* the name Peter becomes—significantly—Marlais. *The Orchards* is a very personal piece, revealing something of Thomas's attitude to himself as a poet and his tendency to be overcome by the welter and conflict of his experience:

The word is too much with us. He raised his pencil so that its shadow fell, a tower of wood and lead, on the clean paper. . . . The tower fell, down fell the city of words, the walls of a poem, the symmetrical letters. . . . 'Image, all image,' he cried to the fallen tower as the night came on. 'Whose harp is the sea? Whose burning candle is the sun?' An image of man, he rose to his feet and drew the curtains open. Peace, like a simile, lay over the roofs of the town. 'Image, all image,' cried Marlais, stepping through the window on to the level roofs. . . . He was a folk-man no longer but Marlais the poet walking, over the brink into ruin, up the side of doom, over hell in bed to the red left, till he reached the first of fields where the unhatched apples were soon to cry fire in a wind from a half-mountain falling westward to the sea.

The impact on the poet of the town which he can see below him, of the nearby country and the sea, is through word and image. The conflict, in his mind, between the reality of the world before him and the reality of the word, is an ever-present one. These early stories present a poetic vision of adolescence and early manhood, with all the beauty and intensity, doubts and fears of that age of self-discovery.

# CHAPTER EIGHT

# PORTRAIT OF THE ARTIST AS A YOUNG DOG

### I

IN *Portrait of the Artist as a Young Dog* Thomas for the first time reveals himself as an artist in comedy. Vernon Watkins has described how he

suddenly abandoned the highly charged, artificial yet impulsive symbolism of such stories as *The Orchards*, *The Lemon* and the unfinished fragment *In The Direction of The Beginning* at about the time of his twenty-fourth birthday. . . . Quite suddenly he began to write about people as they actually were and behaved.[1]

Thomas's eye had now turned outward from his own introspective, obsessive emotions to the world about him. It was the varied and many-coloured life of South Wales that attracted his attention; for he was developing a consuming, though generally unjudging, curiosity about other people's lives. The picture that he gives of Wales is an idealized and exuberant one: *Portrait of the Artist as a Young Dog* is, on the whole, genial in tone. In these stories Thomas drew extensively upon his memories of childhood:

Through the exact memory he had of his childhood and an extraordinary power to recreate it he released a spring of comedy, both of character and situation, which had been hidden from himself because it was at first too close to his experience. These were the stories about Swansea and the surroundings of that, his native town; and very Welsh they were, more true to Swansea than Swansea itself.[1]

The story of the Welsh childhood has become a familiar

genre. In the short story the reader is usually offered an isolated and semi-autobiographical incident. Most Anglo-Welsh writers of this century show, in their early work, this need to record the experiences of their childhood and adolescence. In so doing they lay particular emphasis upon the community in which they were brought up. *Portrait of the Artist as a Young Dog* was among the first of these autobiographical works to blend successfully comedy and nostalgia. The comedy of the book is at once apparent, but its nostalgic mood has received less critical attention. This idealistic looking over the shoulder to a bygone state of innocence and joy is one of Thomas's most characteristic attitudes.

Unlike many other accounts of the Welsh childhood, *Portrait of the Artist as a Young Dog* possesses a unity of structure. That unity is the picture it gives of its author, the delineation of a poet's growing consciousness of himself and of the world in which he lives. It is typical of Thomas that he should have chosen to parody the familiar literary mode, the portrait of the artist. There had been a recent modern example of this literary form in Joyce's *Portrait of the Artist as a Young Man*. Thomas, however, hides the real seriousness of his picture behind the mask of comedy. Too many readers, unfortunately, have not seen beyond the mask. Many critics, too, have over-emphasized the influence of Joyce.

Asked how he came to name his *Portrait of the Artist as a Young Dog*, and whether he had been influenced by James Joyce, he explained very quietly but with firmness that when he wrote the stories that comprise the volume, he had not read a word of Joyce.[2]

He writes, in one of his letters to Vernon Watkins: 'I've just finished my Portrait . . . Young Dog proofs. Out in March. I've kept the flippant title for—as the publishers advised—moneymaking reasons.'[3]

Thomas's volume of stories is carefully planned. Each story deals with a stage in his childhood, youth, or early manhood and he never repeats a situation or experience. Though all the stories are linked and have a tremendous sense of life and movement, each has its own atmosphere and mood. Always, in these tales, Thomas is the observer and interpreter, a little detached from the rest of the group. He is, for example, ever aware of other people's discomfort, and quick to see the pathos of their situation. Though humorous, and sometimes gently satiric, his attitude is compassionate and, despite all their imperfections and oddities, he accepts and delights in the humanity of his characters.

As we have already seen, the opening story, *The Peaches*, tells of a childhood visit to Ann Jones's farm. He reveals at once an uncanny sympathy for his subject: as in the picture of Uncle Jim, who stops for a drink and is a little guilty about his drinking: ' "I'll be out straight away," he said fiercely, as though I had contradicted him, "you stay there quiet." ' In true Welsh style: 'He sang hymns all the way to Gorsehill in an affectionate bass voice, and conducted the wind with his whip.' Thomas records his tendency as a child to dramatize himself:

There was welcome then. The clock struck twelve as she [his aunt] kissed me, and I stood among the shining and striking like a prince taking off his disguise. One minute I was small and cold, skulking dead-scared down a black passage in my stiff, best suit . . . unfamiliar to myself, a snub-nosed storyteller lost in his own adventures and longing to be home; the next I was a royal nephew in smart town clothes, embraced and welcomed, standing in the snug centre of my stories and listening to the clock announcing me.

In stories such as this Thomas reveals himself as extremely sensitive, both to his own feelings and to the feelings of others. He is far from the tough, happy-go-lucky tomboy, unlettered and insensitive, many critics have imagined:

I climbed the stairs; each had a different voice. The house smelt of rotten wood and damp and animals. I thought that I had been walking long, damp passages all my life, and climbing stairs in the dark, alone.

Vividly, too, he describes his youthful, imaginative feeling for nature. By imaginative, in this instance, I refer to his tendency to enlarge upon a particular situation:

On my haunches, eager and alone, casting an ebony shadow, with the Gorsehill jungle swarming, the violent impossible birds and fishes leaping, hidden under four-stemmed flowers the height of horses, in the early evening in a dingle near Carmarthen, my friend Jack Williams invisibly near me, I felt all my young body like an excited animal surrounding me.

Thomas was keenly aware of the way of life peculiar to South Wales. In *The Peaches*, for example, he describes a sermon which his cousin Gwilym, who is studying to be a preacher, gives in the barn. It is an effective parody of the *hwyl* that characterizes Welsh preaching:

I sat on the hay and stared at Gwilym preaching, and heard his voice rise and crack and sink to a whisper and break into singing and Welsh and ring triumphantly and be wild and meek.

Thomas reserves some of his satiric shafts for the well-to-do Mrs. Williams who visits the farm:

She said: 'Please don't put yourself out for me, Mrs. Jones, there's a dear.' She dusted the seat of a chair with a lace handkerchief from her bag before sitting down. . . .

Annie prepares tea for her visitor:

'Now, you must have some peaches, Mrs. Williams, they're lovely . . .'
'No, no, Mrs. Jones, thanks the same', she said. 'I don't mind pears or chunks, but I can't bear peaches.'

Throughout this scene Thomas effectively exposes Mrs. Williams's snobbish insensitivity. She is a proud, vulgar woman, conscious only of her wealth and her consequent importance, and the reader's sympathy goes out to Annie.

In *Where Tawe flows* Thomas satirizes the excesses of Welsh Nationalism: the scene is a meeting of the literary group to which 'young Mr. Thomas' belongs:

'We're looking for seditious literature,' said Mr. Humphries with difficulty, raising his hand in a salute.

'Heil, Saunders Lewis! and we know where to find it,' said Mr. Roberts. Mr. Evans turned off his torch, 'Come in out of the night air, boys, and have a drop of something. It's only parsnip wine,' he added.

Saunders Lewis, the Welsh Nationalist leader, had set fire to an aerodrome in Wales in 1938.

Throughout *Portrait of the Artist as a Young Dog* Thomas is anxious to represent himself as an *enfant terrible*:

I let Edgar Reynolds be whipped because I had taken his homework; I stole from my mother's bag; I stole from Gwyneth's bag; I stole twelve books in three visits from the library, and threw them away in the park; I drank a cup of my water to see what it tasted like; I beat a dog with a stick so that it would roll over and lick my hand afterwards; I looked with Dan Jones through the keyhole while his maid had a bath; I cut my knee with a penknife, and put the blood on my handkerchief and said it had come out of my ears so that I could pretend I was ill and frighten my mother; I pulled my trousers down and showed Jack Williams.

The list of delinquencies need not be taken too seriously and at least saves the account from sentimentality, which is always apt to enter into recollections of childhood. This mischievous desire to shock his more respectable readers gives his writing a certain toughness and honesty.

One of the most delightful scenes in *Portrait of the Artist as a Young Dog* occurs in *A Visit to Grandpa's* and describes a situation that could only be found in Wales, where, by tradition, much emphasis and concern is given to a person's place of burial. The elderly are usually anxious to be buried in their ancestral churchyard, a feeling which, in its philosophical acceptance of death, would attract Thomas's interest. A coffin was sometimes prepared in advance and highly prized by its prospective occupant, and many a bottom drawer contains the 'laying out' clothes. The grandfather in the story one morning disappears. It is soon realized that he has gone to Llangadock—for he has put on his best waistcoat—to be buried. He is discovered, *en route*, in Carmarthen. The final scene has a peculiarly Welsh blend of comedy and high seriousness:

Mr. Griff pointed his coloured stick at him.

'And what do you think you are doing on Carmarthen bridge in the middle of the afternoon,' he said sternly, 'with your best waistcoat and your old hat?'

Grandpa did not answer, but inclined his face to the river wind, so that his beard was set dancing and wagging as though he talked, and watched the coracle men move, like turtles, on the shore.

Mr. Griff raised his stunted barber's pole. 'And where do you think you are going,' he said, 'with your old black bag?'

Grandpa said: 'I am going to Llangadock to be buried.' And he watched the coracle shells slip into the water lightly, and the gulls complain over the fish-filled water as bitterly as Mr. Price complained:

'But you aren't dead yet, Dai Thomas.'

For a moment grandpa reflected, then: 'There's no sense in lying dead in Llanstephan,' he said, 'The ground is comfy in Llangadock; you can twitch your legs without putting them in the sea.'

His neighbours moved close to him. They said:

'You aren't dead, Mr. Thomas.'

'How can you be buried, then?'

'Nobody's going to bury you in Llanstephan.'

'Come on home, Mr. Thomas.'

'There's strong beer for tea.'

'And cake.'

But grandpa stood firmly on the bridge, and clutched his bag to his side, and stared at the flowing river and the sky, like a prophet who has no doubt.

Thomas's grandfather, it seems, was reluctant to be buried in Llanstephan and wanted to be laid to rest in his old home, Llangadock, where 'the ground is comfy'. The closing comparison of the old man to 'a prophet who has no doubt', with its Biblical and druidic associations, is particularly effective.

It was Thomas's habit to note down phrases, even whole sentences, that occurred to him while drinking in a pub or talking with friends. Often, in the middle of a witty story or a literary argument, he would drag a cigarette packet from his pocket, tear off the end, write a few words, and thrust the piece into another pocket. Some phrase, metaphor, or joke had jostled its way through the tobacco haze in the crowded bar-parlour. This note-making seldom caused a break in his discourse: he continued his drinking, smoking, talking, his pockets crammed with hastily written notes and observations. Perhaps surprisingly, he was a good listener, and the embroidered pub-stories of human foibles remained ready for use in his capacious memory. The wealth of objective detail in his prose writing demonstrates his receptiveness to the life around him.

Sense impressions he conveys with remarkable immediacy: a good example being the description of his first pint of Welsh beer:

I liked the taste of beer, its live, white lather, its brass-bright depths, the sudden world through the wet-brown walls of the glass, the tilted rush to the lips and the slow swallowing down to the lapping belly, the salt on the tongue, the foam at the corners.

Thomas usually ends his stories on a note of pathos. Often it is a single sentence which strikes this note, as in the story of Little Cough, where he beautifully conveys the child's sense of life's terrible seriousness. George Hooping (nicknamed Little Cough) has been running on Rhossili sands for hours to prove his toughness to the other boys: 'And when I stared round at George again he was lying on his back fast asleep in the deep grass and his hair was touching the flames.' There is, in each story, a specific, well-defined mood. The Swansea streets are full of emotional connotations for Thomas; a mood of nostalgia always directs the experience.

I was a lonely nightwalker and a steady stander-at-corners. I liked to walk through the wet town after midnight, when the streets were deserted and the window lights out, alone and alive on the glistening tram-lines in dead and empty High Street under the moon, gigantically sad in the damp streets by ghostly Ebenezer Chapel. And I never felt more a part of the remote and overpressing world, or more full of love and arrogance and pity and humility, not for myself alone, but for the living earth I suffered on. . . . I leant against the wall of a derelict house in the residential areas or wandered in the empty rooms, stood terrified on the stairs or gazing through the smashed windows at the sea or at nothing, and the lights going out one by one in the avenues.

Such a paragraph, for all the bravado, is a portrait of the artist.

Thomas grew up in the Swansea of the depression, and this period of poverty and unemployment left its mark on his memory:

Mr. Farr hurried down High Street, savagely refusing laces and matches, averting his eyes from the shabby crowds. He knew that the poor the sick and the ugly, unwanted people were so close around him that, with one look of recognition, one gesture of sympathy, he would be lost among them and the evening would be spoilt for ever.

The story *Who do you wish was with us?* shows his concern with pain and bodily suffering. Dylan's friend Ray, who is accompanying him on a day's outing, keeps remembering his brother, a sufferer from tuberculosis:

I had to change the sheets twice a day for my brother, there was blood on everything. I watched him getting thinner and thinner; in the end you could lift him up with one hand. And his wife wouldn't go to see him because he coughed in her face.

The story which closes the volume, *One Warm Saturday*, was Thomas's favourite and is, perhaps, the most complex and personal in the collection. The poet is wandering by himself about Swansea:

The young man, in his wilderness, saw the holiday Saturday set down before him, false and pretty, as a flat picture under a vulgar sun; the disporting families with paper bags, buckets and spades, parasols and bottles, the happy, hot, and aching girls with sunburn liniments in their bags . . . moved him, he thought dramatically in his isolation, to an old shame and pity; outside all holiday, like a young man doomed for ever to the company of his maggots.

He joins in a game of cricket with a family on the sands, until a dog carries the ball into the sea and swims with it out of reach. He sees Mr. Matthews, a typical Nonconformist 'hell-fire preacher': 'Boys with pea-shooters sat quietly near him. A ragged man collected nothing in a cap.' The day moves to its close: 'the evening dull as a chapel. All his friends had vanished into their pleasures.' Thomas characteristically compares the dull evening to a chapel. He mocks himself, however, poking fun at his self-pity and despair:

He thought: Poets live and walk with their poems; a man with visions needs no other company. . . . I must go home and sit in my bedroom by the boiler. But he was not a poet living and walking, he was a young man in a sea town on a warm bank holiday, with two pounds to spend.

He meets a beautiful young woman, and his conflicting emotions are viewed with the irony of the detached observer:

The young man in the window seat, still bewildered by the first sight of her entering the darkened room, caught the kiss to himself and flushed. He thought to run out of the room and through the miracle-making gardens, to rush into his house and hide his head in the bed-clothes and lie all night there, dressed and trembling, her voice in his ears, her green eyes wide awake under his closed eyelids. But only a sick boy with tossed blood would run from his proper love into a dream, lie down in a bedroom that was full of his shames, and sob against the feathery, fat breast and face of the damp pillow. He remembered his age and poems, and would not move.

Eventually, and inevitably, he gets drunk and goes to a party with the young woman. The story moves to a hazy, dream-like close, as he makes his way home alone. A final, elegiac paragraph suggests man's continuing need for compassion and fuller understanding:

For a long time he waited on the stairs, though there was no love now to wait for and no bed but his own too many miles away to lie in, and only the approaching day to remember his discovery. . . . Then he walked out. . . . The light of the one weak lamp in a rusty circle fell across the brick-heaps and the broken wood and the dust that had been houses once, where the small and hardly known and never-to-be-forgotten people of the dirty town had lived and loved and died and, always, lost.

In *Portrait of the Artist as a Young Dog* the half-mythical Welsh
landscapes of the early stories have been replaced by more
closely observed, often indoor, and always specifically Welsh
scenes charged with comedy and dramatic life.

## II

The opening chapters of Thomas's unfinished novel,
*Adventures in the Skin Trade*, belong to the early period, and
describe young Samuel Bennet's departure from Wales for
London. The first chapter seems to me much superior to the
later ones. Its vein of comedy is richer because it is allied
to a fundamental seriousness. The later chapters present a
chaotic, undiscriminating transcript of experience. The
departure from Wales, however, is well done, with all the
gestures and grief of late adolescence vividly portrayed.
Samuel Bennet creeps downstairs the night before he leaves
and damages papers, china, and furniture in his home so
that he can 'never come back'. The break with his home
costs him some effort; the rebellious gestures are a symbol of
the bond he has to break:

He burnt the edge of his mother's sunshade at the gas mantle,
and felt the tears running down his cheeks and dropping on to his
pyjama collar.
    Even in the first moment of his guilt and shame, he remembered
to put out his tongue and taste the track of his tears. Still crying,
he said, 'It's salt. It's very salt. Just like in my poems.'

On the train journey to Paddington—and to Welshmen
exiled in London how important an emotional experience
this is—he locks himself in the lavatory and destroys all his
useful addresses. In the buffet at Paddington he sits opposite
a woman whom he assumes to be a prostitute. The note of
rebellion again asserts itself:

Dear mother, he wrote with his finger on the back of an
envelope, looking up, between every few invisible words, at the
unnoticing woman opposite, this is to tell you that I arrived
safely and that I am drinking in the buffet with a tart. . . . She
is about thirty-eight years old and her husband left her five years

ago because of her carryings on . . . . And you need not worry
that I shall break my heart trying to reform her, because I
have always been brought up to believe Mortimer Street is
what is right, and I would not wish that on anybody. Besides, I
do not want to reform her.

It is the now familiar rebellion against Nonconformist
morality and teaching that inspires the comedy.

The novel, however, loses its urgency, and the scenes in
London, though entertaining, lack the original quality of
Thomas's best prose. The characterization is also less
individual. Derek Stanford finds that 'Samuel Bennet, his
parents, and sister are well shown; but the off-setting group
of bohemian figures, which the young man encounters in
London, are rather too much to type.'[4] With the possible
exception of the opening chapter, the work is some way below
the standard of *Portrait of the Artist as a Young Dog* and *Under
Milk Wood*. He needed a Welsh setting, which he loved and
hated and understood, to direct and sharpen his imagination.

Thomas abandoned *Adventures in the Skin Trade* at the time
of the war and gave his attention to other work. Vernon
Watkins attributes this to the

impact of war . . . on his appalled and essentially tragic vision.
He was able to reconstruct out of joy the truth of his childhood,
both in his poems and his broadcast scripts, for those experiences
were real; but what was only half real, half fictional, he had to
abandon.[5]

In a mood of reconciliation and devotion, he was beginning
the composition of the later poems.

# DEATHS AND ENTRANCES

ROBERT GRAVES has written:

> An ancient Triad runs;
>> Three sacred things:
>> Poets, graves, kings.

—for an ancient Wales or Ireland a poet was not merely a professional verse-writer: he was acknowledged to exercise extraordinary spiritual power. His person was sacrosanct, like that of the king with whose well-being and well-doing the prosperity of the kingdom was magically bound up, or like the seven prime trees of the sacred grove. When he died the people felt a sudden loss of power and a sorrow stole over them all, even over those who were incapable of understanding the meaning of his simplest poems.[1]

Dylan Thomas, in his later work, drew upon the ancient bardic traditions: assuming, particularly in such poems as 'Author's Prologue', 'Over Sir John's hill', and 'Poem on his birthday', a prophetic role. There is, in this poetry, a typically Welsh blend of Christian and pagan thought and feeling: both attitudes are, however, religious in character. In the later poems he writes generally in a mood of reconciliation and acceptance, having outgrown the earlier rebellious and blasphemous attitudes of the *enfant terrible*. There is an apparent yet profound truth in Gwyn Jones's claim: 'That Dylan Thomas was a preacher in verse is one of the most obvious things about him.'[2] In *Deaths and Entrances* he attains his full stature as a religious poet.

The title of the volume is taken, of course, from Donne's sermon *Deaths Duell*: 'Our very *birth* and entrance into this

life, is *exitus a morte*, an *issue from death*.'³ The poems in this
collection show an advance in sympathy and understanding
due, in part, to the impact of war. Thomas's emotional
concern was turned outward to the sufferings of other people.
There was also a deepening harmony between him and his
Welsh environment. Whereas in the early poems his imagination and energy was sometimes dissipated in introspection,
there is in *Deaths and Entrances* a notable widening of theme
and technique. In this new poetry of spiritual regeneration
he makes greater use of Christian ritual and theology.

'A Refusal to Mourn the Death, by Fire, of a Child in
London' is, perhaps, the best example of Thomas as a
preacher in verse. His incantatory recorded reading of this
poem is strongly reminiscent of the *hwyl* of the Welsh
preacher. Not until the first line of the third stanza does he
permit his voice to fall at the end of a line. This chanting
delivery brings out a rhythmic structure derived from this
tradition of preaching. The poem is ceremonial, ritualistic,
and makes extensive use of sacramental imagery.

> Never until the mankind making
> Bird beast and flower
> Fathering and all humbling darkness
> Tells with silence the last light breaking
> And the still hour
> Is come of the sea tumbling in harness
>
> And I must enter again the round
> Zion of the water bead
> And the synagogue of the ear of corn
> Shall I let pray the shadow of a sound
> Or sow my salt seed
> In the least valley of sackcloth to mourn
>
> The majesty and burning of the child's death.

The opening sentence extends from the first to the thirteenth
line, without intervening punctuation. It is an effective
oratorical opening. Never, until the end of the world, will
he mourn the child's death. The images that build up this
declaration not only create a subtle sound-pattern, but also

define specific concepts. The Bible is the main source of the poem's imagery: 'darkness' is referred to as 'fathering', since it is in darkness that all life begins. Likewise this darkness, which the generative sources of life share, makes all men and all forms of natural life similar in their origin: it is 'humbling'. It fathers both mankind and natural life ('Bird beast and flower'). Early in the poem Thomas suggests the identity of all forms of life. The Biblical source of the imagery of light and darkness and of the sea is the opening chapter of Genesis 2–6;

And the earth was without form, and void; and darkness was upon the face of the deep. . . . And God said, Let there be light: and there was light. And God saw the light, that it was good: and God divided the light from the darkness. . . . And God said, Let there be a firmament in the midst of the waters.

The implication is that the poet will not mourn this death until the end of the world: and this end is seen as a return to the first darkness, the first chaos. The sea, which also will be stilled, is an image that suggests potential life.

In the second stanza Thomas refers specifically to his own death. The water bead and the ear of corn are symbolic primal elements, to which all forms of life, including himself, must return. It is the return from differentiated identity to elemental unity. Significantly, Thomas sees the unity of all existence as sacramental in character ('Zion . . . synagogue'). His sense of the final impersonal identification of all life is closely paralleled by Margiad Evans in her *Autobiography*:

Humanness tells me that . . . death will be lonely. But then, to return to what inhabits and moves me . . . No matter how many people share the earth, solitude is invulnerable. In perception there is no collision. Having once entered it there can be no numbers.[4]

The sterility of grief at such a moment the poet emphasizes in his second stanza by the image of tears as 'salt seed In the least valley of sackcloth'. He may have had in mind the ancient and barbaric custom (referred to in

Judges ix. 45) of scattering salt on an enemy's land to make
it infertile.

Why, we may ask, does the poet refuse to mourn, since he
does, nevertheless, compose a poem on the child's death? The
reason is that Thomas wishes to accept the natural and
inevitable processes of life. He is the religious artist who
celebrates life.

> The religious artist is primarily a celebrator. A celebrator
> in the ritual sense: a maker and performer of a rite. . . . Although
> his ultimate vision is the tragic one of creation through suffering,
> his ultimate sense will be of joy. For in the act of love, the
> central act of Creation, he will see the force of love, in man and
> the world, merge inextricably and mysteriously with the force
> of death.[5]

Thomas would not wish the child to repeat her agony. She
has rejoined the natural forces of life, and if man would see
death in this right perspective, he says, there would be no
cause for sorrow. Nevertheless, the play of emotions in the
poem is subtler than this suggests. As a poet of profound
humanity and compassion, Thomas will not too easily accept
the child's death: he is aware of her suffering and insists
on retaining this awareness:

> I shall not murder
> The mankind of her going with a grave truth
> Nor blaspheme down the stations of the breath
> With any further
> Elegy of innocence and youth.

There is in these lines a certain conflict. The images 'murder . . . mankind . . . blaspheme' suggest, very subtly, that
Thomas, though writing a poem of celebration, will not
allow himself to lose his humanity. He *does* feel pity for the
child's physical suffering. He is deeply moved by the 'mankind of her going' and will not forget her humanity in the
creation of an elegy. The pun in 'grave truth' suggests that
such an elegy would be 'a true thing about the grave' and
also a solemn benediction over the dead child. The phrase
'stations of the breath' refers to the stations of the Cross.

There is a pun also in the line 'Nor blaspheme down the stations of the breath', for the poet has already reached the third stanza without a pause for breath. Such a double meaning, in a profoundly serious setting, is typical of Thomas.

In contrast with the poem's oratorical opening, the last stanza moves, with a slower, meditative, elegiac movement, to a reconciliation of themes:

> Deep with the first dead lies London's daughter,
> Robed in the long friends,
> The grains beyond age, the dark veins of her mother,
> Secret by the unmourning water
> Of the riding Thames.
> After the first death, there is no other.

The child has now rejoined 'the first dead': that is, her body has become part of the natural elements of existence. This is an existence beyond human life, and hence beyond mortality ('The grains beyond age'). The elements are described as 'long friends' because the child was part of them long before taking human form. This is again paralleled by Margiad Evans: 'the earth is the lung by which I breathe —the earth is my greater flesh—the earth is eternity'.[6] There are also, in the image of 'long friends', associations with the worms through which the child returns to the first elements. The paradox of the worm that both 'fathers' life and destroys it Thomas takes from Donne's sermon, *Deaths Duell*: '*Miserable riddle*, when the *same worme* must bee *my mother*, and *my sister*, and *my selfe*. . . . when my *mouth* shall be *filled* with *dust*, and the *worme* shall *feed* . . . the worme is spred *under thee*, and the worme *covers thee*.'[7] Professor Empson has suggested 'she has now a long gown like an angel or like a shroud',[8] and these, too, may be relevant connotations. In particular, the angel reference seems to me to be a likely one, since the child's own conception of immortality would include angels. The water of the 'riding Thames' is 'unmourning' for it accepts the processes of life and death. The last line of the poem has occasioned much critical discussion. Does it posit a belief in immortality in the Christian sense or does it suggest only a return to the first elements? Does it mean there is no other death because there is immortality, or that there is no other death because there is no further life to make such a second death possible? I believe that the line must be interpreted as suggesting a belief in Christian immortality. Thomas's later poems abound in instances of Christian thought and symbol and, unless he himself believed in them, his use of Biblical image and metaphor must be dismissed as ornamentation; which is to misunderstand the religious tradition of his Welsh upbringing.

The final stanza of the poem 'Vision and Prayer' throws interesting light on Thomas's development. The 'meat-eating' sun of the earlier poetry has now become, instead, a metaphor of regeneration and spiritual grace, an image not of mortality but of salvation:

> I turn the corner of prayer and burn
> In   a   blessing   of   the   sudden
> Sun. In the name of the damned
> I would turn back and run
> To  the  hidden  land
> But  the  loud  sun
> Christens down
> The sky.
> I
> Am found.
> O  let  him
> Scald me and drown
> Me in his world's wound.
> His lightning answers my
> Cry. My voice burns in his hand.
> Now  I  am  lost  in  the  blinding
> One. The sun roars at the prayer's end.

In the shaping of this poem he has been influenced by George Herbert's poem 'Easter Wings', and the lucidity of Thomas's language brings to mind his later statement: 'It is impossible to be too clear. I am trying for more clarity now. At first

I thought it enough to leave an impression of sound and feeling and let the meaning seep in later.'[9]

In his later work he increasingly makes direct use of particular Welsh landscapes. A loved and familiar scene becomes the object around which his ideas evolve, and in *Deaths and Entrances* there are many poems which draw their inspiration from a particular place rich in childhood associations. Cwmdonkin Park, for example, is described in 'The Hunchback in the Park', and the chained cups in the fountain basin, the rockery, and the willow groves are still to be seen there:

> The hunchback in the park
> A solitary mister
> Propped between trees and water
> From the opening of the garden lock
> That lets the trees and water enter
> Until the Sunday sombre bell at dark
>
> Eating bread from a newspaper
> Drinking water from the chained cup
> That the children filled with gravel
> In the fountain basin where I sailed my ship
> Slept at night in a dog kennel
> But nobody chained him up.

Compassion for the hunchback is linked to a nostalgia for the poet's own youth, when 'the groves were blue with sailors' and 'the wild boys innocent as strawberries'. It is typical of Thomas's tendency to think in sexual terms that the hunchback should have

> Made all day until bell time
> A woman figure without fault
> Straight as a young elm
> Straight and tall from his crooked bones
> That she might stand in the night
> After the locks and chains

Perhaps the most celebrated of Thomas's poems on the theme of childhood is 'Fern Hill'. Whereas for Shakespeare or Keats life progresses towards a serene consummation where 'ripeness is all', for Vaughan, Traherne, and Thomas childhood, with its intimations of immortality, is the ideal age. The attempt to recreate this childhood state of innocence and grace produces a visionary, mystical poetry. The word mysticism is, of course, derived from a Greek word meaning 'to shut the eyes'. Rimbaud wrote to a friend: '*Le Poëte se fait* voyant *par un long, immense et raisonné* dérèglement *de* tous les sens.' This 'reasoned derangement of all the senses' is, as we have seen, a characteristic of Thomas's poetry: indeed he once referred to himself as 'the Rimbaud of Cwmdonkin Drive'.[10] In his *Centuries of Meditations* Traherne has, in a similar manner, registered the feelings of innocence and holiness that he associates with childhood.

All appeared new, and strange at first, inexpressibly rare and delightful and beautiful. I was a little stranger, which at my entrance into the world was saluted and surrounded with innumerable joys. My knowledge was divine. I knew by intuition those things which since my Apostasy, I collected again by the highest reason. My very ignorance was advantageous. I seemed as one brought into the Estate of Innocence. All things were spotless and pure and glorious: yea, and infinitely mine, and joyful and precious. I knew not that there were any sins, or complaints or laws.[11]

In this state of vision all creation is seen in its original innocence and joy. It is the innocence and holiness of Eden, with no consciousness of sin or death. In Thomas's visionary poetry his feeling for the natural world is linked with the nostalgia for childhood and his love for Wales. Elder Olson said that Thomas 'recaptured, in the charming natural world of Wales, something of the lost Eden and something of a foretoken of Heaven'.[12] In 'Fern Hill' the poet again draws upon his childhood experiences at the farm of his aunt Ann Jones.

'Fern Hill' shows Thomas's original use of the stanza form. A complex structure of assonance and alliteration, internal rhyme, recurring rhythms, and an elaborate consonantal harmony, provides the technical framework of the poem. I consider 'Fern Hill' in some detail, since it reveals what is perhaps Thomas's major contribution to the development of technique in English poetry. Whether in this he was consciously employing the metrical patterns of Welsh poetry it is not possible to determine; but it seems that, in so far as he has repeated loose forms of these metrical patterns in his own work, it is meaningful to speak of a racial influence. Probably he had discussed these traditional verse forms with his father, who knew Welsh and had tried himself to write poetry in English. Throughout his career Thomas placed great emphasis upon the craft of the poet:

The writing of a poem is, to me, the physical and mental task of constructing a formally watertight compartment of words . . . To me, the poetical 'impulse' or 'inspiration' is only the sudden, and generally physical, coming of energy to the constructional, craftsman ability. The laziest workman receives the fewest impulses. And vice versa.[13]

Gwyn Jones says that Thomas is

Welsh in the cunning complexity of his metres, not only in the loose *cynghanedd*, the chime of consonants and pealing vowels, but in the relentless discipline of his verse, the hierarchic devotion to the poet's craft, the intellectual exactitude and emotional compression of word and phrase and stave and poem.[14]

The fact that Thomas's poetry is more easily understood after one has heard him read it aloud proves the importance of the aural pattern in its structure. Sound and rhythm frequently indicate which words and which ideas are linked. The structure of the poem was often musical rather than syntactical, and Thomas often began a poem with a phrase or rhythm. This would be modulated, extended and brought into a longer sequence of verbal patterns. He would then start another, go back to the first, start a third; shaping the whole into a pattern of sounds. Of 'Fern Hill', for example, there were over two hundred manuscript versions. Brinnin reports a discussion with Thomas on the subject of composition:

We began to speak of working methods. I had noticed that on many of his manuscripts Dylan would add a single word or a phrase, or a new punctuation, then recopy the whole poem in longhand. When another addition or revision was made, no matter how minor or major, he would then copy the whole poem again. When I asked him about this laborious repetition, he showed me his drafts of 'Fern Hill'. There were more than two hundred separate and distinct versions of the poem. It was, he explained, his way of 'keeping the poem together', so that its process of growth was like that of an organism. He began almost every poem merely with some phrase he had carried about in his head. If this phrase was right, which is to say, if it were resonant or pregnant, it would suggest another phrase. In this way a poem would 'accumulate'. Once 'given' a word (sometimes the prime movers of poems were the words of other poems or mere words of the dictionary that called out to be 'set') or a phrase or a line (or whatever it is that is 'given' when there is yet a poem to 'prove') he could often envision or 'locate' it within a pattern of other words or phrases or lines, that, not given, had yet to be discovered: so that sometimes it would be possible to surmise accurately that the 'given' unit would occur near the end of the poem or near the beginning or near the middle or somewhere between.[15]

The process described here is rather like that of a jig-saw, whose various pieces are filled in to make up a general unified pattern. The way in which a poem was built up can be seen from the facsimiles of the manuscript versions of 'Poem on his birthday' on pages 150-53. Vernon Watkins says that Thomas

was a slow and patient craftsman, and he had become slower since the early poems. His method of composition was itself painfully slow. . . . He used separate work-sheets for individual lines, sometimes a page or two being devoted to a single line, while the poem was gradually built up, phrase by phrase. He usually had beforehand an exact conception of the poem's length, and he would decide how many lines to allot to each part of its development.[16]

This method of composition is not quite the same as that in the early work, in which there was more insistence on conflict and paradox.

The discussion of the prosody and technique of Welsh poetry on pp. 8 and 127 may help to clarify the following analysis of the sound structure of 'Fern Hill'. This poem

consists of six stanzas, each of nine lines. The table below
indicates the number of syllables in each line of each stanza.
A close pattern is maintained:

|          |     | | St. 1 | St. 2 | St. 3 | St. 4 | St. 5 | St. 6 |
|----------|-----|-|-------|-------|-------|-------|-------|-------|
| Line 1 . | .   | . | 14 | 14 | 14 | 14 | 14 | 14 |
| Line 2 . | .   | . | 14 | 14 | 14 | 14 | 14 | 14 |
| Line 3 . | .   | . | 9  | 9  | 9  | 9  | 9  | 9  |
| Line 4 . | .   | . | 6  | 6  | 6  | 6  | 6  | 6  |
| Line 5 . | .   | . | 9  | 9  | 9  | 9  | 9  | 9  |
| Line 6 . | .   | . | 15 | 14 | 14 | 14 | 14 | 14 |
| Line 7 . | .   | . | 14 | 14 | 15 | 14 | 14 | 15 |
| Line 8 . | .   | . | 7  | 7  | 9  | 9  | 9  | 7  |
| Line 9 . | .   | . | 9  | 9  | 6  | 6  | 6  | 9  |

The corresponding lines in every stanza have the same
number of syllables, until the sixth and seventh, where
there is some relaxation. On three occasions fifteen syllables
are used, whereas in the other nine lines there are fourteen
syllables. In three stanzas lines 8 and 9 follow a 7/9 pattern;
in the other three the pattern is 9/6. This elaborate sound-
structure, which links stanza to stanza as well as line to line,
is not maintained at the expense of meaning, but is, rather,
a method of shaping and controlling the sense.

'Fern Hill' opens:

Now as I was young and easy under the apple boughs
About the lilting house and happy as the grass was green,
        The night above the dingle starry,
            Time let me hail and climb
        Golden in the heydays of his eyes,
And honoured among wagons I was prince of the apple towns
And once below a time I lordly had the trees and leaves
        Trail with daisies and barley
        Down the rivers of the windfall light.

And as I was green and carefree, famous among the barns
About the happy yard and singing as the farm was home,
        In the sun that is young once only,
            Time let me play and be
        Golden in the mercy of his means,
And green and golden I was huntsman and herdsman, the calves

Sang to my horn, the foxes on the hills barked clear and cold,
And the sabbath rang slowly
In the pebbles of the holy streams.

The scene is, of course, Ann Jones's farm, where in his
childhood the poet was a 'prince', 'lordly' in his happiness
and freedom. Time was then kind to him, for he was unaware
of his mortality. There is a consistent development of
metaphor: 'apple boughs' . . . 'apple towns' . . . 'windfall
light'. The intoxication of the senses is conveyed by an
ordered derangement of sensory perception. Experience is
seen in a state of visionary flux: the calves sang, the foxes
barked, and the sabbath rang in the 'pebbles of the holy
streams'. Thomas was then 'below a time' because, in his
innocence, he was ignorant of mutability and death. Yet,
he tells us in the second stanza, the sun is young once only:
that is to say, the sun, which is here a symbol of the boy's
innocence and joy, is only once seen with the eyes of childhood. The reference to the 'holy streams' suggests the holiness of creation. Green, throughout the poem, symbolizes
growth and life as well as innocence (in the colloquial sense
of 'inexpert'). The word 'easy' has perhaps overtones of the
colloquial 'I'm easy': there is also the sense of 'easy-going'.

The poem cannot be fully appreciated without some
understanding of its sound patterns. In the following
analysis related sounds are printed in italic. This is not an
entirely adequate method of suggesting their subtle inter-
play, but it has the advantage of simplicity.

In the first stanza, there is a chiming of consonants and
vowels: the *a* of 'apple' at the end of line 1 is repeated in the
*A* of 'About' in line 2, while the diphthong in *bou*ghs is
repeated in A*bout*. There are many examples of assonance
and alliteration: *h*ouse . . . *h*appy; *gr*ass . . . *gr*een; eas*y* . . .
happ*y* . . . starr*y*; *t*ime . . . c*lim*b (there is also a repetition of
'l' sounds in this line); am*ong* . . . wag*on*; lor*dly* . . . bar*ley*;
*tr*ees . . . *l*eaves . . . dais*ies*; *tr*ees . . . *tr*ail. In the second stanza
some of the related sound patterns are: *fam*ous . . . am*ong*;
*b*arns . . . *ab*out . . . *h*appy; s*un* . . . y*oung*; *m*erc*y* . . . *m*eans;
*s*ang . . . *r*ang. Throughout the poem certain rhythms are

repeated: 'young and easy'/'trees and leaves'/'green and carefree'/'green and golden'/'green and dying'; likewise, 'Golden in the heydays'/'Golden in the mercy'. Sometimes alliteration and assonance are neatly balanced within the line; often they continue into the following line. Thomas employs a looser form of *cynghanedd* than is used in medieval Welsh poetry. For example, he does not have a division in the middle of the line, with a cross-balance of alliterated syllables, but instead allows his alliterative effects to follow a freer pattern, which is built up within the whole stanza. *Cynghanedd gytsain*, the repetition of a series of consonants, is found in line 4, where the *t*, *m*, and *l* sounds are repeated: '*Time let me* hail and *climb*'. In Thomas's poetry the repeated consonants are sometimes widely separated. His frequent mingling of rhyme and alliteration, as in '*heaven* . . . *heron* . . . beckon' is similar to the Welsh *cynghanedd sain*. Another device used by Thomas is *cymeriad*: that is, the repetition of the first letter of one line at the beginning of successive lines. There is an example of this in the second stanza of 'Fern Hill'. Another device of Welsh prosody, *cyrch-gymeriad* (link-taking), a form of verbal repetition between stanzas, he uses in a looser form. It must be remembered, however, that in Thomas we have a 'loose *cynghanedd*',[14] following the spirit rather than the letter of the bardic tradition.

Even in this later verse Thomas permits himself such a lyrical, rhapsodic, flight as 'it was running, it was lovely . . .'. In the third stanza of 'Fern Hill', by a conscious derangement of the senses to convey the boy's excitement, the landscape becomes a fiery vision ('fire green as grass'):

All the sun long it was running, it was lovely, the hay
Fields high as the house, the tunes from the chimneys, it was air
        And playing, lovely and watery
           And fire green as grass.
        And nightly under the simple stars
As I rode to sleep the owls were bearing the farm away,
All the moon long I heard, blessed among stables, the night-jars
        Flying with the ricks, and the horses
          Flashing into the dark.

The ricks and the horses are, of course, a familiar part of the farm scene. Thomas's recording of his impressions as he falls asleep is closely paralleled in his description of a visit to the farm in *The Peaches*:

The candle flame jumped in my bedroom where a lamp was burning very low, and the curtains waved; the water in a glass on a round table by the bed stirred, I thought, as the door closed, and lapped against the sides. There was a stream below the window; I thought it lapped against the house all night until I slept.

With the new day the world returns in all its pristine, primeval glory and appears to the boy as Eden did to Adam. It is as though he sees Creation spinning from the hand of God the Creator ('the first, spinning place'), and all created things sing His praises ('the fields of praise').

> And then to awake, and the farm, like a wanderer white
> With the dew, come back, the cock on his shoulder: it was all
>             Shining, it was Adam and maiden,
>                 The sky gathered again
>             And the sun grew round that very day.
> So it must have been after the birth of the simple light
> In the first, spinning place, the spellbound horses walking warm
>             Out of the whinnying green stable
>                 On to the fields of praise.

This closely resembles Traherne's: 'I saw all in the peace of Eden; Heaven and Earth did sing my Creator's praises, and could not make more melody to Adam, than to me. All Time was Eternity and a perpetual Sabbath.'[17] There is a quicker movement in the opening line of Thomas's stanza as the child wakes to a new day. There is, too, a subtle play of sounds in the phrase 'Adam and maiden'.

Throughout the poem Thomas selects his imagery from the farm and the countryside around it; the apple trees, the grass and flowers, the barn, the farmyard, the ricks, the horses and stables. He makes extensive use, in particular, of images drawn from natural life, animal and vegetable, such as the fox and the cockerel, daisies and barley. The farm landscape is seen as Eden before the Fall, and the very horses are held in this spell of innocence and grace. In the middle of the fifth stanza the tide of ecstatic recollection begins to turn:

And honoured among foxes and pheasants by the gay house
Under the new made clouds and happy as the heart was long,
            In the sun born over and over,
                  I ran my heedless ways,
            My wishes raced through the house high hay
And nothing I cared, at my sky blue trades, that time allows
In all his tuneful turning so few and such morning songs
            Before the children green and golden
                  Follow him out of grace,

Here again are echoes of Traherne:

The corn was orient and immortal wheat, which never should be reaped, nor was ever sown. I thought it had stood from everlasting to everlasting ... The green trees when I saw them first ... transported and ravished me, their sweetness and unusual beauty made my heart to leap, and almost mad with ecstasy.[17]

The opening of Thomas's stanza has a rhapsodic lilt: 'happy as the heart was long'. The sun is born over and over; that is, it is recreated each day in its original splendour. For the child, however,—unlike the sun—there are intimations of mortality, for time allows so few 'morning songs'. The days of innocence—'lamb white days' is a Biblical image —give way to experience, and in the closing stanza the moon, an image of mortality, appears:

Nothing I cared, in the lamb white days, that time would take me
Up to the swallow thronged loft by the shadow of my hand,
            In the moon that is always rising,
                  Nor that riding to sleep
            I should hear him fly with the high fields
And wake to the farm forever fled from the childless land.
Oh as I was young and easy in the mercy of his means,
            Time held me green and dying
            Though I sang in my chains like the sea.

The farm, a symbol of youth, is 'forever fled'. It is now a 'childless land'. The poet says that Time held him, always, 'green and dying', a characteristic paradox. It implies that the child had within him the potentiality not only of life but of death. He was both innocent and passing from innocence. His chains are, of course, the chains of mortality. As I have already suggested, it is possible that Thomas's tubercular symptoms induced the intense, Keatsian awareness of mortality that informs his poetic imagination.

In a letter to Vernon Watkins written in August 1944 Thomas mentioned 'Poem in October', which he had just completed: 'The other [new poem] is a Laugharne poem.'[18] The letter is written from Llangain, a nearby Carmarthenshire village, where Thomas was staying with his parents; and it also mentions his intended move to New Quay, Cardiganshire (where he was to live for several months). He continued to spend much time in Wales, usually at his parents' home, even during his two years' stay in Oxfordshire. Frequently, he returned to Laugharne with its cliffside castle and hillsides sweeping to the sea's edge. It is this Laugharne seascape which inspires 'Poem in October'. Related in theme and technique to 'Fern Hill', it, too, is concerned with the visionary experience associated with childhood.

Early on the morning of his thirtieth birthday, he is walking on the hillside above the village and the harbour. 'The poem proceeds so resonantly that one scarcely sees, for the sound of the calling gulls and knocking boats, the simple fisher scene with its flying birds, rocking masts and quiet "net webbed wall" ':[19]

> It was my thirtieth year to heaven
> Woke to my hearing from harbour and neighbour wood
> And the mussel pooled and the heron
> Priested shore
> The morning beckon
> With water praying and call of seagull and rook
> And the knock of sailing boats on the net webbed wall
> Myself to set foot
> That second
> In the still sleeping town and set forth.

Here is Thomas's characteristic use of sacramental imagery, suggesting the holiness of this Welsh landscape; 'the heron

Priested shore . . . With water praying'. Vernon Watkins
has told me how, if Thomas described a heron, it was
described as a creation of God. So, in Watkins's own poem
'The Heron', the bird seems sacerdotal in its meditative
isolation:

> Yet no distraction breaks the watch
> Of that time-killing bird . . .
> Calamity about him cries,
> But he has fixed his golden eyes
> On water's crooked tablet,
> On light's reflected word.[20]

Likewise, we may compare Thomas's 'With water praying'
with Watkins's line: 'I watch the inquisitive cormorant pry
from the praying rock of Pwlldu'[21] Both poets suggest the
sacramental nature of the universe. Brinnin remarked on
visiting Laugharne:

now that I have seen herons along the very shore where Thomas
sees them . . . my new impression is based on the observation
that herons *do* stand in sacerdotal attitudes, as if they were
perpetually extending benediction, and that, when they are
surrounded by kittywakes and oyster-catchers, they do recall
priests crowded about by parishioners.[22]

The syllabic sound-structure of 'Poem in October' is
similar to that of 'Fern Hill'. Alliterative consonants, rhymes
and half-rhymes, and echoed vowels punctuate the poem,
and these rather than normal syntax suggest the sense-
structure. In the opening stanza, 'heaven' and 'hearing',
and later 'heaven' and 'heron' alliterate; while 'beckon' and
'second' continue the chiming pattern; likewise 'harbour
and neighbour'; while the *h* in 'harbour' is linked with that
in 'heaven' and 'hearing'. 'Woke', 'wood', 'rook' and 'foot';
'hearing', 'praying', 'sailing', and 'sleeping' interweave
their harmonies. In the syllabic structure of each stanza
there is an even more controlled patterning than in 'Fern
Hill'. As the following table indicates, only in the sixth line
of stanza six, does Thomas vary his basic pattern:

|          | St. 1 | St. 2 | St. 3 | St. 4 | St. 5 | St. 6 | St. 7 |
|----------|-------|-------|-------|-------|-------|-------|-------|
| Line 1 . | 9     | 9     | 9     | 9     | 9     | 9     | 9     |
| Line 2 . | 12    | 12    | 12    | 12    | 12    | 12    | 12    |
| Line 3 . | 9     | 9     | 9     | 9     | 9     | 9     | 9     |
| Line 4 . | 3     | 3     | 3     | 3     | 3     | 3     | 3     |
| Line 5 . | 5     | 5     | 5     | 5     | 5     | 5     | 5     |
| Line 6 . | 12    | 12    | 12    | 12    | 12    | 13    | 12    |
| Line 7 . | 12    | 12    | 12    | 12    | 12    | 12    | 12    |
| Line 8 . | 5     | 5     | 5     | 5     | 5     | 5     | 5     |
| Line 9 . | 3     | 3     | 3     | 3     | 3     | 3     | 3     |
| Line 10 .| 9     | 9     | 9     | 9     | 9     | 9     | 9     |

I have indicated the pattern of syllables in order to suggest the ideal of craftsmanship that Thomas maintained. These poems, which run so easily off the tongue, which seem such rhapsodic flights of lyricism, were the result of hard and devoted work.

In this mood of exultation, he crosses the border of time and sees in a vision his lost childhood:

> Pale rain over the dwindling harbour
> And over the sea wet church the size of a snail
> With its horns through mist and the castle
> Brown as owls
> But all the gardens
> Of spring and summer were blooming in the tall tales
> Beyond the border and under the lark full cloud.
> There could I marvel
> My birthday
> Away but the weather turned around.

The poet turns from the 'dwindling harbour', the church, Laugharne Castle which is as brown as the owls that frequent it, to see the visionary landscapes of youth, those earlier gardens of spring and summer. The 'But' in line 5 of this stanza points the contrast between the actual weather (which is rainy) and the ideal, 'summer' weather of the childhood vision. The word 'tall', used in its colloquial sense, suggests the extravagance of these 'tall' tales his memory tells him. He sees again the little boy that once he was:

And down the other air and the blue altered sky
 Streamed again a wonder of summer
 With apples
 Pears and red currants
And I saw in the turning so clearly a child's
Forgotten mornings when he walked with his mother
 Through the parables
 Of sun light
And the legends of the green chapels

 And the twice told fields of infancy
That his tears burned my cheeks and his heart moved in mine.

During the moment of vision the whole creation appears infinite and holy. T. S. Eliot has said of the poetry of vision:

Dante's is a *visual* imagination. It is a visual imagination in a different sense from that of a modern painter of still life: it is visual in the sense that he lived in an age in which men still saw visions. It was a psychological habit, the trick of which we have forgotten, but as good as any of our own. We have nothing but dreams, and we have forgotten that seeing visions—a practice now relegated to the aberrant and uneducated—was once a more significant, interesting, and disciplined kind of dreaming.[23]

Significantly, innocence and joy are associated in the poet's mind with Sunday school and its Biblical stories. The New Testament imagery of 'Fern Hill' and 'Poem in October' is strikingly different from the Old Testament metaphors of the early poetry. Thomas now speaks of 'the parables Of sun light', rather than 'the meat-eating sun'.

It is interesting to see that, in recapturing his childhood experience, he places such emphasis upon the influence of nature. The child, it seems, was already a pantheist and his mystical sense of communion is repeated in the adult poet's vision:

 These were the woods the river and sea
 Where a boy
 In the listening
Summertime of the dead whispered the truth of his joy

To the trees and the stones and the fish in the tide.
And the mystery
Sang alive
Still in the water and singingbirds.

The word 'dead' refers to those inanimate things which,
though not conscious, seem to be listening to the boy in the
quiet season of summer. The poem closes in a mood of
typically Welsh *hiræth* or nostalgia. It is impossible, the
poet tells us, to remain in the country of childhood, and he
expresses the longing that he may, in a year's time ('turning')
celebrate the 'heart's truth' on this same hill:

And there could I marvel my birthday
Away but the weather turned around. And the true
Joy of the long dead child sang burning
In the sun.
It was my thirtieth
Year to heaven stood there then in the summer noon
Though the town below lay leaved with October blood.
O may my heart's truth
Still be sung
On this high hill in a year's turning.

In his later work Thomas employed increasingly elaborate
verse forms and his finest poems are those built on a
strict technical framework. Nevertheless, he seldom repeats
in one poem the formal structure of another. His development as a poet is marked by continued technical experiment.
In the 'Ballad of the Long-legged Bait' he was influenced by
Vernon Watkins's use of the looser ballad form. This poem has
easy, flexible rhythms and an immediate play of sound and
colour. The opening lines describe the fisherman's departure:

The bows glided down, and the coast
Blackened with birds took a last look
At his thrashing hair and whale-blue eye;
The trodden town rang its cobbles for luck.

Then good-bye to the fishermanned
Boat with its anchor free and fast
As a bird hooking over the sea,
High and dry by the top of the mast,

> Whispered the affectionate sand
> And the bulwarks of the dazzled quay.
> For my sake sail, and never look back,
> Said the looking land.

Words are enjoyed for their sensuous qualities: this is a poetry of verbal intoxication:

> Sails drank the wind, and white as milk
> He sped into the drinking dark;
> The sun shipwrecked west on a pearl
> And the moon swam out of its hulk.

We learn that it is a woman who is to be sacrificed. She is the bait whereby, through the celebration of the flesh, new life and spiritual regeneration is to be obtained:

> For we saw him throw to the swift flood
> A girl alive with his hooks through her lips;
> All the fishes were rayed in blood,
> Said the dwindling ships . . .
>
> . . . Oh all the wanting flesh his enemy
> Thrown to the sea in the shell of a girl.

Thomas refers to the 'wanting flesh' as his enemy, associating the ideas of sex and sin. Because of the loose verbal structure, however, the imagery in the poem becomes diffuse and the narrative thread is lost. There are whole stanzas whose meaning is obscure and some could be omitted without apparent loss. Both the language and the narrative lack organization, and it is significant that Thomas never used this loose ballad form again. His imagination, in itself fiery and intense, required a strong formal discipline to achieve its most satisfactory expression.

Frequently, in this later work, a person known and dear to the poet is taken as the subject of a poem. In 'This Side of the Truth', addressed to his son Llewelyn, he defines his moral attitudes. The poem, which is dedicated to Llewelyn, opens:

> This side of the truth,
> You may not see, my son,
> King of your blue eyes
> In the blinding country of youth,
> That all is undone,
> Under the unminding skies,
> Of innocence and guilt
> Before you move to make
> One gesture of the heart or head,
> Is gathered and spilt
> Into the winding dark
> Like the dust of the dead.

Being in the 'country of youth' the child is 'blind' to good and evil, a state the poet compares to kingship ('King of your blue eyes'). But, he goes on, all good and evil is already determined. Yet the notions of good and evil evaporate:

> Good and bad, two ways
> Of moving about your death . . .
> Into the innocent
> Dark, and the guilty dark, and good
> Death, and bad death,

There is no moral decision in conventional terms. Good and evil are seen not as ultimate antinomies, but as expressions of a higher force that comprehends both. This force is 'unjudging love':

> And all your deeds and words,
> Each truth, each lie,
> Die in unjudging love.

The greater lucidity of these later poems, a lucidity accompanied nevertheless by increased profundity and insight, is at once evident. Gwyn Jones has said that 'this corner [Laugharne] of Wales raised him [Thomas] to his full Merlin-height of poetry'.[24] The next chapter, dealing with Thomas's last years at Laugharne, where he lived from 1948 until his death, considers the poems written in those years and describes the final phase of his development.

As surely his last evangelism, the poems to 'great and fabulous dear God' (Hail to His beasthood!), belonged to Wales. Ask any of his generation of Welsh writers what their mothers hoped for them, and they will confess: the pulpit. Dylan's pulpit was the Carmarthenshire countryside, God's rough tumbling ground.[25]

The nature of this evangelism and its place in this countryside the present chapter has, to some degree, already shown.

# CHAPTER TEN

# COLLECTED POEMS

YLAN THOMAS's *Collected Poems* was published in
November 1952. In addition to previously published
work it contained eight new poems. In a *Note* to this
volume he wrote:

> I read somewhere of a shepherd who, when asked why he
> made, from within fairy rings, ritual observances to the moon to
> protect his flocks, replied: 'I'd be a damn' fool if I didn't!' These
> poems, with all their crudities, doubts, and confusions, are
> written for the love of Man and in praise of God, and I'd be a
> damn' fool if they weren't.

It might be said that Thomas's own work contains 'ritual
observances', in that it expresses the religious artist's celebration of man and God and natural life. The Carmarthen
countryside is the scene of this celebration.

The fishing village of Laugharne has always been popular
with Welsh artists and writers. Augustus John, Richard
Hughes, and Keidrych Rhys, as well as Thomas have, at
various times, made their home there. The village is built
on hill-slopes which descend to the seashore, hills that almost
meet as they sweep down on either side of the horseshoe bay.
The town square is bordered on one side by the stretches
of sand and mud flats. In the square is the Cross House Inn
and close by Brown's Hotel, the two pubs that Thomas
frequented. Just off the square, and looking out to sea across
the long stretches of mud flats, stands Laugharne Castle.
Further along the bay, perched on the cliffside like a bird's
nest, is the Boat House.[1] Halfway up the cliff path, which

leads from the village to the Boat House, is Thomas's
workshop—called by him affectionately 'the shack'. It
looks from the outside much like a garage perched pre-
cariously on the cliff, exposed to the storms and sea-noises,
winds and weathers of the bay. Furnished with bare wooden
table, chair, and anthracite stove, it was apt to become itself
a sea of manuscripts, discarded drafts of poems, empty
cigarette packets, literary periodicals, and books.

The path at this point slopes steeply to the Boat House,
and is flanked on one side by the trees and bushes growing
out of the cliff-face. In summer wild flowers crowd this side
of the path. On its other side, below the narrow ledge, the
sea laps against this mountain wall. The pathway everywhere overlooks the sea and seems hewn out of the mountain-
side. A garden slopes down to the Boat House, which is
built halfway up the cliff. The house with its veranda over
the sea wall, seems to grow out of the rock. Walking on
this veranda, which runs along two sides of the house,
Brinnin likened to 'walking on deck. Lights in the distance
that seemed as though they might belong to passing ships
were really lights in farmhouses across the mouth of the
river Taf where it flowed into the estuary.'[2] The farms on
the surrounding hills Thomas described in his poem 'Author's
Prologue' as 'the wound asleep Sheep white hollow farms'.
The Boat House can also be reached by a seaside path which
the tide washes over at certain times of the day, a route which
passes below the walls of the castle. One enters the small
backyard of the house through an opening in the breakwater
which fences it. The Boat House is 'as much given to the sea
as sequestered against it'.[3]

I have described the Laugharne setting in some detail,
since it is directly related to the genesis of the later work.
The seascape visible from the poet's home is the source of
theme and image for example, in 'Over Sir John's hill',
'Author's Prologue', and 'Poem on his birthday'. 'Over
Sir John's hill' is on one level a narrative poem describing
a hawk killing its prey. One would hardly expect to find in
such a subject a statement of the poet's attitude to mortality,

God, sin, and redemption, but into his narrative Thomas
has woven a whole pattern of concepts. It is important,
therefore, to interpret the action in terms of ideas; for the
poet has used the particular scene to embody his own
personal religious and philosophical beliefs.

It is clear how the poem began: a hawk seeking its prey
must have been a common enough event. Thomas's workshop windows

on two sides brought in sunlight and sealight, saving it from
seeming cramped. One window looked upon a watery vista—
shallows between long sloping hills—terminating in the Irish
Sea; the other looked out across the narrow part of Carmarthen
Bay towards Sir John's Hill.[4]

Sir John's Hill is also known in Laugharne as St. John's
Hill.

'Over Sir John's hill' has the elaborate formal
structure characteristic of the later work. It is composed of five twelve-line stanzas, each with the rhyme
scheme AABCCBDEAEDD. Thomas accomplished the
considerable task of maintaining this scheme by employing
such near-rhymes as: 'hedges' . . . 'heron' . . . 'headstone'
(stanza 1), and 'whistles' . . . 'windows' . . . 'whispering'
(stanza 4). The opening lines describe the hawk waiting
for its prey: it is 'on fire', a phrase suggesting both the
process of destruction and the sunlight on its wings. The
hawk

> . . . pulls to his claws
And gallows, up the rays of his eyes the small birds of the bay
And the shrill child's play
Wars
Of the sparrows and such who swansing, dusk, in wrangling
    hedges.

The word 'gallows' seems to suggest a certain guilt on the
part of the birds: as if, with their warring and wrangling,
they are, in allegorical terms, heirs of original sin. The
doomed birds 'swansing'—a further instance of the poet's
preoccupation with death—

And blithely they squawk
To fiery tyburn over the wrestle of elms until
The flash the noosed hawk
Crashes, and slowly the fishing holy stalking heron
In the river Towy below bows his tilted headstone.

The hill is called 'fiery tyburn' since it is the place of execution, and the verb 'noosed' continues the metaphor of guilt
and punishment. There is ambiguity in the metaphor of
the hawk as executioner, since that, too, it is implied, is a
prey to mortality. The movement of the verse here enacts
the swoop of the hawk, but after the kill moves to an elegiac
rhythm. A new figure, the heron, now enters the scene.
Thomas, as we have seen, always associates holiness with
this bird. It remains outside the present action, like the poet
an observer, and later mediator. The hill, covered with
jackdaws, is said to wear the black cap of a judge passing
sentence of death, an image which operates both on the visual
and allegorical level. The hill is therefore described as 'just'.
The epithet 'gulled' in the phrase 'gulled birds' refers to
their complete passivity. They are following a prescribed
existence, and are bound to it. The second stanza concludes:

There
Where the elegiac fisherbird stabs and paddles
In the pebbly dab-filled
Shallow and sedge, and 'dilly dilly', calls the loft hawk,
'Come and be killed,'
I open the leaves of the water at a passage
Of psalms and shadows among the pincered sandcrabs
    prancing.

The 'elegiac fisherbird' is the heron, and there is in this
phrase a special religious significance since it derives from
the New Testament description of Christ as the fisher of
men.

At this point the poet enters the narrative. The language
has further Biblical echoes: 'water', one of Thomas's favourite
symbols, is associated with birth and with the concept
of existence as a state of flux. Life does not end, but changes
its form. Water, in terms of New Testament theology,

contains also the idea of absolution. The 'psalms' continue
the devotional imagery. The act of killing that the poet
witnesses is itself the way to a new form of existence. He is
reading—to paraphrase crudely—'a passage' on 'leaves' of
the book of life: 'leaves of the water' also suggests the leaves
of a tree, so that there is a characteristic merging and
uniting of the forms of natural life. Shadows imply distance:
the actors in this drama are to the poet, by reason of their
mortality, distant, shadowy creatures. The invitation 'Come
and be killed' suggests the inevitability of the action.
He probably had in mind here the familiar nursery rhyme:

> O what have you got for dinner, Mrs. Bond?
> There's beef in the larder, and ducks in the pond.
> Crying, Dilly, dilly, dilly, dilly, dilly, come to be killed
> For you must be stuffed, and my customers filled. [5]

The poet is reconciled to death:

And read, in a shell,
Death clear as a buoy's bell:
All praise of the hawk on fire in hawk-eyed dusk be sung,
When his viperish fuse hangs looped with flames under the brand
Wing, and blest shall
Young
Green chickens of the bay and bushes cluck, 'dilly dilly,
Come let us die.'
We grieve as the blithe birds, never again, leave shingle and elm,
The heron and I,
I young Aesop fabling to the near night by the dingle
Of eels, saint heron hymning in the shell-hung distant. . . .

A shell, the husk of a once-living creature, speaks of
mortality: one, literally, listens to it. So, too, the sea-sound
of the buoy's bell at this moment suggests a funeral bell. The
birds, whom the poet later deems 'led-astray' are, however,
holy ('blest') in their mortality. 'All praise' is given to 'the
hawk on fire', for it is performing its natural function, a
function that the poet accepts and celebrates. 'Green' in the
phrase 'Green chickens' symbolizes life and also, by implication, death, which co-exists with life; a usage comparable

with the 'green and dying' of 'Fern Hill'. It carries, too, the idea of pristine innocence. In comparison with the earlier work, Thomas is building this paradoxical conception of existence into a more philosophic, ordered, pattern.

Often in Anglo-Welsh writing animal life is closely linked with human. 'A marked feature . . . in the stories of the early Celtic church', writes Eiluned Lewis, 'is the place accorded to birds and animals, which seems to belong to an ancient and primitive way of life.'[6] In contemporary Anglo-Welsh writing, human, animal and vegetal life is viewed as part of a sacramental whole, and animal life plays an important part in Thomas's later verse. 'Over Sir John's hill' is a bestiary fable with direct reference to the human condition.

The bardic and prophetic stance Thomas adopts in these later poems is related to the idea of the *dyn hysbys* or wise man, a tattered version of the early druid, found in Anglo-Welsh fiction. In his statements concerning the nature of the poet and the function of poetry Thomas was careful to foster this bardic myth in relation to his own poetic personality. So, in 'Over Sir John's hill', the poet is a mediator standing aside from immediate mortality. Like the heron, he remains outside the action. As a religious artist his function is to celebrate life, but he also intercedes on its behalf:

It is the heron and I, under judging Sir John's elmed
Hill, tell-tale the knelled
Guilt
Of the led-astray birds whom God, for their breast of whistles,
Have mercy on,
God in his whirlwind silence save, who marks the sparrows hail,
For their souls' song.

There are obvious Biblical echoes and rhythms in the supplication, 'whom God, for their breast of whistles, Have mercy on', and in the reference to the sparrows.

Death dominates the final stanza, slowing the cadences of the verse and determining the selection of image: 'tear of the Towy', 'Wear-willow river'. The elms are 'looted' now that life has been destroyed, and the poet acknowledges himself no less vulnerable than the birds to 'the lunge of night':

> Only a hoot owl
> Hollows, a grassblade blown in cupped hands, in the looted elms
> And no green cocks or hens
> Shout
> Now on Sir John's hill. The heron, ankling the scaly
> Lowlands of the waves,
> Makes all the music; and I who hear the tune of the slow,
> Wear-willow river, grave,
> Before the lunge of the night, the notes on this time-shaken
> Stone for the sake of the souls of the slain birds sailing.

Also inspired by Laugharne, and even more remarkable in its scrupulous craftsmanship, is the poem 'Author's Prologue', which consists of 102 lines, the first rhyming with the last, the second with the last but one, the third with the last but two, and so on until the middle where two rhymes meet:

> Sheep white hollow farms
> To Wales in my arms.

In addition to this, the first three and the last three lines end with the same words: 'now', 'end', 'sun': 'sun', 'end', 'now'. Thomas has himself commented on the poem's artifice in a letter to his publishers:

> I intended, as you know, to write a more-or-less straight-forward intimate prose preface and then funked it. And then I began to write a prologue in verse which has taken the devil of a time to finish. Here it is, only a hundred and two lines, and pathetically little, in size and quality, to warrant the two months and more I've taken over it. To begin with, I set myself . . . a most difficult technical task: the Prologue is in two verses—in my manuscript a verse to a page—of 51 lines each. And the second verse rhymes backward with the first. The first and last lines of the poem rhyme; the second and the last but one; and so on and so on. Why I acrosticked myself like this, don't ask me. [7]

Relevant to this concern with form, so central to Welsh bardic poetry, is David Jones's comment on Hywel the poet warrior, who was evidently moved by the natural beauty of the terrain through which he moved his fierce war-bands, and he loved the dapple of that landscape and the beauty of bright foam and bright weapons and saffron gowns and white limbs and white gulls, but none of this vivid awareness would have given us a single line of his famous poem in praise of North Wales unless he had first loved an art-form, and had mastered that form or rather had himself been mastered by the elusive constraints of that very specialised art, Welsh 12th-century prosody. But the principle I wish to bring to your attention is the same whatever the art-form. The artist, no matter of what sort or what his medium, must be *moved by the nature of whatever art he practises.* . . . The artist is *not*, necessarily, a person vastly more aware than his friends and relations of the beauties of nature, but rather he is the person most aware of the nature of an art.[8]

There were 160 manuscript versions of the 'Prologue' and 106 of 'Over Sir John's hill', so relentlessly did Thomas correct and recorrect his work. He wrote:

To me, the poetical 'impulse' or 'inspiration' is only the sudden, and generally physical, coming of energy to the con-structional, craftsman ability. The laziest workman receives fewest impulses. And vice versa.[9]

In these later years he composed less in any given period of time, owing to the greater critical effort he put into his work. Some critics have mistakenly assumed that his slower process of composition was the result of diminishing inspira-tion. Thomas was aware that his writing was costing him more effort, and in a letter to Vernon Watkins expressed his satisfaction at this:

I'm so glad you wrote the last bit about the poems: how you so much more liked the latest to the earliest. Wouldn't it be hell if it was the other way around, and the words were coming quicker & slicker and weaker and wordier every day and, by compari-son, one's first poems in adolescence seemed, to one, like flying-fish islands never to be born in again? Thank God, writing is daily more difficult, less passes Uncle Head's blue-haired pencil that George Q. Heart doesn't care about, and that the result, if only to you and me, is worth all the discarded shocks, the reluctantly shelved grand moony images, cut-&-come again cardpack of references.[10]

'Author's Prologue' uses the Old Testament imagery of the Flood 'to express the poet's apprehension of a second inundation, a new chaos. . . . Wales becomes a sanctuary for all loved things'.[11] He is looking out at sunset from his home above the bay:

> This day winding down now
> At God speeded summer's end
> In the torrent salmon sun,
> In my seashaken house . . .
> Out there, crow black, men
> Tackled with clouds, who kneel
> To the sunset nets,
> Geese nearly in heaven, boys
> Stabbing, and herons, and shells
> That speak seven seas,

Though the poet writes 'at poor peace', his art is sacred:

> At poor peace I sing
> To you strangers (though song
> Is a burning and crested act . . .)

Thomas compares himself to Noah: he is building an ark of poetry into which he invites all the creatures of Wales, of its seas, its woods and its countryside. This ark is a symbol of Love:

> . . . I, a spinning man,
> Glory also this star, bird
> Roared, sea born, man torn, blood blest.
> Hark: I trumpet the place,
> From fish to jumping hill! Look:
> I build my bellowing ark
> To the best of my love
> As the flood begins,

The poet, 'a spinning man', glories in the world, which is man-torn yet blessed by his blood. It was also, according to Genesis i. 9-10, 'sea born':

And God said, Let the waters under the heaven be gathered together unto one place, and let the dry land appear: and it was so. And God called the dry land Earth; and the gathering together of the waters called he Seas. . . .

Thomas's detailed reference to all animal life illustrates that affection for—and sensitivity towards—animals that has characterized Welsh literature from the time of the *Mabinogion*:

> Huloo, on plumbed bryns,
> O my ruffled ring dove
> In the hooting, nearly dark
> With Welsh and reverent rook . . .
> But animals thick as thieves
> On God's rough tumbling grounds
> (Hail to His beasthood!) . . .
> O kingdom of neighbours, finned
> Felled and quilled, flash to my patch
> Work ark and the moonshine
> Drinking Noah of the bay,
> With pelt, and scale, and fleece.

*Bryn* is the Welsh word for hill. The poem closes with a description of the Ark riding out under the stars of Wales that further proves the truth of Renan's observation that animals are 'transformed by the Welsh imagination into intelligent beings. No race conversed so intimately as did the Celtic race with the lower creation, and accorded it so large a share of moral life.'[12]

> We will ride out alone, and then,
> Under the stars of Wales . . .
> Huloo, my prowed dove with a flute!
> Ahoy, old, sea-legged fox,
> Tom tit and Dai mouse!
> My ark sings in the sun
> At God speeded summer's end
> And the flood flowers now.

In 'Lament' Thomas returns to satire on Nonconformist traditions. It is more controlled and well directed than the earlier satire and rather more lewd. The

poem has five stanzas, each of twelve lines, with nine
or ten syllables to the line. The rhyme scheme follows
a regular pattern—ABCDABCDEFEF—but each stanza
has a slightly varied refrain. The poem tells the story of a
'roaring boy'; and each stanza describes a certain period of
his lively, lecherous career. It opens:

> When I was a windy boy and a bit
> And the black spit of the chapel fold,
> (Sighed the old ram rod, dying of women),
> I tiptoed shy in the gooseberry wood,
> The rude owl cried like a telltale tit,
> I skipped in a blush as the big girls rolled
> Ninepin down on the donkeys' common,
> And on seesaw sunday nights I wooed
> Whoever I would with my wicked eyes,
> The whole of the moon I could love and leave
> All the green leaved little weddings' wives
> In the coal black bush and let them grieve.

Throughout this poem Thomas draws his imagery, satirically, from the chapel: 'black spit of the chapel fold'; 'the
black beast of the beetles' pews'; 'the black cross of the holy
house'. The word 'gooseberry' suggests the gooseberry
bushes under which children are often said to be found, and
it also echoes the expression to 'play gooseberry'. 'Donkeys'
common' almost certainly refers to Cwmdonkin Park, since
*cwmdonkin* is the Welsh for 'donkey valley'. The 'old ram rod'
recalls the summer of his lusty career when he cared little
about his 'coal black soul':

> To the sultry, biding herds, I said,
> Oh, time enough when the blood creeps cold,
> And I lie down but to sleep in bed,
> For my sulking, skulking, coal black soul!

The poet directly mocks the conventional Nonconformist
code:

> When I was a half of the man I was
> And serve me right as the preachers warn,
> (Sighed the old ram rod, dying of downfall)

He describes his downfall to a state of physical exhaustion with powerful sexual imagery: 'crumpled horn', 'limp time', 'slunk pouting out'. 'The idea and image of the soul's eye ("blind" and "slashed") as the male member is especially audacious':[13]

> . . . a black sheep with a crumpled horn,
> At last the soul from its foul mousehole
> Slunk pouting out when the limp time came;
> And I gave my soul a blind, slashed eye,
> Gristle and rind, and a roarers' life,
> And I shoved it into the coal black sky
> To find a woman's soul for a wife.

Broken-heartedly the poet concludes:

> For, oh, my soul found a sunday wife
> In the coal black sky and she bore angels! . . .
> Chastity prays for me, piety sings,
> Innocence sweetens my last black breath,
> Modesty hides my thighs in her wings,
> And all the deadly virtues plague my death!

Helpless, he is surrounded by chastity, piety, innocence, modesty—all the 'deadly virtues'. 'Sunday wife', like the phrase 'sober as Sunday', is a thrust at the solemnity of the Welsh Sunday when, until very recently, all public houses, cinemas and shops were closed. The only respectable Sunday pursuit was Chapel.

'Poem on his birthday' was also written towards the end of Thomas's life, and, like 'Poem in October', 'Over Sir John's hill' and 'Author's Prologue', was prompted by his contemplation of the Laugharne scene. The illustrations of selected work-sheets of this poem (which I number Folios 1-4) indicate the jigsaw-like pattern of Thomas's method of composition. Occasional words and phrases are altered to fit the pattern of thought; thus, 'shambling sky' (F.1) becomes 'seizing sky' in the finished poem; 'spiralling cloud' (F.1) becomes 'serpent cloud'; 'Herons, on one leg, bless' (F.2) becomes, 'Herons, steeple stemmed, bless'. On the working sheets are word lists which Thomas employed

Poem On His Birthday

In the mustardseed sun,
By eely river and switchback sea
    where the cormorants scud,
In his house on stilts high among beaks
    And palavers of birds
This sandgrain day in the bent bay's grave
    He celebrates and spurns
His driftwood thirty fifth wind-turned age;
    Herons spire and spear.

    Under and round him go
Flounders, gulls, on their cold dying trails,
    Doing what they are told,
Curlews aloud in the congered waves
    Work at their ways to death,
And the rhymer in the long tongued room, ✓
    Who tolls his birthday bell,
Tolls ~~~~ the ambush of his wounds;
    ~~~~ for leg, bless.
    In the whistledown fall
He sings towards anguish; finches fly
    In the claw tracks of hawks
On a shambling sky; small fishes glide
~~~~through the waves of the drowned
~~~~ to the islands of otters. He
    In his cool unsteepled room
And the hewn coils of his trade perceive ●
    Herons walk in their shroud,
    ~~~~ riddled
The people's river's robe
Of minnows rippling around their prayer;
    And far at sea he knows,
Who slaves afraid to his fury and
    In a spiralling cloud,
Dolphins dive in their turnturtle pill,
    Seafoxes and scaowls
(Dales) Taste the flesh of their death as the trawled
    ~~~~ as they pounce and mouth.

    Thirty five bellnotes ~~~~

Working sheet F.1 of 'Poem on his birthday'

caves    muzzee
combes   gullet
scallops  isle,
whorls   a...

wheels
oriels
domes
arches

2 23
161
... 24

eyelids
doors
nets
folds
gardens
orchards
islands
tilting
townships
yards
acres
moors
prairies
fabric
structures

189
2-60

Poem On His Birthday

In the mustardseed sun,
By full tilt river and switchback sea
    Where the cormorants scud,
In his house on stilts high among beaks
    And palavers of birds
This sandgrain day in the bent bay's grave
    He celebrates and spurns
His driftwood thirty fifth wind turned age;
    Herons spire and spear.

Under and round him go
Flounders, gulls, on their cold, dying trails,
    Doing what they are told,
Curlews aloud in the congered waves
    Work at their ways to death,
And the rhymer in the long tongued room,
    who tolls his birthday bell,
Toils towards the anguish of his wounds.
    Herons, on one leg, bless.

In the thistledown fall
He sings towards anguish; finches glide
    Through the ... of the drowned
Towns to the ... of otters. He
    pastures
    In his winged, racking house
And the turn coils of his trade perceives
    Herons walk in their shroud,

The livelong river's robe
Of minnows wreathing around their prayer;
    And far at sea he knows,
Who slaves afraid to his deathless end
    In a spiralling cloud,
Dolphins dive in their turnturtle dust,
    The rippled seals streak down
To kill and their own tide daubing blood
    Slides good in the sleek mouth.

Through the lanes of the drowned
Sea towns to pastures of otters. He

doors

Working sheet F.2 of 'Poem on his birthday'

And far at sea he knows,
who slaves afraid to his ~~fiery~~ end
In a spiralling cloud,
Dolphins dive in their turnturtle fall

The ~~seagulls swoop &~~ pounce            Dive, x
In ~~green wood~~ seafowl pounce

Seabears go ~~killing down~~
And ~~taste the flesh of their own death~~, salt
And good in the dark mouth

The flesh they pounce
Upon is the flesh of their own dark, salt
And good in the dark mouth.

And the ~~fish~~ that ~~dread~~ down
To kill, taste the flesh of their own salt
Death good in the ~~dark~~ mouth.

Seafoxes pouncing down

_____

thresh deep                              Crater mouth        and
                                                             for
seal.        death            'bor.     ◡                    awe
                                                             or
loom                                                         moor
tower                                                        moored
swinging                                                     more

142                                                          animal
                        fleshing
And the seals that flesh down
To kill, taste the flesh of their own salt raw unbor
Death, good in the dark mouth.

Vas'    whales mar dome down                    oven

Dolphins in their turnturtle fall dive deep
And the seals that flesh down
To k                                            hale.

bell call crawl haul squall trawl wall halt    Gaia
caught drawn gorge horde howler jaw law paw port raw
Sword tall  YAWN
                        funeral  bull mill

Working sheet F.3 of 'Poem on his birthday'

At half his billd span,
A man of words who'd drawn down the stars to his lyric oven,
He looks back at his years.

§    A lyrical man

At half his billd span,
A lyrical man ~~who'd~~ who'd pull the stars
~~And the~~ And the

And the ~~up~~ years ~~spun~~ spinning back to the dark,

The dead ~~& years~~ spinning back to the dark
gong,

The cocklesucked  Thirty five

H                                                    ransacked love

The ~~dead~~ spent lovers spinning back to the

Thirty five ways to death                d
                                         Keening
                                         requiem
Bygone love makes a sound               Jeremiad
like a ~~bell~~                          dirge
        bell ducked in the foam         sackcloth
gong                                     coronach  Koronah
                                         a cypress bell
            deep                         sacring bell
Long gongs ducked in the foam           angelus

                                         550
                                         363
Thirty five ~~stages~~ to                412
            sounds like
Bygone love ~~makes a sound~~ a cypress bell
       ~~Swung~~ in fanes of the foam
                  chantries of.
nelled                    minsters
wung in sea minsters

Working sheet F.4 of 'Poem on his birthday'

for his selection of image; unwanted words in the catalogue are frequently crossed out (as in F.2). Similarly, another manuscript page lists words which have the meaning of dwellings: aires, boroughs, harbours, dwellings, quarters, arbours, lair, buildings, tenements, alleys, galleries, cellars bowers. Sometimes the word-lists catalogue possible rhymes: ball, call, crawl, haul, squall, trawl, wall (F.3). It is clear, too, that he explores and toys with certain images and words. The original version tends to differ from the final one in terms of stylistic expression, rather than theme. In F.4, for example, most of the expressions were rejected, though they conform with the rest of the poem in terms of idea, such as the lines:

> At half his bible span,
> A man of words who'd drag down the stars to his lyric oven,
> He looks back at his years.

On this page the poet followed a blind alley. F.3 provides a good illustration of the growth of one passage in particular:

> Seabears go killing down
> And taste the flesh of their own death, salt
> And good in the dark mouth.

becomes:

> The flesh they pounce
> Upon is the flesh of their own death, salt
> And good in the dark mouth.

It is then modified to:

> And the fish that . . . down
> To kill, taste the flesh of their own salt
> Death good in the dark mouth.

Lower on the page we have:

> And the seals that sleek down
> To kill, taste the flesh of their own salt raw
> Death, good in the dark mouth.

The next version reads:

> Dolphins in their turnturtle pall dive deep
>  And the seals that sleek down
> To k

The final version in the *Collected Poems* reads:

> Dolphins dive in their turnturtle dust,
>  The rippled seals streak down
> To kill and their own tide daubing blood
>  Slides good in the sleek mouth.

Throughout these changing versions the basic ideas informing the lines remain the same. It is the expression that is
modified, extended, and improved. Caitlin Thomas said of
her husband's method of composition:

And dear God, when I think of that concentrated muttering,
and mumbling, and intoning; the realms of discarded lists of
rhyming words; the innumerable repetitions and revisions; and
how at the end of an intensive five-hour stretch (from two to
seven prompt as clockwork) Dylan would come out very pleased
with himself, saying he had done a good day's work—and present
me proudly with two, or three perhaps, fiercely belaboured
lines.[14]

'Poem on his birthday' opens:

> In the mustardseed sun,
> By full tilt river and switchback sea
> Where the cormorants scud,
> In his house on stilts high among beaks
> And palavers of birds
> This sandgrain day in the bent bay's grave
> He celebrates and spurns
> His driftwood thirty-fifth wind turned age;
> Herons spire and spear.

This, like the subsequent stanzas, consists of alternating
lines of six and nine syllables. The epithet 'mustardseed'
refers both to the yellow colour of the sun and to the New
Testament parable in which the kingdom of heaven is
compared to a grain of mustardseed. 'On stilts' is an apt
description of the poet's Laugharne home on its cliffside
vantage-point. He watches the herons and gulls, the hawks

and fishes, all hunting for their prey, whose death is shown
as part of the scheme of things. This particular day is a
'sandgrain' beside the total immensity of time, and the world
is viewed as a graveyard in which everything living moves
toward death. Thomas, on one occasion, said that his poetry
had become 'statements made on the way to the grave'.[15]
The herons once again are holy witnesses of the scene;
the poet also, as in 'Over Sir John's hill' and 'Author's
Prologue', is a witness and mediator:

> Under and round him go
> Flounders, gulls, on their cold, dying trails,
>     Doing what they are told,
> Curlews aloud in the congered waves
>     Work at their ways to death,
> And the rhymer in the long tongued room,
>     Who tolls his birthday bell,
> Toils towards the ambush of his wounds;
>     Herons, steeple stemmed, bless.

There are many similarities, both in theme and expression,
between 'Poem on his birthday' and some of the poems in
Vernon Watkins's *The Lady with the Unicorn*, published in
1948. Since Thomas was closely acquainted with Watkins's
work it is likely he was influenced by these. The idea of the
curlews 'working their way towards death' is paralleled in
'Fidelity to the Living': 'The light, the bird at peace in
the sky, though pulled by a plummet of lead.'[16] Likewise
Thomas's later line 'Dolphins dive in their turnturtle dust'[17]
resembles in attitude and image a passage in Watkins's
poem 'Rhossili':

> . . . the long flat beach, no bend, no break in the dance
> Of sandgrains and seawaves, drenched in gold spray, where
>     the downs fly on to Llangennith:
> Dolphins, plunging from death into birth, you are held by the
>     Sibyl's trance![18]

There is a marked similarity of language: 'sandgrains and
seawaves'/'sandgrain day'; 'overhead wheel the herring gulls,
each with a plummet'/'gulls on their cold, dying trails'.

Of the two poems, 'Poem on his birthday' is technically more accomplished.

The 'ambush of his wounds' towards which 'the rhymer ... toils' refers to the act of redemption that the poet, in his art, performs. He redeems, it is implied, both himself and the world by his dedication. The third stanza continues:

> In the thistledown fall,
> He sings towards anguish; finches fly
>     In the claw tracks of hawks
> On a seizing sky; small fishes glide
>     Through wynds and shells of drowned
> Ship towns to pastures of otters. He
>     In his slant, racking house
> And the hewn coils of his trade perceives
>     Herons walk in their shroud.

'The rhymer' 'sings towards anguish' as finches and fishes pass before him inexorably to their death: 'wynds', 'drowned Ship towns' suggest the ancient life of the world. There is a similar vision of time past in a later stanza:

> There he might wander bare
> With the spirits of the horseshoe bay
>     Or the stars' seashore dead,
> Marrow of eagles, the roots of whales
>     And wishbones of wild geese. . . .
>
> Who knows the rocketing wind will blow
>     The bones out of the hills,
> And the scythed boulders bleed. . . .

Vernon Watkins shows a similar perception of the continuity of historical time, with its 'shored up' past life, in 'Fidelity to the Dead':

> The withered leaf is blest, and the bird with shrunk claw in the shingle.
> Under the shawl the life-yielding hand has caught the passionate thread.[19]

Watkins's poem closes with the line, 'Love is fidelity to the unfortunate dead', which suggests the nature of these poets' concern with death; for both seem to write, at times, 'to set the dead at rest'.[20] The following lines from Vernon Watkins's poem 'Rhossili' also resemble, both in theme and image, the early stanzas of 'Poem on his birthday':

> Tide-blown the castaways lie
> Peeled to the parched and weary grains where the beaked
>   ships spin and are gone.[21]

I think that Thomas, in his movement towards a more philosophic acceptance of Christian faith and teaching, was deeply influenced by Vernon Watkins, who has himself told me that Thomas latterly tested every argument by reference to the Christian faith. Elsewhere he has said that Thomas's poetry represents

the work of a poet who was able to live Christianity in a public way, and whose work distilled it—a poet narrow and severe with himself and wide and forgiving in his affections. Innocence is always a paradox, and Dylan Thomas presents, in retrospect, the greatest paradox of our time.[22]

This does not, of course, imply an orthodox and conventional acceptance of the Christian Church; certainly not Church-going orthodoxy and practice.

In the later stanzas of 'Poem on his birthday' Thomas's movement towards this spiritual faith is presented in philosophic terms:

> Oh, let me midlife mourn by the shrined
>         And druid herons' vows
> The voyage to ruin I must run,

This voyage, however, is redeemed by the knowledge of certain blessings; the fact of humanity and the spirit of love:

> Yet, though I cry with tumbledown tongue,
>         Count my blessings aloud:
>
> Four elements and five
> Senses, and man a spirit in love.

The poet has learned to accept even the terror of his own inner conflict; he has learned 'to praise in spite of'. The ideas of original sin, salvation, and damnation, are the natural outcome of the attempt to face the world, and in Thomas's final poems there is no retreat into childhood. Not only does the poet claim an increasing faith as he approaches death, but the world, too, seems to sing its Creator's praises more joyously:

>          That the closer I move
> To death, one man through his sundered hulks,
>          The louder the sun blooms
> And the tusked, ramshackling sea exults . . .
>                    . . . the whole world then,
>          With more triumphant faith
> Than ever was since the world was said,
>          Spins its morning of praise . . . .
>
>                              . . . Oh,
>          Holier then their eyes,
> And my shining men no more alone
>          As I sail out to die.

Before turning to Thomas's later prose it would be as well to look at his last years in Laugharne, and to consider the impact of this particular Welsh village upon his everyday life. Caitlin Thomas in her book *Leftover Life to Kill* has attempted to show the close bond between the poet and his Welsh environment:

> And I did all I could to make him work, at his own special work, and not public money-making work. And it was only with our kind of purely vegetable background, which entailed months on end of isolated, stodgy dullness and drudgery for me, that he was flattened out enough to be able to concentrate.[23]

During the long concentrated, isolated months of composition in Laugharne Thomas produced his poetry, deriving his inspiration from this environment. It was the visits to the United States—and he seems to have been aware of this—which distracted him from his work. As he wrote in a letter:

> Then I went to the States with my luggage of dismays and was loudly lost for months, peddling and bawling to adolescents the romantic agonies of the dead. . . .

About another visit to the States, I don't know. Though I can only play a poet there, and not make poetry.[24]

Caitlin Thomas has said that:

For Dylan, more than anybody, this [America] was a poisonous atmosphere: he needed opposition, gentle, but firm, constant curbing, and a steady dull, homely bed of straw to breed his fantasies in. Nobody ever needed encouragement less, and he was drowned in it. He gave to those wide-open-beaked readings the concentrated artillery of his flesh and blood, and, above all, his breath. I used to come in late and hear, through the mikes, the breath-straining panting:[25]

In her book his wife has given an account of Thomas's daily routine in Laugharne, describing the steady, regularly industrious life he enjoyed there:

So he was much better than me at contenting himself with the very simple, I might justly say moronic, life. Because, there is no other possible explanation, he lived in a world of his own: 'out of this world', as they so succinctly put it in America. Thus: the best part of the morning in the kitchen of this same high class establishment [the Brown's Hotel, Laugharne], putting bets on horses, listening, yes, actually listening for once, open mouthed, to local gossip and scandal, while drinking slow consecutive pints of disgustingly flat, cold-tea, bitter beer. Muzzily back to late lunch, of one of our rich fatty brews, always eaten alone, apart from the children. . . . Then, blown up with muck and somnolence, up to his humble shed, nesting high above the estuary; and bang into intensive scribbling, muttering, whispering, intoning, bellowing and juggling of words; till seven o'clock prompt.
Then straight back to one of the alternative dumps [the pubs]: we had long discussions as to which was the deadliest; to spend the rest of the evening in 'brilliant repartee'.[26]

Thomas's interests were not those of the intellectual or cosmopolitan bohemian poet: literary parties, the theatre, discussions—there were none of these in Laugharne. Few contemporary poets can have lived such a humdrum, non-literary existence.

He had the same dislike, amounting to superstitious horror, of philosophy, psychology, analysis, criticism; all those vaguely termed ponderous tomes; but most of all, of the gentle art of discussing poetry.[27]

His way of life followed a working-class rather than middle-class pattern, though it should be remembered that the social structure of Wales differs from that in England. Brinnin thought 'Dylan's manner in his own village seemed to be directed toward looking and acting as much like everyone else as possible'.[28] He fitted easily, and in later years with something of a patriarchal dignity, into the Laugharne setting: and his

home was to Dylan . . . a private sanctum, where for once he was not compelled, by himself admittedly, to put on an act, to be amusing, to perpetuate the myth of the *Enfant Terrible*: one of the most damaging of myths, and a curse to grow out of.[29]

Both his wife and mother were anxious that he should not undertake another trip to the U.S.A., realizing that his health was far from good and that in America he needed to be kept from proffered whiskies like a child from free sweets: in Wales he usually drank beer. Just before his final visit to America he had had one or two blackouts—on one occasion collapsing while at the cinema in Carmarthen.

Despite lucrative offers of permanent work in America, he knew that he could not leave Laugharne.

The calmest and happiest days of his life were probably those he spent in Wales. The chief part of his creative writing was done in the landscape and among the people to whom he was most deeply attached. He was able in Laugharne to work continuously almost every afternoon. In London, where he had so many social contacts and where so many dramatic masks were expected of him, he could not work at all![30]

London had entertained and distracted him, but America was to kill him.

# CHAPTER ELEVEN

# THE ARTIST IN COMEDY

## I

THE prose written in the last ten years of his life reveals Thomas's maturing powers as an artist in comedy. It is more varied than the early work, more certain yet more subtle in its effect. Most of it was commissioned work, much of it for the B.B.C., and while it is true that he regarded these excursions into prose as a means of earning money, and something entirely subsidiary to the task of writing poetry, what is abundantly clear is the pleasure he took in their composition and the consistently high quality of the writing.

Three very different items in *A Prospect of the Sea* illustrate Thomas's range as a prose writer in these years. In *The Followers* he depicts the odd, self-conscious feelings and behaviour of late adolescence. A scene is presented swiftly and sharply:

> It was six o'clock on a winter's evening. Thin, dingy rain spat and drizzled past the lighted street lamps. The pavements shone long and yellow. In squeaking goloshes, with mackintosh collars up and bowlers and trilbies weeping, youngish men from the offices bundled home against the thistly wind.

The older men return home 'to safe, hot, slippered, weatherproof hearths, and wives called Mother, and old, fond, fleabag dogs, and the wireless babbling'. The reader, however, is left in the cold, wet, sad evening, the shops closing, 'a newsboy . . . in a doorway, calling the news to nobody, very softly'. The young man, our anti-hero, awaiting his friend Leslie at the corner of Crimea Street, emerges from the grey rain, self-consciously moved by the bedraggled scene:

It was the saddest evening I had ever known. A young man, with his arm round his girl, passed by me, laughing; and she laughed back, right into his handsome, nasty face. That made the evening sadder still.

This is comedy in a low key, veined with irony rather than sentiment, wit, or robust bawdy.

Leslie carried his umbrella which he used only to press doorbells; he was also 'trying to grow a moustache'. The two young men whistle admiringly at passing girls, while assessing whether they can afford a pint. They decide to visit 'The Marlborough', which, like the night, is cold and damp: 'that evening it was the saddest room I had ever known'. The eye is sympathetic but critical that records their adolescent attitudes, observes the 'barmaid with gold hair and two gold teeth in front, like a well-off rabbit's . . . She looked up as we came in, then blew on her nails again and polished them without hope.' Even Swansea is this evening 'the dizzy, ditchwater town at the end of the railway lines'. 'Oh, for our vanished youth,' exclaims the narrator. The tone is ironic, realistic, disenchanted. Eventually 'a wet girl brushed by' and without a word they followed her, despite the reflection, 'I wonder what's the point in following people, it's kind of daft'. Peeping through the curtains of her home, they observe a disappointingly domestic scene: 'Everything there in the warm kitchen, from the tea-caddy and the grandmother clock, to the tabby that purred like a kettle, was good, dull and sufficient'. Then the ghostly voice of Auntie Katinka, whose picture in the album mother and daughter have been secretly smiling over, exclaims 'Why are those two boys looking in at the window?' At once the oppressive atmosphere is pricked like a balloon and the boys run off on their different ways, unspeaking but gripped by the experience. Compared with Thomas's earlier study of adolescence, *One Warm Saturday*, this is less consciously poetic in style, and the comedy stems from the author's increased detachment.

In *How to be a Poet* Thomas satirizes by exaggeration certain types of would-be poets. The ridicule is intended to mock and destroy: he has little time for the Civil Service 'week-end' poet who assiduously cultivates his way to promotion through poetry. This rather Georgian, 'lyrical' poet, he tells us, 'dropped into the Civil service at an age when many of our young poets are now running away to Broadcasting House, today's equivalent of the Sea'.

It is a savage portrait:

> His ears are uncannily sensitive, he can hear an opening being opened a block of offices away. And soon he learns that a poem in a Civil Service magazine is, if not a step up the ladder, at least a lick in the right direction.

Having published some slim volumes, Cribbe—whose name, Thomas sharply comments, 'goes the small, foetid rounds'—decides he must write a novel:

> He soon comes to the conclusion that only quick sales and ephemeral reputations are made by tough novels with such titles as *I've Got It Coming* or *Ten Cents a Dice*; by proletarian novels about the conversion to dialectical materialism of Palais-de wide boys, entitled, maybe, *Red Rain On You, Alf*; by novels called maybe, *Melody In Clover,* about dark men with slight limps, called Dirk Conway and their love for two women, lascivious Ursula Mountclare and little, shy Fay Waters.

Thomas concludes caustically that when the whole of Cribbe's trilogy has appeared, he 'rises, like scum, to the N.I.B. committee.'

The next target is a rather 'sensitive', effeminate young man, also aspiring to the status of poet. His name is Cedric:

> To follow in Cedric's footsteps—(he'd love you to, and would never call a policeman unless it was that frightfully sinister sergeant you see sometimes in Mecklenburgh Square, just like an El Greco)—you must...arrive at the University with your reputation already established as a coming poet and looking, if possible,

something between a Guard's officer and a fashionable photographer's doxy.

The picture of Cedric shows Thomas's ultimate mastery of innuendo and irony, the sentence with a scorpion sting in its tail. He mocks his social-political concerns as a poet of the thirties in a passage of high comedy: the precious conversation between Cedric and Rodney swells to a fine crescendo that is neatly pricked by the comic bathos of Cedric's final decision.

Social awareness! That was the motto. He would talk over coffee—('Adrian makes the best coffee in the whole of this uncivilized island.' 'Tell me, Rodney, where *do* you get these delicious pink cakes?' 'It's a secret.' 'Oh, *do* tell. And I'll give you that special receipt that Basil's Colonel brought back from Ceylon . . .')—of spending the long vacation in 'somewhere *really* alive. I mean, but really. Like the Rhondda Valley or something. I mean, I know I'll feel really *orientated* there. . . . Books, books. It's people that count. I mean, one's got to know the miners.' And he spends the long vacation with Reggie, in Bonn.

A very different kind of comedy is that of *A Story*, where Thomas's attitude to his subject is completely sympathetic. It describes 'a day's outing, by charabanc, to Porthcawl, which, of course, the charabanc never reached, and it happened when I [Dylan] was so high and much nicer'. This tale of a typically Welsh drinking trip Thomas wrote for television just after going on such an outing from Laugharne. As so often in his stories he gives a child's-eye view:

The first I heard of the annual outing was when I was sitting one evening on a bag of rice behind the counter, under one of my uncle's stomachs, reading an advertisement for sheep-dip, which was all there was to read.

There is some difficulty before departure:

'If you go on that outing on Saturday, Mr. Thomas,' she [Mrs. Thomas] said to my uncle in her small, silk voice, 'I'm going home to my mother's.'
Holy Mo, I thought, she's got a mother. . . .
'It's me or the outing, Mr. Thomas.'

I would have made my choice at once, but it was almost half a minute before my uncle said: 'Well, then, Sarah, it's the outing, my love.' He lifted her up, under his arm, on to a chair in the kitchen, and she hit him on the head with the china dog. Then he lifted her down again, and then I said goodnight.

The narrative moves as leisurely as the charabanc passing from pub to pub, and ends on a characteristic note of comic pathos, pointed by alliteration: 'And dusk came down warm and gentle on thirty wild, wet, pickled, splashing men without a care in the world at the end of the world in the west of Wales.' *A Story* is more true to Wales than Wales itself. Many Welshmen have known the drinking trip—on Sundays it was always to England while it was still 'stop tap' in Wales that day—which never reached its destination. This exuberant tale, perhaps one of Thomas's most successful, certainly his most amusing and popular, was one of the last he wrote. He moves easily and quickly from the robust comedy of the drinkers to the touching, solitary musings of the boy: his handling of dialogue, for which he obviously has an acute ear and a retentive memory, is as clear and dramatic as his delineation of character.

II

During the final years of his life Thomas wrote many broadcast scripts. They have been collected in the volume *Quite Early One Morning*; and their chronological presentation indicates how they became more outward-looking in subject matter and more dramatic in form. The early broadcasts such as *Reminiscences of Childhood*, are dominated by the voice of the narrator; there is little dialogue except for the occasional comments and exchanges of children. Each script, however, is carefully constructed, and although most are built up by selection of incident and episode from the past, there is usually a formal pattern. In the first broadcast the narrator begins with a general recollection of Swansea, which is followed by his view of Wales and the outside world as a child:

This sea town was my world; outside, a *strange* Wales, coal-pitted, mountained, river run, full, so far as I knew, of choirs and sheep and story-book tall hats, moved about its business which was none of mine; beyond that unknown Wales lay England, which was London, and a country called 'The Front' from which many of our neighbours never came back.

Then, like a television shot, his picture narrows and focuses on the lost world of childhood when he 'carried a wooden rifle in Cwmdonkin Park and shot down the invisible, unknown enemy like a flock of wild birds. And the park itself was a world within the world of the sea town . . . that park grew up with me.' The poet's eye then looks outward to the 'dame school' of his infancy and ends—as often in these broadcasts—on an image of fantasy, whereby the child alive now in the grown man boasts that he can fly:

I say to the children of my class: 'At last I have a secret.'
'What is it? What is it?'
'I can fly!' And when they do not believe me . . . I fly, like Dracula in a schoolboy cap, level with the windows of the school, peering in until the mistress at the piano screams, and the metronome falls with a clout to the ground, stops, and there is no more Time.

Similarly Thomas uses the image of the snowball to link his *Memories of Christmas*:

All the Christmases roll down the hill towards the Welsh-speaking sea, like a snowball growing whiter and bigger and rounder . . . and I plunge my hands in the snow and bring out whatever I can find.

He continues this use of an image for formal structure: 'In goes my hand into that wool-white bell-tongued ball of holidays. . . .' 'Now out of that bright white snowball of Christmas gone comes the stocking. . . .' Out of the snowball of childhood emerge the voices of Mrs. Prothero and the firemen:

I was in Mrs. Prothero's garden, waiting for cats, with her son Jim. It was snowing. . . . Patient, cold and callous, our hands wrapped in socks, we waited to snowball the cats. . . . We were

so still, Eskimo-footed arctic marksmen in the muffling silence of
the eternal snows—eternal, ever since Wednesday—that we
never heard Mrs. Prothero's first cry from her igloo at the
bottom of the garden.

Imagination heightens the joyous comedy of recollection:

'Fire!' cried Mrs. Prothero, and she beat the dinner-gong.
And we ran down the garden, with the snowballs in our arms,
towards the house, and smoke, indeed, was pouring out of the
dining-room, and the gong was bombilating, and Mrs. Prothero
was announcing ruin like a town-crier in Pompeii. This was
better than all the cats in Wales standing on the wall in a row.

Mr. Prothero laments the untimely fire 'standing in the
middle of the room, saying "A fine Christmas!" and smack-
ing at the smoke with a slipper'. Having discharged their
snowballs into the clouds of smoke, missing Mr. Prothero,
Dylan and his friend rush to telephone:

'Let's call the police as well,' Jim said.
'And the ambulance.'
'And Ernie Jenkins, he likes fires.'

Excitedly the two boys watch the arrival of Jim's aunt, Miss
Prothero, and the incident ends on a note of touching
absurdity:

Jim and I waited, very quietly, to hear what she would say to
them. She said the right thing, always. She looked at the three
tall firemen in their shining helmets, standing among the smoke
and cinders and dissolving snowballs, and she said: 'Would you
like something to read?'

It is an ending that vividly brings to mind the poet's skill as
a broadcaster, exploiting the aural and visual resources of
language to the full.

This later prose records Thomas's impassioned search for
a bygone innocence and happiness as his life grew ever more
chaotic in a present harassed by debts, responsibilities, and
despairs. As small boy or vanished provincial youth, he
escapes into the past. In *Conversation about Christmas* (from *A*

*Prospect of the Sea*) he refuses to break the childlike vision of Christmas in this dialogue between Self and Small Boy:

*Small Boy.* But Christmas when you were a boy wasn't any different to Christmas now.
*Self.* It was, it was.
*Small Boy.* Why was Christmas different then?
*Self.* I mustn't tell you.
*Small Boy.* Why mustn't you tell me? Why is Christmas different for me?
*Self.* I mustn't tell you.
*Small Boy.* Why can't Christmas be the same for me as it was for you when you were a boy?
*Self.* I mustn't tell you. I mustn't tell you because it is Christmas now.

Similarly, *Return Journey* is the search for a lost self. Walking through Swansea, the poet looks 'for someone after fourteen years'. The script has a dramatic structure, based on the narrator's questioning of several distinct groups—the pub clientele, reporters, passers-by, teachers. Asked whether she remembers 'young Thomas', the barmaid replies only 'Lots of Thomases come here; it's a kind of home from home for Thomases'. He moves through the town, where

the voices of fourteen years ago hung silent in the snow and ruin, and in the falling winter morning I walked on through the white havoc'd centre where once a very young man I knew had mucked about as chirpy as a sparrow after the sips and titbits and small change of the town.

The poet's search leads him through the bombed sites of former haunts, to the shore, the Uplands where 'the journey had begun of the one I was pursuing through his past'. Inevitably the pilgrimage ends in Cwmdonkin Park as 'dusk was folding the Park around, like another, darker snow. . . . We had reached the last gate. Dusk drew around us and the town. I said: 'What has become of him now?' The Park-Keeper replies: 'Dead. . . . Dead. . . . Dead.' So ends the journey whose theme is the cry, 'Come back, come back,' the cry of Captain Cat in *Under Milk Wood*.

### III

*Under Milk Wood*, a radio play for voices, reveals Thomas's full development as an artist in comedy. The form of the play is the passage of one day in the lives of the inhabitants of the village. There is no plot, no action, no development of incident, for time sequence has taken the place of narrative sequence. The characters remain basically the same—they come to no deeper knowledge of themselves than they possessed at the outset—as we meet them at different times of the day. As in the other broadcast scripts, it is the language, the selection of metaphor and image, that shows development. At the beginning the village and its people are evoked in images of dream and darkness:

FIRST VOICE

Come now, drift up the dark, come up the drifting sea-dark street now in the dark night seesawing like the sea, to the bible-black airless attic over Jack Black the cobbler's shop where alone and savagely Jack Black sleeps in a nightshirt tied to his ankles with elastic and dreams of

SECOND VOICE

chasing the naughty couples down the grassgreen gooseberried double bed of the wood. . . .

A little later the characters are shown at their morning activities and chores:

The Reverend Eli Jenkins, in Bethesda House, gropes out of bed into his preacher's black, combs back his bard's white hair, forgets to wash, pads barefoot downstairs, opens the front door . . . and hearing the sea break and the gab of birds, remembers his own verses and tells them softly to empty Coronation Street that is rising and raising its blinds.

In the afternoon the movement of the play becomes slower, the rhythms and images appropriate to that time of day: 'The sunny slow lulling afternoon yawns and moons through the dozy town. The sea lolls, laps and idles in, with fishes sleeping in its lap.' Mr. Pugh sleepily nods at table, and

Mrs. Pugh nags him for it. With evening comes imagery of dusk and darkness:

Jack Black prepares once more to meet his Satan in the wood. He grinds his night-teeth, closes his eyes, climbs into his religious trousers, their flies sewn up with cobbler's thread, and pads out, torched and bibled, grimly, joyfully, into the already sinning dusk.

In this way the time sequence of a day is used to explore and define character: though it is essentially the same uncaring Mr. Waldo as earlier shocked the gossips, who now, 'in the dusky wood hugs his lovely Polly Garter under the eyes and rattling tongues of the neighbours and the birds, and he does not care'. And it is the same Polly Garter who makes love to him but longs for a dead lover, for 'it is not *his* [Mr. Waldo's] name that Polly Garter whispers as she lies under the oak and loves him back. Six feet deep that name sings in the cold earth.'

The play has a strict formal development, as the First and Second Voice, like all-seeing television cameras, spot and bring on stage the people of this village who have fallen (and there is surely a pun here) 'head over bells in love'. By comparison, the earlier broadcast talk *Quite Early One Morning* (1945), in which the poet walks through a small Welsh town by the sea and describes its inhabitants and their dreams—a script clearly related to the idea and genesis of *Under Milk Wood*—is less dramatized: all is seen, acted out, and presented through the poet-narrator. Consequently it lacks the dramatic qualities of variety, movement, comedy, the full and vivid realization of character that we find in *Under Milk Wood*.

What then is the picture of life offered in the play, and how is it used for purposes of comedy? Undoubtedly, the comedy stems from Thomas's acute but compassionate observation of the habits and foibles of the Welsh scene. In a letter the poet registers his impressions of those idiosyncrasies and deeply rooted habits of thought and feeling that are the raw material of his vision of Welsh life:

It is hysterical weather where I am writing, BlaenCwm, Llangain, Carmarthenshire, Wales, in a breeding-box in a cabbage valley, in a parlour with a preserved sheepdog, where mothballs fly at night, not moths, where the Bible opens itself at Revelations; and is there money still for tea? . . . Gladys's pet lamb-now-sheep follows her maaa-ing for poor, unloved Gladys's unmade milk. . . . Up the hill-lane behind this house too full of Thomases, a cottage row of undeniably mad unpossessed peasantry of the inbred crooked county, my cousins, uncles, aunts, the woman with the gooseberry birthmark who lies with dogs, the farmlabourer who told me that the stream that runs by his cottage side is Jordan water and who can deny him, the lay preacher who believes that the war was begun only to sell newspapers which are the devil's sermon-sheets.[1]

The remark that 'the Bible opens itself at Revelations', the references to 'Jordan water' and the lay preacher's views on war, show the wealth that Thomas's background offered him and which he was not slow to exploit.

*Under Milk Wood* grew directly from his impressions of his Welsh environment. Similarly, rhythm and phrase, especially in the dialogue, belong essentially to the South Wales dialect of English:

FIRST NEIGHBOUR

Poor Mrs. Waldo

SECOND NEIGHBOUR

What she puts up with

FIRST NEIGHBOUR

Never should of married

SECOND NEIGHBOUR

If she didn't had to

FIRST NEIGHBOUR

Same as her mother

SECOND NEIGHBOUR

There's a husband for you

FIRST NEIGHBOUR

Bad as his father

A 'play for voices', it must be read aloud for its verbal harmonies to be fully appreciated; yet the buoyant and imaginative movement of the lines is kept under the strictest control:

Listen. It is night moving in the streets, the processional salt slow musical wind in Coronation Street and Cockle Row, it is the grass growing on Llaregyb Hill, dewfall, starfall, the sleep of birds in Milk Wood. Listen. It is night in the chill, squat chapel, hymning in bonnet and brooch and bombazine black, butterfly choker and bootlace bow, coughing like nannygoats, sucking mintoes, fortywinking hallelujah; night in the four-ale, quiet as a domino; in Ocky Milkman's lofts like a mouse with gloves; in Dai Bread's bakery flying like black flour. It is to-night in Donkey Street, trotting silent, with seaweed on its hooves, along the cockled cobbles, past curtained fernpot, text and trinket, harmonium, holy dresser, watercolours done by hand, china dog rosy tin teacaddy.

After the first lyrical sentence a note of comedy creeps in: it is night in the chapel, where mintoes are sucked during sermons; and in the four ale, where dominoes are played, the night is 'quiet as a domino'. There follow other apt and beautiful evocations of the quiet and softness of night: it is 'like a mouse with gloves', it is 'flying like black flour', it is a donkey trotting silent 'with seaweed on its hooves'—we are near the harbour of this sea-town.

A basic stylistic device is the accumulation of words similar in sound and associations: 'the sloeblack, slow, black, crowblack, fishingboat-bobbing sea'. The catalogue of words employed for comic or incantatory effect is a common feature of Anglo-Welsh speech and writing. Thomas controls these verbal compilations, however, with rhythms cunningly varied. His selection of word is never arbitrary: in the dreams of boys the sea becomes 'jollyrodgered' and they sleep in the 'bucking ranches of the night'—pirates and cowboys being appropriate boyish associations. Thomas often uses the transferred epithet: 'dogs sleep in the wetnosed yards' and cats 'lope sly, streaking' on the 'one cloud of the roofs'.

The imagery of the play is as Welsh as its cadences: Ocky

Milkman weeps 'like a funeral'; the Reverend Eli Jenkins dreams of eisteddfodau and 'intricately rhymes, to the music of crwth [an old Welsh stringed instrument] and pibgorn' [a form of pipe]. A knowledge of Welsh customs often helps to explain an image's significance, as when Evans the Death

sees, upon waking fifty years ago, snow lie deep on the goosefield behind the sleeping house; and he runs out into the field where his mother is making welshcakes in the snow, and steals a fistful of snowflakes and currants and climbs back to bed to eat them cold and sweet under the warm, white clothes while his mother dances in the snow kitchen crying out for her lost currants.

What, one may ask, has snow to do with welshcakes? The dream experience is not entirely fantasy, for it was the custom in Wales when making welshcakes to use snow in the mixture, since this gave them an exquisite lightness. Consequently welshcakes came to be associated with snow, as the one provided an excuse for the other. The particular form of welshcake Thomas refers to is the 'pic'—from the Welsh *pice ar y maen*—which contains currants and is made on an iron bakestone placed over the open fire.

Thomas had learned by this time to make full use of Welsh literary and social traditions. For example, the Reverend Eli Jenkins's description of 'Llaregyb Hill, that mystic tumulus, the memorial of peoples that dwelt in the region of Llaregyb before the Celts left the Land of Summer and where the old wizards made themselves a wife out of flowers', echoes a passage in Gwyn Jones's book *A Prospect of Wales* (published in 1948): 'As soon as I saw anything I saw Twm Barlwm, that mystic tumulus, the memorial of peoples that dwelt in that region before the Celts left the Land of Summer.'[2] The 'Land of Summer' is of course England, which was nostalgically so termed by the Welsh after they had been driven into the mountains of Wales; and Thomas's reference to the creation of a wife out of flowers has its source in the *Mabinogion*:

'Aye,' said Math, 'let us seek, thou and I, by our magic and enchantment to conjure a wife for him out of flowers.' . . . And then they took the flowers of the oak, and the flowers of the broom, and the flowers of the meadowsweet, and from those they called forth the very fairest and best endowed maiden that mortal ever saw, and baptized her with the baptism they used at that time.[3]

Such sources show how Thomas came to use his Welsh literary and cultural background without satiric intent.

*Under Milk Wood* is of course imaginative rather than realistic. In its fantasy and optimism, its conscious delight in the beauty of language, and its genial view of character, it is directly related to the *Mabinogion*: and like the *Mabinogion* it is saved from sentimentality by a certain earthy, colloquial humour. There is no real sense of evil in the world of *Under Milk Wood*: vice and virtue are seen as attributes of individuality.

Thomas, in a letter, throws valuable light on his increasingly tolerant view of character. That he conceived his play in terms of a particular place, Laugharne, is clearly shown by the opening sentence:

But out of my wórking, however vainly, on it, came the idea of *Llareggub* . . . Out of it came the idea that I write a piece, a play, an impression for voices, an entertainment out of the darkness, of the town I live in, and to write it simply and warmly and comically with lots of movement and varieties of moods, so that, at many levels, through sight and speech, description and dialogue, evocation and parody, you came to know the town as an inhabitant of it. . . .

Let me particularize, and at random. As the piece goes on, two voices will be predominant: that of the preacher, who talks only in verse, and that of the anonymous exhibitor and chronicler called, simply, First Voice. And the First Voice is really a kind of conscience, a guardian angel. Through him you will learn about Mr. Edwards, the draper, and Miss Price, the sempstress, and their odd and, once it is made clear, most natural love. Every day of the week they write love letters to each other, he from the top, she from the bottom, of the town: all their lives they have known of each other's existence, and of their mutual love: they have seen each other a thousand times, and never spoken: easily they could have been together, married, had children: but that is not the life for them: their passionate love, at just this distance, is all they need. And Dai Bread the baker, who has two wives: one is loving and mothering, sacklike and jolly: the other is gypsy slatternly and, all in love, hating: all three enjoy it. And Mrs. Ogmore-Pritchard who, although a boardinghouse keeper, will keep no boarders because they cannot live up to the scrupulous and godlike tidiness of her house and because death can be the only boarder good enough for her in the end. And Mr. Pugh, the schoolmaster, who is always nagged by his wife and who is always plotting her murder. This is wellknown to the town, and to Mrs. Pugh. She likes nagging; he likes plotting, in supposed secrecy, against her. He would always like plotting, whoever he lived with; she would always like nagging, whoever she lived with. How lucky they are to be married. And Polly Garter has many illegitimate babies because she loves babies but does not want only one man's. And Cherry Owen the soak, who likes getting drunk every night; and his wife who likes living with two men, one sober in the day, one drunk at night. And the cobbler who thinks the town is the wickedest place to live in in the world, but who can never leave it while there is a hope of reforming it; and, oh, the savour his cries of Gomorrah add to the pleasures of the little town wicked. And the old woman who every morning shouts her age to the heavens; she believes the town is the chosen land, and the little river Dewi the River of Jordan; she is not at all mad; she merely believes in heaven on earth. And so with all of them, all the eccentrics whose eccentricities, in these first pages, are but briefly and impressionistically noted: all, by their own rights, are ordinary and good; and the First Voice, and the poet preacher, never judge nor condemn but explain and make strangely simple and simply strange.[4]

Thomas's moral attitude in *Under Milk Wood* closely resembles that in his poem 'This Side of the Truth': it is one of 'unjudging love'. He understands and accepts the foibles of his characters, hinting at a basic innocence beneath all their eccentricities. Even Mr. and Mrs. Pugh, he says, are suited to each other. Though there are signs of the severe Nonconformist code in Jack Black's denunciations of the town, these only add to the 'pleasures of the little town wicked'. Clearly Thomas has a deep affection for Mary Ann Sailor's conviction that Llaregyb is the chosen land: 'she is not at all mad; she merely believes in heaven on earth'. This recalls his comment in the letter about 'the farm-labourer who told me that the stream that runs by his cottage side is Jordan water and who can deny him'.

The Reverend Eli Jenkins is Thomas's most kindly portrait of the Welsh minister, though the Reverend's poems to some extent parody the naïve and sentimental aspects of Nonconformist piety, and also the eisteddfod literary traditions:

> We are not wholly bad or good
> Who live our lives under Milk Wood,
> And Thou, I know, wilt be the first
> To see our best side, not our worst.

I well remember the murmurings of assent and approval that these sentiments received from the audience when the play was performed at Swansea: the conventional piety of the stanza obviously appealed to them. There was no hint of the amusement that the lines tended to elicit from London audiences. I suspect the Welsh reaction was truer to the feelings of the play: Nonconformity possesses its gentler traditions. Thomas is not entirely satirical and mocking here, for he interprets the life of this town on different levels of emotional truth: 'at many levels, through sight and speech . . . evocation and parody, you come to know the town'.

Much use is made of music to create the atmosphere and assist the changing moods of the play. The teasing song of the children with its echoes of children's games and rhymes, helps to evoke the lively morning 'that is all singing':

> GIRL
>
> Kiss me in Milk Wood
> Or give me a penny.
> What's your name?
>
> THIRD BOY
>
> Dicky.

GIRL

Kiss me in Milk Wood Dicky
Or give me a penny quickly.

THIRD BOY

Gwennie Gwennie
I can't kiss you in Milk Wood.

GIRLS' VOICES

Gwennie ask him why.

GIRL

Why?

THIRD BOY

Because my mother says I mustn't.

GIRLS' VOICES

Cowardy cowardy custard
Give Gwennie a penny.

By contrast there is the haunting nostalgia of Polly Garter's
song for her dead lover:

Now when farmers' boys on the first fair day
Come down from the hills to drink and be gay,
Before the sun sinks I'll lie there in their arms
For they're *good* bad boys from the lonely farms,

But I always think as we tumble into bed
Of little Willy Wee who is dead, dead, dead . . .

A vein of lewd comedy salts the play, and many of the
songs, in particular, have a *double entente*. Polly Garter's
song of sexual reminiscence is leavened with appropriate
reflections: for Thomas 'cherry' had phallic associations
(cf. 'cherry capped dangler'):

I loved a man whose name was Tom
He was strong as a bear and two yards long
I loved a man whose name was Dick
He was big as a barrel and three feet thick
And I loved a man whose name was Harry
Six feet tall and sweet as a cherry

Praise the Lord! We are a musical nation.

The Reverend Eli Jenkins's innocent comment on this song illustrates both the irony and assured modulation of feeling that characterize the play. Mr. Waldo's ditty about the chimney sweep is a version of a stock pub ballad:

> Poor little chimbley sweep she said
> Black as the ace of spades
> O nobody's swept my chimbley
> Since my husband went his ways.
> Come and sweep my chimbley
> Come and sweep my chimbley
> She sighed to me with a blush
> Come and sweep my chimbley
> Come and sweep my chimbley
> Bring along your chimbley brush!

As Thomas well knew, pub singing in Wales can move with complete ease from bawdy to a favourite hymn or folk-song.

The characters express their sexual feelings with disarming and generally comic frankness. Gossamer Beynon does not care if Sinbad Sailors '*is* common, I want to gobble him up. I don't care if he *does* drop his aitches . . . so long as he's all cucumber and hooves'. Mae Rose Cottage 'listens to the nannygoats chew, draws circles of lipstick round her nipples' and confides to the unlistening goats, 'I'm fast. I'm a bad lot. God will strike me dead. I'm seventeen. I'll go to hell. . . . I'll sin till I blow up' and 'lies deep, waiting for the worst to happen'. Equally obsessed, Jack Black nightly 'climbs into his religious trousers, their flies sewn up with cobbler's thread, and pads out, torched and bibled, grimly, joyfully, into the already sinning dusk'. Certain words, such as 'martyr' recur as sexual puns: 'I saw you talking to a saint this morning. Saint Polly Garter. She was martyred again last night. Mrs. Organ Morgan saw her with Mr. Waldo.' And again:

And how's Organ Morgan, Mrs. Morgan?

N

FIRST WOMAN

you look dead beat

SECOND WOMAN

it's organ organ all the time with him

THIRD WOMAN

up every night until midnight playing the organ.

MRS. ORGAN MORGAN

Oh, I'm a martyr to music.

Natural life plays an important role in *Under Milk Wood* as in the later poems, and animals in particular are part of the natural background: through them the impressions of morning, afternoon or evening are often registered:

The owls are hunting. Look, over Bethesda graveyard one hoots and swoops and catches a mouse by Hannah Rees, Beloved Wife.

There's the clip clop of horses on the sunhoneyed cobbles of the humming streets, hammering of horse-shoes, gobble, quack and cackle, tomtit twitter from the bird-ounced boughs, braying on Donkey Down.

The following evocation of milking time is characteristic of Anglo-Welsh literature, and part of a tradition as old as the *Mabinogion*:

SECOND VOICE

Farmer Watkins in Salt Lake Farm hates his cattle on the hill as he ho's them in to milking.

UTAH WATKINS (*in a fury*)

Damn you, you damned dairies!

SECOND VOICE

A cow kisses him.

UTAH WATKINS

Bite her to death!

SECOND VOICE

he shouts to his **deaf dog** who smiles and licks his hands. . . .

SECOND VOICE

he bawls to the cow who barbed him with her tongue, and she
moos gentle words as he raves and dances among his summer-
breathed slaves walking delicately to the farm. The coming of
the end of the Spring day is already reflected in the lakes of their
great eyes. Bessie Bighead greets them by the names she gave them
when they were maidens.

*Under Milk Wood* describes the natural world with the
freshness and pristine innocence of an Eden before the Fall.
Throughout the play Thomas uses sacramental imagery to
suggest the holiness of 'this place of love': 'And in Coronation
Street, which you alone can see it is so dark under the
chapel in the skies. . . . Time passes. Listen. Time passes.
An owl flies home past Bethesda, to a chapel in an oak.' The
word 'chapel' is not now accompanied by a sneer as in his
early work, but is used as an image of holiness and grace.

The handling of themes in *Under Milk Wood* tends to be
nostalgic. The characters, at the moments of greatest
intensity, frequently look back with a sense of longing to the
past. Consequently, there is a tendency to idealize this
remembered experience, as when the voices of the dead
recall the sweetness of life:

FIRST DROWNED

How's it above?

SECOND DROWNED

Is there rum and laverbread? . . .

FIRST DROWNED

Fighting and onions?

SECOND DROWNED

And sparrows and daisies?

THIRD DROWNED

Tiddlers in a jamjar?

FOURTH DROWNED

Buttermilk and whippets?

**FIFTH DROWNED**

Rock-a-bye baby?

**FIRST DROWNED**

Washing on the line?

**SECOND DROWNED**

And old girls in the snug?

**THIRD DROWNED**

How's the tenors in Dowlais?

**FOURTH DROWNED**

Who milks the cows in Maesgwyn?

Laverbread, which is made from seaweed, is a food peculiar to South Wales and in particular to the Swansea area, since the seaweed is gathered from the nearby Gower coast. Whippet racing, mentioned by the Fourth Drowned, became a popular pastime in South Wales during the years of the depression. The snug was a small room in the public house where women used to drink before it was respectable for them to drink at all, and they had to do so in relative secrecy.

Although the nostalgia is often veined with comedy, at times—as in dead Rosie Probert's speech—it is presented with a seriousness that is by contrast the more moving:

> Remember her.
> She is forgetting.
> The earth which filled her mouth
> Is vanishing from her.
> Remember me.
> I have forgotten you.
> I am going into the darkness of the darkness for ever.
> I have forgotten that I was ever born.

Though many of the characters in *Under Milk Wood* speak of death, there is no terror in the play, no painful encounters with reality, such as Polly Garter, Mr. Pugh, or Captain Cat might be expected to have known. Nor are there echoes of the doubts and despairs that haunted Thomas's life and found expression in his poetry. The Reverend Eli Jenkins's prototype in *Quite Early One Morning* was 'troubled by one thing only, and that, belief': Thomas chooses to explore no such doubts in his later portrayal of a Nonconformist minister. For it is in the '*White* Book of Llaregyb' that the poet is celebrating—for the last time—'the *innocence* of men' and the '*kind* fire' of God in 'this place of love'.*

IV

Several of Thomas's radio broadcasts are critical introductions to such poets as Sir Philip Sidney, Henry Vaughan, Edward Thomas, and Wilfred Owen. These are informative, accurate, and sympathetic; and one is struck by the depth and sharpness of Thomas's appreciation of a variety of other men's poetic worlds. It is impressionistic criticism, finely sensitive in its response to the poet—as when he speaks of the sudden maturing of Owen's poetry under the impact of war:

> To see him in his flame-lit perspective, against the background, now of the poxed and cratered war-scape, shivering in the snow under the slitting wind, marooned on a frozen desert, or crying, in a little oven of mud, that his 'senses are charred', is to see a man consigned to articulate immolation. He buries his smashed head with his own singed hands, and is himself the intoning priest over the ceremony, the suicide, the sunset. He is the common touch. He is the bell of the church of the broken body. He writes love letters home for the illiterate dead . . . the unhonoured prophet in death's country. [5]

Always Thomas is aware of the common humanity of the poet, for he is 'a poet for such a very tiny bit of his life; for the rest, he is a human being, one of whose responsibilities is to know and feel, as much as he can, all that is moving around and within him'. [6]

I have, in this book, tried to show how Thomas's needs as an artist became increasingly rooted in his love for Wales. A few days before his final departure for America he discussed with Phillip Burton, formerly a drama producer on the

---

* My italics.

B.B.C. Welsh Region, a projected play describing Welsh life. The play

was to be set in a small industrial town in South Wales, and it would tell of the lives of two families who live unknown to each other in neighbouring streets. The play would begin with the birth of the boy in one family and the girl in the other. . . . There was to be little realism in the presentation, and the families would live their separate but unconsciously interwoven lives at separate ends of the stage, until at last the boy and the girl met in the middle.[7]

Not long after discussing his plans for this play Thomas died, in New York, in November 1953, while on a poetry recital tour. Shortly before his death, and aware of the seriousness of his condition, he spoke of his longing (*hiraeth*) for Wales and home. 'He opened his eyes and, calmly, sadly, said: "Tonight in my home the men have their arms around one another, and they are singing." '[8] He was thinking of the traditional Welsh Saturday evening that he had depicted so often in his stories, evenings in Laugharne at Brown's Hotel or the Cross House Inn, a short walk from his 'sea-shaken' home. Just before the final coma, in the terror and wretchedness of his illness and loneliness

turning on his bed, he awoke to speak, sometimes in tears, of his wife, of the misery of his existence, and of his wish to die. 'I want to go to the Garden of Eden,' he said, 'to die . . . to be for ever unconscious.'[9]

A few days later he died, in exile. Two years before he had written a poem for his dying father: a last cry addressed to a God as real and present as an enemy or friend. That cry still rings:

> And you, my father, there on the sad height,
> Curse, bless, me now with your fierce tears, I pray.
> Do not go gentle into that good night.
> Rage, rage against the dying of the light.

# NOTES

## CHAPTER ONE: THE WELSH BACKGROUND

1. Dylan Thomas: quoted by Geoffrey Moore in 'Dylan Thomas', *Kenyon Review*, vol. xvii (Spring 1955), p. 261.
2. Dylan Thomas: *New Verse*, no. 11 (October 1934), p. 9. Thomas was then nineteen years old.
3. Gwyn Jones: 'Welsh Dylan', *Adelphi*, vol. 30, no. 2 (February 1954), p. 115.
4. Karl Shapiro: 'Dylan Thomas', *Poetry*, vol. 87, no. 2 (November 1955), p. 105.
5. Vernon Watkins: comment on a review of J. M. Brinnin: *Dylan Thomas in America* in *Encounter*, vol. VI, no. 6 (June 1956), p. 78.
6. Geoffrey Moore: 'Dylan Thomas', *Kenyon Review*, vol. xvii (Spring 1955), pp. 264–5.
7. Robert Graves: Foreword to Alun Lewis: *Ha! Ha! Among the Trumpets* (London, 1945), p. 7.
8. A. G. Prys-Jones: 'Death Shall Have No Dominion', *Dock Leaves* (Dylan Thomas Memorial Number), vol. 5, no. 13 (Spring 1954), p. 27.
9. See David Williams: *A History of Modern Wales* (London, 1950), p. 272.
10. Thomas Parry: *A History of Welsh Literature*, translated by H. Idris Bell (London, 1955), p. 48.
11. See Gwyn Williams: *An Introduction to Welsh Poetry* (London, 1953), pp. 243–5.
12. Gwyn Jones: 'Welsh Dylan', *Adelphi*, vol. 30, no. 2 (Spring 1954), p. 115.
13. Matthew Arnold: *On the Study of Celtic Literature* (London, 1919), p. 83.
14. Ibid., p. 110.
15. Geraint Goodwin: *The Heyday in the Blood* (London, 1954), p. 124.
16. Caitlin Thomas: *Leftover Life to Kill* (London, 1957), pp. 73–74.
17. Rhys Davies: *The Story of Wales* (London, 1943), p. 24.
18. T. Rowland Hughes: *From Hand to Hand*, translated from the Welsh by R. C. Ruck (London, 1950), p. 27.
19. Gwyn Jones: Introduction to *Welsh Short Stories* (London, 1956), p. xiii.

## CHAPTER TWO: THE INTRUDERS: INFLUENCES AND RELATIONSHIPS

1. Stephen Spender: *Spectator* (5 December 1952), pp. 780–1.
2. Dylan Thomas in a letter to Stephen Spender (9 December 1952), quoted by Derek Stanford: *Dylan Thomas* (London, 1954), p. 25.
3. Gwyn Thomas: quoted in 'Language, Style, and the Anglo-Welsh' by Gwyn Jones, *Essays and Studies* (1953), p. 107.
4. Dylan Thomas: *Quite Early One Morning* (London, 1954), pp. 147–8.
5. Ibid., p. 148.
6. Alun Lewis: 'The Mountain Over Aberdare', from *Raiders' Dawn* (London, 1942), p. 87:

From this high quarried ledge I see
The place for which the Quakers once
Collected clothes, my fathers' home,
Our stubborn bankrupt village sprawled
In jaded dusk beneath its nameless hills;
The drab streets strung across the cwm,
Derelict workings, tips of slag
The gospellers and gamblers use
And children scrutting for the coal
That winter dole cannot purvey;
Allotments where the collier digs
While engines hack the coal within his brain;
Grey Hebron in a rigid cramp,
White cheap-jack cinema, the church
Stretched like a sow beside the stream;
And mourners in their Sunday best
Holding a tiny funeral, singing hymns
That drift insidious as the rain. . . .

And in a curtained parlour women hug
Huge grief, and anger against God. . . .

7. Vernon Watkins: 'Innovation and Tradition', unsigned Obituary Notice, *The Times* (10 November 1953).
8. A. G. Prys-Jones: 'Death Shall Have No Dominion', *Dock Leaves*, vol. 5 (Spring 1954), no. 13, p. 26.
9. *Collected Poems*, p. 13.
10. Henry Vaughan: *The Works of Henry Vaughan*, vol. 1, Edited by L. C. Martin (Oxford, 1957), pp. 419–20.
11. Thomas Traherne: *Centuries of Meditations* (London, 1908), pp. 156–7.
12. Dylan Thomas: 'On Reading One's Own Poems', *Quite Early One Morning*, p. 131.
13. Vernon Watkins: a short autobiographical note in *Twentieth Century Authors*: First Supplement, Edited by Stanley J. Kunitz (New York, 1955), p. 1,052.
14. Dylan Thomas: *Letters to Vernon Watkins* (London, 1957), p. 64.
15. Ibid., pp. 17–18.

CHAPTER THREE: EARLY YEARS

1. *The Mabinogion*, translated by Gwyn Jones and T. Jones (London, 1949), pp. 63–64.
2. Edward Thomas: *The Life and Letters of Edward Thomas*, Edited by John Moore (London, 1939), pp. 156 and 168.
3. Dylan Thomas: 'Reminiscences of Childhood' (First Version), *Quite Early One Morning*, p. 1.
4. I am indebted for much information concerning Dylan Thomas's early years to Mrs. D. J. Thomas, the poet's mother, Glyn Jones, a close friend of Thomas in his late teens, and Mr. David Richards.
5. Mrs. D. J. Thomas: in an interview reported in *Everybody's* (21 April 1956), pp. 23 and 39. The article, entitled 'Go and Write, Boy!', was written by Paul Ferris.
6. Caitlin Thomas: *Leftover Life to Kill*, p. 56.
7. J. M. Brinnin: *Dylan Thomas in America* (London, 1956), p. 92.
8. Dylan Thomas: 'Modern Poetry', *Swansea Grammar School Magazine*, vol. 26, no. 3 (December 1929), pp. 82–84.

9. Ibid., vol. 27, no. 3, p. 112.
10. Dylan Thomas: 'Reminiscences of Childhood', *Quite Early One Morning*, pp. 5–6.
11. Dylan Thomas: *Portrait of the Artist as a Young Dog* (London, 1940), p. 13.
12. Ibid., pp. 9–10
13. Dylan Thomas: *Swansea Grammar School Magazine*, vol. 27, no. 3 (December 1930), pp. 87–89.
14. Ibid., p. 82.
15. Dylan Thomas: *Quite Early One Morning*, p. 81.
16. Dylan Thomas: *Portrait of the Artist as a Young Dog*, pp. 186–7.
17. Augustus John: 'The Monogamous Bohemian', *Adam* (Dylan Thomas Memorial Number), no. 238 (December 1953), p. 10.
18. J. M. Brinnin: *Dylan Thomas in America*, p. 26.
19. Dylan Thomas: quoted in *Adam*, no. 238 (December 1953), p. 68.
20. Dylan Thomas: *Portrait of the Artist as a Young Dog*, pp. 129–30.
21. Ibid., pp. 195–6.
22. Gwyn Jones: 'Welsh Dylan', *Adelphi*, vol. 30, no. 2 (February 1954), p. 112.
23. Geoffrey Moore: 'Dylan Thomas', *Kenyon Review*, vol. xvii (1955), p. 264.
24. Dylan Thomas: 'Tragedy of Swansea's Comic Genius', *Herald of Wales* (23 January 1932), p. 6.
25. Dylan Thomas: 'A Modern Poet Of Gower: Anglo-Welsh Bards', *Herald of Wales* (25 June 1932), p. 8.
26. Dylan Thomas: *Quite Early One Morning*, pp. 75–76.
27. Dylan Thomas: quoted in *Adam*, no. 238, p. 68.

CHAPTER FOUR: *18 POEMS*

1. Vernon Watkins: Introduction to Dylan Thomas: *Letters to Vernon Watkins*, pp. 12–13.
2. Vernon Watkins: 'Innovation and Tradition', unsigned Obituary Notice, *The Times* (10 November 1953).
3. Dylan Thomas: *Letters to Vernon Watkins*, p. 49.
4. T. S. Eliot: *After Strange Gods* (London, 1934), p. 38.
5. Ibid., pp. 19–20.
6. Vernon Watkins: Comment on a review of J. M. Brinnin: *Dylan Thomas in America* in *Encounter*, vol. vi, no. 6 (June 1956), p. 77.
7. Dylan Thomas: quoted by Geoffrey Moore in 'Dylan Thomas', *Kenyon Review*, vol. xvii, p. 261.
8. Caitlin Thomas: *Leftover Life to Kill*, p. 57.
9. V. S. Pritchett: 'The English Puritan', *New Statesman and Nation*, vol. liii, no. 1,350 (26 January 1957), p. 103.
10. Margiad Evans: *Autobiography* (London, 1952), p. 158.
11. 'Hymne to God, my God, in my sicknesse', *Donne's Poetical Works*, vol. i, Edited by H. J. C. Grierson (London, 1912), p. 368.
12. Robert Martin Adams: 'Taste and Bad Taste in Metaphysical Poetry', *Hudson Review*, vol. viii, no. 1, p. 73.
13. Karl Shapiro: 'Dylan Thomas', *Poetry*, vol. 87, no. 2 (November 1955), p. 106.
14. Dylan Thomas: *Adventures in the Skin Trade and other stories* (New York, 1955), pp. 129–30.
15. Ibid., p. 136.
16. R. B. Marriott: *Adam*, no. 238, p. 32.
17. Karl Shapiro: 'Dylan Thomas', *Poetry*, vol. 87, no. 2, p. 110.
18. Francis Scarfe: *Auden and After* (London, 1945), pp. 112–13.

o

19. Dylan Thomas: quoted in Henry Treece: *Dylan Thomas* (London, 1949), p. 48.

20. Ibid., pp. 47–48.

21. Dylan Thomas: *Letters to Vernon Watkins*, p. 38.

22. *Collected Poems*, p. 4.

23. Ibid., p. 15.

24. Ibid., p. 37.

25. Ibid., p. 38.

26. Dylan Thomas: *Portrait of the Artist as a Young Dog*, p. 30.

27. Margiad Evans: *Autobiography*, p. 26.

28. Ibid., pp. 46 and 47.

CHAPTER FIVE: *TWENTY-FIVE POEMS*

1. *Collected Poems*, p. 73.

2. Derek Stanford: *Dylan Thomas*, p. 24.

3. Dylan Thomas: *Portrait of the Artist as a Young Dog*, pp. 21–22.

4. Karl Shapiro: 'Dylan Thomas', *Poetry*, vol. 87, no. 2, p. 104.

5. T. S. Eliot: *After Strange Gods*, p. 53.

6. Dylan Thomas: *Under Milk Wood*, p. 81.

7. Karl Shapiro: 'Dylan Thomas', *Poetry*, vol. 87, no. 2, p. 106.

8. Matthew Arnold: *On the Study of Celtic Literature*, p. 116.

9. Lawrence Durrell: *Poetry London—New York*, no. 1 (March-April,1956), p. 34.

CHAPTER SIX: *THE MAP OF LOVE*

1. Vernon Watkins: 'Dylan Thomas', unsigned Obituary Notice, *The Times* (10 November 1953).

2. Karl Shapiro: 'Dylan Thomas', *Poetry*, vol. 87, no. 2, p. 108.

3. David Richards: Preface to an unpublished manuscript by Dylan Thomas.

4. Dylan Thomas: quoted by Henry Treece: *Dylan Thomas*, p. 47.

5. Dylan Thomas: 'On Reading One's Own Poems', *Quite Early One Morning*, p. 137.

6. Dylan Thomas: *Portrait of the Artist as a Young Dog*, pp. 23–24.

7. John Donne: *Deaths Duell, Sermons of John Donne*, vol. x, Edited by E. M. Simpson and G. R. Potter (California, 1961), pp. 232–3.

8. Ibid., p. 238.

9. Babette Deutsch: 'The Orient Wheat', *Virginia Quarterly Review*, vol. 27, no. 2 (Spring 1951), p. 224.

10. William Blake: *Poetry and Prose*, Edited by G. Keynes (London, 1946), p. 187.

11. Vernon Watkins: Introduction to Dylan Thomas: *Letters to Vernon Watkins*, p. 13.

12. David Aivaz: 'The Poetry of Dylan Thomas', *The Hudson Review*, Vol. iii, no. 3 (Autumn 1950), p. 394.

13. *Collected Poems*, p. 86.

14. John Donne: *Deaths Duell, Sermons of John Donne*, vol. x, Edited by E. M. Simpson and G. R. Potter, p. 234.

15. Dylan Thomas: quoted by J. M. Brinnin in *Dylan Thomas in America*, p. 212.

16. Dylan Thomas: 'Book Review', *Adelphi*, vol. viii (September 1934), pp. 418–19.

17. Lawrence Durrell: *Poetry London—New York*, no. 1 (March-April 1956), p. 35.

18. Vernon Watkins in a note to Dylan Thomas: *Letters to Vernon Watkins*, p. 30.

19. Ibid., p. 19.

20. Ibid., p. 54.

21. Ibid., p. 101.

CHAPTER SEVEN: A PROSE INTERLUDE: THE EARLY STORIES

1. Dylan Thomas: *A Prospect of the Sea* (London, 1955), p. 20.
2. Vernon Watkins: 'Dylan Thomas', unsigned Obituary Notice, *The Times* (10 November, 1953).
3. Margiad Evans: *Autobiography*, pp. 45–46.
4. Dylan Thomas: *The Enemies, A Prospect of the Sea*, p. 40.
5. Dylan Thomas: *The Orchards, A Prospect of the Sea*, p. 90.
6. Dylan Thomas: 'This bread I break', *Collected Poems*, p. 39.
7. Dylan Thomas: 'To Others than You', *Collected Poems*, p. 107.
8. T. S. Eliot: *After Strange Gods*, p. 46.
9. See Rhys Davies: *The Story of Wales*, (London, 1943).
10. Dylan Thomas: *Adventures in the Skin Trade and other stories* (New York, 1955), p. 128.

CHAPTER EIGHT: *PORTRAIT OF THE ARTIST AS A YOUNG DOG*

1. Vernon Watkins: Foreword to *Adventures in the Skin Trade* (London, 1955), pp. 8–9.
2. William Griffiths: *Adam*, no. 238, p. 30.
3. Dylan Thomas: *Letters to Vernon Watkins*, p. 79.
4. Derek Stanford: *Dylan Thomas*, p. 165.
5. Vernon Watkins: Foreword to *Adventures in the Skin Trade* (London, 1955), p. 12.

CHAPTER NINE: *DEATHS AND ENTRANCES*

1. Robert Graves: Foreword to Alun Lewis: *Ha! Ha! Among the Trumpets*, p. 7.
2. Gwyn Jones: *The First Forty Years, Some Notes on Anglo-Welsh Literature* (Cardiff, 1957), p. 12.
3. John Donne: *Sermons of John Donne*, vol. x, Edited by E. M. Simpson and G. R. Potter, pp. 231–7.
4. Margiad Evans: *Autobiography*, p. 112.
5. W. S. Merwin: 'The Religious Poet', *Adam*, no. 238, p. 73.
6. Margiad Evans: *Autobiography*, p. 88.
7. John Donne: *Sermons of John Donne*, vol. x, Edited by E. M. Simpson and G. R. Potter, p. 238.
8. William Empson: 'To Understand a Modern Poem', *Strand* (March 1947), p. 64.
9. Dylan Thomas: *Quite Early One Morning*, p. vii.
10. Dylan Thomas: *Letters to Vernon Watkins*, p. 104.
11. Thomas Traherne: *Centuries of Meditations* (London, 1908), p. 157.
12. Elder Olson: *The Poetry of Dylan Thomas* (Chicago, 1954), p. 20.
13. Dylan Thomas: *New Verse*, no 11 (October 1934), p. 8.
14. Gwyn Jones: 'Welsh Dylan', *Adelphi*, vol. 30, no. 2 (February 1954), p. 115.
15. J. M. Brinnin: *Dylan Thomas in America*, pp. 103–4.
16. Vernon Watkins: Introduction to Dylan Thomas: *Letters to Vernon Watkins*, p. 17.
17. Thomas Traherne: *Centuries of Meditations*, p. 157.
18. Dylan Thomas: *Letters to Vernon Watkins*, p. 114.
19. Babette Deutsch: 'The Orient Wheat', *Virginia Quarterly Review*, vol. 27, no. 2, p. 223.
20. Vernon Watkins: *The Death Bell* (London, 1954), p. 47.
21. Ibid., p. 60.
22. J. M. Brinnin: *Dylan Thomas in America*, p. 99.
23. T. S. Eliot: 'Dante', *Selected Essays* (London, 1934), p. 243.

24. Gwyn Jones: 'Welsh Dylan', *Adelphi*, vol. 30, no. 2, p. 114.
25. Ibid., p. 116.

CHAPTER TEN: *COLLECTED POEMS*

1. I visited Mrs. Caitlin Thomas at the Boat House in 1955, and the late Mrs. D. J. Thomas, who was staying there, during a second visit in 1957.
2. J. M. Brinnin: *Dylan Thomas in America*, p. 83.
3. Ibid., p. 82.
4. Ibid., p. 93.
5. *Songtime*, Edited by Percy Dearmer and Martin Shaw (London, 1915), p. 37.
6. Eiluned Lewis: *Honey Pots and Brandy Bottles* (London, 1954), p. 10.
7. Dylan Thomas: Letter to E. F. Bozman, *Books*, no. 282 (December 1953), pp. 114–15.
8. David Jones: 'Self-Portrait'. This was broadcast from the Swansea station of the B.B.C. in August 1955. The quotation from this talk is published in Gwyn Jones's lecture, *The First Forty Years*, p. 20.
9. Dylan Thomas: *New Verse*, no 11 (October 1934), p. 8.
10. Dylan Thomas: *Letters to Vernon Watkins*, p. 131.
11. Raymond Garlick: *Dock Leaves*, vol. 5, no. 13, p. 2.
12. Ernest Renan: *Poetry of the Celtic Races* (London, 1896), p. 21.
13. Derek Stanford: *Dylan Thomas*, p. 140.
14. Caitlin Thomas: *Empire News*, Article on Dylan Thomas.
15. Dylan Thomas: quoted by J. M. Brinnin: *Dylan Thomas in America*, p. 147.
16. Vernon Watkins: 'Fidelity to the Living', *The Lady with the Unicorn* (London, 1948), p. 40.
17. *Collected Poems*, p. 171.
18. Vernon Watkins: *The Lady with the Unicorn*, p. 48.
19. Ibid., p. 40.
20. Ibid., p. 63.
21. Ibid., p. 47.
22. Vernon Watkins: 'Dylan Thomas', unsigned Obituary Notice, *The Times* (10 November 1953).
23. Caitlin Thomas: *Leftover Life to Kill*, p. 35.
24. Dylan Thomas: 'Letter II' *Botteghe Oscure*, vol. xiii, pp. 99–100.
25. Caitlin Thomas: *Leftover Life to Kill*, pp. 58–59.
26. Ibid., pp. 36–37.
27. Ibid., p. 53.
28. J. M. Brinnin: *Dylan Thomas in America*, p. 86.
29. Caitlin Thomas: *Leftover Life to Kill*, p. 34.
30. Vernon Watkins: Introduction to *Letters to Vernon Watkins*, p. 20.

CHAPTER ELEVEN: THE ARTIST IN COMEDY

1. Dylan Thomas: 'Letter to Oscar Williams', *New World Writing*, Seventh Mentor Selection (New York, 1955), pp. 130–2.
2. These words by Arthur Machen are quoted by Gwyn Jones: *A Prospect of Wales* (London, 1948), p. 17.
3. *The Mabinogion*, translated by Gwyn Jones and T. Jones, p. 68.
4. Dylan Thomas: 'Letter', *Botteghe Oscure*, vol. ix, pp. 154–5.
5. Dylan Thomas: 'Wilfred Owen', *Quite Early One Morning*, p. 102.
6. Dylan Thomas: 'On Poetry', *Quite Early One Morning*, p. 170.
7. Phillip Burton: *Adam*, no. 238, p. 36.
8. J. M. Brinnin: *Dylan Thomas in America*, p. 211.
9. Ibid., p. 227.

# SELECT BIBLIOGRAPHY

## WORKS BY DYLAN THOMAS

### Unpublished Material

(i) Manuscript Poems (*c.* 1931–3): MS. 48,217, British Museum. There are 79 pages.

(ii) An unpublished manuscript, consisting of nine pages, which Dylan Thomas gave to Mr. David Richards, The Cross House, Laugharne. The manuscript contains the written answers by Dylan Thomas to various questions put to him by Mr. Richards.

(iii) Four notebooks of manuscript poems covering the years 1930–4 (although there are gaps), now in the Lockwood Memorial Library, State University of New York at Buffalo.

### Published Works

#### BOOKS

*18 Poems*, London, 1934.
*Twenty-Five Poems*, London, 1936.
*The Map of Love*, London, 1939.
*Portrait of the Artist as a Young Dog*, London, 1940.
*Deaths and Entrances*, London, 1946.
*Collected Poems*, London, 1952.
*The Doctor and the Devils*, London, 1953.
*Under Milk Wood*, London, 1954.
*Quite Early One Morning*, London, 1954.
*A Prospect of the Sea*, London, 1955.
*Adventures in the Skin Trade*, London, 1955.
*Adventures in the Skin Trade and other stories*, New York, 1955.
*Letters to Vernon Watkins* (edited, with an Introduction, by Vernon Watkins), London, 1957.

#### ARTICLES AND LETTERS

##### referred to in the text

Seven Letters to Oscar Williams (1945–1953), *New World Writing*, Mentor Selection, no. 7 (New York, 1955), pp. 128–40.

'Modern Poetry', *Swansea Grammar School Magazine*, vol. 26, no. 3 (December 1929), pp. 82–84.

'Children's Hour', *Swansea Grammar School Magazine*, vol. 27, no. 3 (December 1930), pp. 87–89.

'Three Nursery Rhymes', *Swansea Grammar School Magazine*, vol. 27, no. 3 (December 1930), p. 82.

'Tragedy of Swansea's Comic Genius', *Herald of Wales* (23 January 1932), p. 6.

'A Modern Poet Of Gower: Anglo-Welsh Bards', *Herald of Wales* (25 June 1932), p. 8.

'An Enquiry', *New Verse*, no. 11 (October 1934), pp. 8–9.

'Book Review', *Adelphi*, vol. viii, no. 6 (September 1934), pp. 418–20.

'Address to a Scottish Society of Writers in Edinburgh', quoted in *Adam*, no. 238 (December 1953), p. 68.

'Insults', *Strand* (March 1947), p. 65.

Letter to E. F. Bozman, *Books*, No. 282 (December 1953), pp. 114–15.

Two Letters in *Botteghe Oscure*, vol. ix, pp. 154–5, and vol. xiii, pp. 97–100.


J. A. Rolph: *Dylan Thomas: A Bibliography* (London, 1956) provides a complete (up to the date of its publication) list of Thomas's published work, both in books and periodicals.

# WORKS ABOUT DYLAN THOMAS

### BOOKS

Treece, Henry: *Dylan Thomas*, London, 1949.

Olson, Elder: *The Poetry of Dylan Thomas*, Chicago, 1954.

Stanford, Derek: *Dylan Thomas*, London, 1954.

Brinnin, J. M.: *Dylan Thomas in America*, London, 1956.

Thomas, Caitlin: *Leftover Life to Kill*, London, 1957.

Tedlock, E. W.: *Dylan Thomas: The Legend and the Poet*, London, 1960.

Holbrook, David: *Llareggub Revisited: Dylan Thomas and the state of modern poetry*, Cambridge, 1962.

Tindall, W. York: *A Reader's Guide to Dylan Thomas*, London, 1962.

Jones, T. H.: *Dylan Thomas*, London, 1963.

ARTICLES

*(Including reviews) on Dylan Thomas referred to in the text*

Adams, Robert Martin: 'Taste and Bad Taste in Metaphysical
Poetry', *Hudson Review*, vol. viii, no. 1, pp. 61–77.

Aivaz, David: 'The Poetry of Dylan Thomas', *Hudson Review*,
vol. iii, no. 3 (Autumn 1950), pp. 382–404.

Burton, Phillip: Article on Dylan Thomas in *Adam*, no. 238
(December 1953), pp. 36–37.

Deutsch, Babette: 'The Orient Wheat', *Virginia Quarterly Review*,
vol. 27, no. 2 (Spring 1951), pp. 221–36.

Durrell, Lawrence: 'Letter' on Dylan Thomas in *Poetry London—
New York*, no. 1 (March-April 1956), pp. 34–35.

Empson, William: 'To Understand a Modern Poem', *Strand*
(March 1947), pp. 61–64.

Ferris, Paul: 'Go and Write, Boy', an interview with Mrs. D. J.
Thomas, reported by Paul Ferris in *Everybody's* (21 April
1956), pp. 23 and 39.

Garlick, Raymond: 'Editorial', *Dock Leaves*, vol. 5, no. 13, pp. 1–5.

Griffiths, William: Article on Dylan Thomas in *Adam*, no. 238,
p. 30.

John, Augustus: 'The Monogamous Bohemian', *Adam*, no. 238,
pp. 9–10.

Jones, Gwyn: *The First Forty Years, Some Notes on Anglo-Welsh
Literature*, (Cardiff, 1957).

—— 'Language, Style, and the Anglo-Welsh', *Essays and Studies*,
1953, pp. 102–14.

—— 'Welsh Dylan', *Adelphi*, vol. 30, no. 2 (February 1954),
pp. 108–17.

Maud, R. N.: 'Dylan Thomas' Collected Poems: Chronology of
Composition', Publications of the Modern Language
Association, vol. lxxvi (June 1961), pp. 292–7.

Merwin, W. S.: 'The Religious Poet', *Adam*, no. 238, pp. 73–78.

Moore, Geoffrey: 'Dylan Thomas', *Kenyon Review*, vol. xvii,
no. 2 (Spring 1955), pp. 258–77.

Prys-Jones, A. G.: 'Death Shall Have No Dominion', *Dock
Leaves*, vol. 5, no. 13, pp. 26–29.

Shapiro, Karl: 'Dylan Thomas', *Poetry*, vol. 87, no. 2 (November
1955), pp. 100–10.

Spender, Stephen: Review of *Collected Poems*, *Spectator* (5 December 1952), pp. 780–1.

Watkins, Vernon: Comment on a review of *Dylan Thomas in
America*, *Encounter*, vol. vi, no. 6 (June 1956), pp. 77–79.

—— 'Innovation and Tradition', unsigned Obituary Notice,
*The Times* (10 November 1953).

Watkins, Vernon: Introduction to *Letters to Vernon Watkins* (London, 1957), pp. 11–21.
—— Notes to *Letters to Vernon Watkins*. These precede the letters to which they refer.
—— Foreword to *Adventures in the Skin Trade* (London, 1955), pp. 7–14.

### Other Books to which Reference has been made

Arnold, Matthew: *On the Study of Celtic Literature* (London, 1919).
Davies, Rhys: *The Story of Wales* (London, 1943).
Jones, Gwyn: *Welsh Short Stories* (London, 1956).
*Mabinogion, The*, translated by Gwyn Jones and T. Jones (London, 1949).
Parry, Thomas: *A History of Welsh Literature*, translated from the Welsh by H. Idris Bell (London, 1955).
Renan, Ernest: *Poetry of the Celtic Races* (London, 1896).
Williams, David: *A History of Modern Wales* (London, 1950).
Williams, Gwyn: *An Introduction to Welsh Poetry* (London, 1953).
—— *The Burning Tree*, translations from early Welsh poetry (London, 1956).

### Anglo-Welsh Literary Periodicals

*Wales*, edited by Keidrych Rhys (Carmarthen, 1937–9, 1943–8, 1958–60).
*The Welsh Review*, edited by Gwyn Jones, (Cardiff, 1939, 1944–8).
*Dock Leaves*, edited by Raymond Garlick (Pembroke Dock, 1949—). This is now *The Anglo-Welsh Review*.

# INDEX

## DATE DUE

DEMCO INC 38-2971